Kel Richards' Dictionary of Australian PhraseandFable

KEL RICHARDS is an Australian author, journalist and radio personality. He presents Sydney radio station 2CH's *Sunday Night Open Line* show. He has written a series of crime novels and thrillers for adult readers, including *The Case of the Vanishing Corpse, Death in Egypt* and *An Outbreak of Darkness*. Richards presented ABC News Radio's weekend afternoons, which included regular *Wordwatch* segments, a feature he introduced. Initially developed as a filler program to allow time for changes of people or locations between programs, *Wordwatch* aired its thousandth episode in November 2003. Kel now presents the 2CH *Word of the Day* daily at breakfast time.

Kel Richards' Dictionary of Australian Phrase and Fable

NEWSOUTH

A NewSouth book

Published by
NewSouth Publishing
University of New South Wales Press Ltd
University of New South Wales
Sydney NSW 2052
AUSTRALIA
newsouthpublishing.com

© Kel Richards 2013
First published 2013

10 9 8 7 6 5 4 3 2 1

National Library of Australia Cataloguing-in-Publication entry
Author: Richards, Kel, 1946 –
Title: Kel Richards' dictionary of Australian phrase and fable/
Kel Richards.
ISBN: 9781742233734(pbk.)
      9781742241128(epub)
      9781742243863(mobi)
      9781742246291(epdf)
Subjects: English language – Australia – Terms and phrases.
Australian literature – Dictionaries.
Mythology, Aboriginal Australian – Dictionaries.
Dewey Number: 423.1

Design Di Quick
Printer Griffin Press

Preface

It's late at night and you reach out for a good book to read at bedtime. What sort of book do you reach for? A thriller? A biography? A travel book? Or a dictionary?

A what! Who would pick up a dictionary for a little light reading? Well, I confess that I would. In fact, I have done. Often. (I can particularly recommend *A Dictionary of Austral English* by E. E. Morris – great fun and a delightful late night read.) If you think a dictionary is just for quickly consulting to check a spelling or settle an argument with the idiot at the next desk over the meaning of 'aggravate', you need to discover a different sort of dictionary – a dictionary designed for reading and browsing. Some words and expressions have stories to tell, and this *Dictionary of Australian Phrase and Fable* records (for the most part) a string of short stories in which the heroes are colourful words or phrases whose adventures have won them a place in Aussie English.

Now at this point I have to acknowledge that I'm just a journalist who delights in telling these stories, but I have stories to tell only because of the hard work done by a host of serious word researchers: Australia's real linguists, lexicographers and editors. Over the years I have met, or chatted to, or interviewed on my radio show, a string of serious academic wordies: Dr Bruce Moore (of the Australian National Dictionary Centre); his predecessor, Dr Bill Ramson; Professor Roly Sussex; Professor Pam Peters; Sue Butler (of the *Macquarie Dictionary*), and a host of others I would remember if my brain was younger and sharper. They have patiently answered my questions and explained the puzzles posed by the most colourful form of English on the planet – Aussie English.

The books they (and their colleagues) have written or edited have also been vitally important for a journalist digging around in our rich linguistic goldfield. For example, I have learned much about the spectrum of the Australian vocabulary, both from the series of books on regional Australian terms published by the *Australian National Dictionary* team and from writing my own book, Word Map, based on research done by the *Macquarie Dictionary*, in association with ABC Online. And of course I owe a massive debt to every dictionary ever published in Australia – from the first edition of the *Macquarie* onwards, including that great bicentenary volume, *The Australian National Dictionary*.

I also had the pleasure of being for some years a member of SCOSE – the ABC's Standing Committee on Spoken English. Those debates, discussions and conversations at SCOSE meetings have richly fed my understanding of our language at work. (The very first SCOSE meeting I ever attended, many years ago, was chaired by the legendary Arthur Delbridge, founder of the Macquarie Dictionary.)

I also have to acknowledge the contributions of thousands of listeners who have emailed or phoned with either questions or answers about the latest bits of flotsam and jetsam being carried along in the ever-changing flood of Australian slang. If you are one of these, you should go through this book with a highlighter in your hand marking your contributions. Then you can show them to all your friends saying, 'I told him that!' (And you did, too. Thank you.)

Introduction

'Reports of my death have been greatly exaggerated', Mark Twain is supposed to have said when his obituary was published somewhat prematurely. Something similar has happened to Aussie English: reports of its death have been greatly exaggerated. From time to time newspaper columns contain an obituary for our language, usually naming American television shows and the global youth culture as the chief suspects in the verbicide. However, such lamentations are premature, to say the least – Aussie English is alive and well and as fit as a Mallee bull.

While we Aussies are fascinated by words and language in general, it seems we are particularly fascinated by our own words – from the inventive coinages of earlier generations to the latest word play: everything from 'stone the crows' to 'budgie smugglers', and beyond.

And it's not just us.

Some time ago I had reason to greet a visiting American couple at the airport. When I met them for the first time, almost the first thing they said to me was, 'Go on … say it for us.' Say what? I thought to myself. And then the penny dropped, and I said, 'G'day'. 'He said it!' they squealed with delight. 'He said "G'day"!'

Americans are increasingly attracted to Aussie English and, far from them swamping us, there are signs that the reverse is happening (or, at the very least, that it's a two-way street). This trend quite possibly began when American commentators and television crews were here during the 2000 Sydney Olympics. We, of course, heard the Australian commentary, but apparently many

American commentators peppered their broadcasts with bits of Aussie English they had picked up (and been delighted by).

And some of these expressions then caught on and became embedded in American English. For instance, the latest edition of the *Merriam-Webster Dictionary* includes the Aussie word 'bludge'. They define the verb 'to bludge' as meaning 'to avoid responsibilities or hard work', adding: 'transitive verb, slang, chiefly Australia: to take advantage of: impose on'. One American dictionary for college students says that to bludge means 'to goof off'.

And it's not just the Yanks who appreciate our verbal inventiveness. When Philip Hensher was reviewing Tim Winton's novel *Breath* in the British weekly *The Spectator* he wrote: 'Australian English must be the most consistently inventive and creative arm of the language.' And then he added, 'I would rather be shipwrecked with a good dictionary of Australian slang than with any other reference work.'

And Michael Quinion, in his review of Gerry Wilkes's *A Dictionary of Australian Colloquialisms*, describes Aussie English as 'a colloquial language unlike any other'. This is because, he writes, Aussie English is influenced by 'the cant and slang of criminal transportees … the dialect of immigrants' home areas … contact with many Aboriginal languages … a characteristically sardonic sense of humour and an enviable ability to turn a phrase in a moment.'

So, then, Aussie English is as bright as a box of budgies – and is being seen as such around the world.

But why this book? Well, dictionaries of phrase and fable have been appearing since 1870. Such books are not dictionaries of definitions so much as of information: they focus on language, but (in most entries) they go beyond simply explaining the meaning to also telling the story behind the expression. A quick search of the World Wide Web shows well over a dozen dictionaries of phrase and fable, from various authors and various publishers, some general and some specialised. But none of these deal with that most vigorous and vivid branch of the English language: Aussie English.

This book aims to fill that gap.

Abdul

The nickname Aussie soldiers (see **Digger**) used for the Turkish soldiers they were fighting at Gallipoli in World War I. The equivalent of calling a German soldier 'Jerry' in World War II.

Aboriginal

The original inhabitants of Australia. The word is first recorded with this meaning from 1829. Aboriginal comes from the same Latin source word from which we get 'original'. Hence, the *Oxford English Dictionary* defines Aboriginal as the 'First or earliest so far as history or science gives record'. The Australian Government's *Style Manual* recommends using Aborigine as the noun and Aboriginal as the adjective. However, Stephen Murray-Smith finds this unnecessary, and suggests that the simplest thing to do is to use Aboriginal(s) as both the noun and the adjective, for both the singular and the plural. He asserts that this is strictly correct, as well as uncomplicated. His advice is probably sound. The word always takes a capital letter. (See also **Koori** and **Indigenous**.)

Aboriginalities

The title of a column appearing in the *Bulletin* magazine during the height of its influence as 'the Bushman's Bible'. The column consisted of contributions from readers (usually submitted under pseudonyms) containing tall tales, bush yarns and odd paragraphs about aspects of Australiana. It began in 1898 and a selection of items from the column was published as *Aboriginalities from The Bulletin* in 1913. (See also **Bulletin**.)

Above-ground pool

A domestic swimming pool that sits on the ground, rather than being dug into it. Usually constructed from a frame with a rubberised, waterproof lining. Popular because cheaper to install than an in-ground pool and, hey, Australia's a hot country.

Ack-willie

While there is slang common to English-speaking armies around the world, Aussie soldiers appear to have been especially verbally inventive. For instance, it's common to speak of soldiers who go A.W.L. or A.W.O.L. ('absent without leave') but only Aussies called doing so 'going ack-willie'. This comes from military signalling code – a set of phonetic elaborations for letters of the alphabet (referring to 'AM' as 'ack emma' and 'PM' as 'pip emma' – that sort of thing). Hence the quaint expression 'going ack-willie'. The earliest citation is from 1943.

A couple of lamingtons short of a CWA meeting

Not fully informed, a bit slow on the uptake (particularly at getting jokes) or a bit light-on in the intelligence department. This is one of scores of variations on 'not the full quid' – the variations providing Aussies with wide scope for linguistic invention. The CWA is the Country Women's Association.

Act, to bung on an

To spit the dummy, to turn on a tantrum. The implication is that there is a degree of pretence or overacting going on here.

Adelaide food

For some reason Adelaide seems to be the home of a number of idiosyncratic examples of Australian food terms. For instance, there is the pie floater – a hot meat pie upside-down on pea soup, with a generous dollop of tomato sauce. Then there's the savoury slice: a pastry slice with savoury mince filling, topped with cheese and bacon. If you have a sweet tooth you could try a frog cake – a small cake shaped like a frog with an open mouth and covered in icing (usually green, although pink and chocolate are also available), invented by Balfours bakery of Adelaide in 1922. Or, perhaps, a sinker – a solid fruit square with flaky pastry on the top and bottom, and topped with pink icing. Or, perhaps, a German cake – a yeast cake with a crumble topping, sometimes with fruit (either apple or apricot) under the crumble. All are among South Australia's great contributions to the dictionary of Australian gastronomy.

Adrian Quist

Drunk. Rhyming slang ('Adrian Quist' = 'pissed'). And no, it's not a made-up name: Adrian Quist (1913–91) was a champion Australian tennis player.

Advance Australia Fair

Peter Dodds McCormick was born in Glasgow in 1834. In 1855 he arrived, as a young immigrant, in Australia. And a little over twenty years after his arrival he composed the song that was to become our national anthem 'Advance Australia Fair'. The first public performance is thought to have been given in Sydney on

30 November (St Andrew's Day) in 1878 at the St Andrew's Day concert of the Highland Society. The song was later published by W. J. Paling and Company with the subtitle: 'Respectfully dedicated to the sons and daughters of Australia'. In 1974 'Advance Australia Fair' was chosen to be the Aussie national anthem (replacing 'God Save the Queen'). Most Aussies can remember the first verse, but here are two verses, so that you won't have to make silent goldfish mouthing actions should they ever play the second verse in your presence:

> Australians all let us rejoice,
> For we are young and free;
> We've golden soil and wealth for toil,
> Our home is girt by sea;
> Our land abounds in Nature's gifts
> Of beauty rich and rare;
> In history's page, let every stage
> Advance Australia fair!
> In joyful strains then let us sing,
> 'Advance Australia fair!'
>
> Beneath our radiant Southern Cross,
> We'll toil with hearts and hands;
> To make this Commonwealth of ours
> Renowned of all the lands;
> For those who've come across the seas
> We've boundless plains to share;
> With courage let us all combine
> To advance Australia fair.
> In joyful strains then let us sing
> 'Advance Australia fair!'

The first line originally read 'Australia's sons let us rejoice.' The above is the politically correct, and now official, version.

Peter Dodds McCormick was paid £100 for his composition by the Australian government in 1907. He died in Sydney in 1916. His claim to fame, perhaps, is that he has given us the only national anthem in the world containing the word 'girt'. (The *Aunty Jack* team of Grahame Bond and Rory O'Donoghue once composed a 'national anthem' for Wollongong which included the immortal line 'Girt by sea – on one side'.)

Akubra

The brand name of the iconic Aussie bush hat. The brand has been in use since 1912. The classic Akubra is made from rabbit fur. According to legend, a broad-brimmed Akubra can take up to 15 rabbit skins. Mind you, there is a saying in the bush: 'The broader the brim, the smaller the property'. (See also **Baggy Green** and **Slouch hat**.)

Alcheringa

See **Dreamtime**.

Amber fluid, the

An older slang term for beer. First recorded in 1906, perhaps less common now.

Ambo

A paramedic – Aussie abbreviation of 'ambulance officer'.

Ankle biters

In Aussie English small children (toddlers) have been known as ankle biters for some time now. It's in *The Australian National Dictionary* as a distinctively Aussie expression, first recorded in 1981. However, according to American language expert William Safire, ankle biter is also a bit of American Army slang – with an entirely different meaning. It appears that in the US Army ankle biters are 'people who criticize one's position but offer no constructive alternative'. While the Australian slang use is simply a reference to toddlers being close to the ground, the American term seems to suggest a small dog that keeps nipping at your heels and worrying you. The message is: be careful when describing your children as ankle biters to visiting Americans. They might be surprised to hear that your toddlers are 'critical of your position while offering no constructive alternative'. What was that you muttered? Something about 'two nations divided by a single language'?

Anythink

Quite commonly you will hear Australians turn a terminal 'g' into a 'k'. It happens most often at the end of the word 'thing'. Thus 'something' becomes 'somethink' and 'anything' becomes 'anythink'. Why does it happen? People who would never spell 'anything' with a 'k' insist on saying it with a 'k' – why? What is happening in their brains (or their mouths) to make them produce the sounds they do? The best guess I can offer is that this expresses a need for sharper, more definite endings to these words. The terminal 'g' tails away, while the terminal 'k' ends the word with a clear and definite clunk. (But that's still not a good excuse for doing it!)

Anzac

Did you realise that the word 'Anzac' is copyright? Originally, of course, it simply meant the 'Australian and New Zealand Army Corps'. But so deeply has this word entered into the consciousness of our nation that there are laws, passed way back in 1920, that control and protect its use. The Minister for Veterans' Affairs administers the protection of the word 'Anzac', and the minister's approval is needed for the use of the word in connection with any 'trade, business, calling or profession, any entertainment, lottery or art union, any building, private residence, boat or vehicle, or any charitable or other institution'. Even Anzac biscuits are protected by law. Well, not so much the biscuits as the name of the biscuits. And, by the way, 'Anzac' is no longer an acronym – it is now officially a word: that means the 'A' is upper-case and the rest of the letters should be lower-case.

Anzac biscuit

This is a biscuit made with rolled oats, golden syrup and coconut; one of Australia's national foods. During World War I the wives, girlfriends and mums of the Australian soldiers used to make these biscuits to ship over to their blokes. They were originally called Soldiers' Biscuits, but after the landing on Gallipoli, they were given their present name. And any entry on Anzac biscuits would be incomplete without a recipe, so here's one from the Australian War Memorial:

Ingredients
1 cup each of plain flour, sugar, rolled oats and coconut
4 oz butter
1 tablespoon golden syrup
2 tablespoons boiling water
1 teaspoon bicarbonate of soda
(add a little more water if mixture is too dry)

Method
1. Grease biscuit tray and pre-heat oven to 180°C.
2. Combine dry ingredients.
3. Melt together butter and golden syrup. Combine water and bicarbonate of soda, and add to butter mixture.
4. Mix butter mixture into dry ingredients.
5. Drop teaspoons of mixture onto tray, allowing room for spreading.
6. Bake for 10–15 minutes or until golden. Allow to cool on tray for a few minutes before transferring to cooling racks.

And why are there no eggs? Because apparently in the war, most poultry farmers had joined the army, so eggs were scarce. Golden syrup took the place of eggs as the binding agent in Anzac biscuits.

Anzac Day

Every year on 25 April Australia stops to celebrate Anzac Day. It marks the anniversary of the first major military action fought by Australian and New Zealand forces during World War I. The diggers landed at Gallipoli on 25 April 1915, meeting fierce resistance from the Turkish defenders. They were evacuated at the end of that year after eight months of stalemate, fierce fighting, and appalling losses. Over 8000 Australian soldiers were killed. The legend of Anzac was born on the beaches of Gallipoli. April 25th was officially named Anzac Day in 1916 as an occasion of national commemoration. Every year on this date commemorative services are held at dawn – the time of the original landing. Later in the morning, across the nation, Anzac Day marches are held in every major city and many smaller centres.

Archibald Prize

An annual prize for portraiture funded from a bequest by Jules François Archibald (1856–1919). It has been won over the years by some of Australia's leading painters. Often controversial, it attracts a great deal of publicity each year and gives the art of portraiture a high profile in Australia. The bequest requires that portraits submitted are 'preferentially of some man or woman distinguished in Arts, Letters, Science or Politics'. The Archibald's reputation for controversy and headlines was cemented in 1943 when William Dobell was awarded the prize for his portrait of Joshua Smith. Two unsuccessful competitors challenged the trustees' decision in the New South Wales Supreme Court, arguing that the painting was not a portrait but a caricature. The court, however, after hearing evidence from artists and critics, upheld the original judges' decision. J. F. Archibald's other notable bequest funded the Archibald Fountain (at the northern end of Sydney's Hyde Park. Archibald was for many years proprietor and editor of the *Bulletin*. (See **Bulletin**.)

Arcing up

1. Crying.
2. Launching a verbal attack.
3. Reacting angrily (perhaps parallel to the expression 'bridle up').

Possibly the expression comes from welders starting to weld steel, the cry 'Arcing up!' being a warning to look away.

Aristotle

Rhyming slang for 'bottle'. There was a time when you could go to your local bottle shop and order 'an Aristotle of the **amber fluid**, please, love'.

Artist

Not someone who's slapping paint on canvas, but a negative way of describing a person with an unattractive speciality. So an exaggerator full of tall tales is a 'bull artist'. The bloke who's full of rip-off schemes is a 'con artist'. A heavy drinker is a 'booze artist'. And so on.

Art union

An art union is something like a lottery, except that it is usually run to raise money for a charity, and the prize is usually not money but a house on the Gold Coast or a car, or both. But art union? It doesn't seem to have anything to do with any union, and art doesn't seem to come into it. Well, the story is this: art unions were formed in Britain and Europe in the 19th century as associations to promote art by purchasing paintings and other works of art and dispensing these things among their members by lottery. Over time in Australia and New Zealand (but only here) things changed. All kinds of prizes, not just paintings and other works of art, came to be offered, and consequently the name 'art union' came to be applied to any lottery with prizes in kind rather than cash.

Arvo

This means, of course, the afternoon – Aussies love to shorten words like this: 'this afternoon' becomes 'sarvo; 'Saturday afternoon' becomes Sat'dee arvo. Perhaps abbreviations such as this were born in the dust storms of the outback – the shorter you made your words, the less dust you swallowed!

As full as ...

When an Aussie is full of either food ('I couldn't eat another bite, love') or grog ('I think I've got me wobbly boots on') there are a number of ways of saying just how full:

as full as a goog (where 'goog' means egg – an item that is
    always completely full, packed to the shell)
as full as a state school
as full as a boot
as full as the fat lady's sock
as full as a stripper's dance card
as full as a stuffed pig
as full as the family dunny
as full as Santa's sack on Christmas eve
as full as the family album
as full as the last bus (or last tram)
as full as a public school's hat rack
as full as a cattle tick (picturing a cattle tick swollen with blood).

Ashes

Not a reference to bushfires, but to the trophy played for by England and Australia in Test cricket: an urn containing a cremated cricket stump, which is kept permanently in England. It's also the title of the continuing competition between the English and Australian national cricket teams. *The Australian National Dictionary* lays claim to this as an Aussie word, even though it's based on a mock obituary that first appeared in an English newspaper:

In Affectionate Remembrance of English Cricket, which died at the Oval on 29th August, 1882, Deeply lamented by a large circle of sorrowing friends and acquaintances. R.I.P.

N.B.—The body will be cremated and the ashes taken to Australia.

Sporting Times (London), 2 September 1882

Despite this, the *Australian National Dictionary* says of 'Ashes': 'Recorded earliest in Aust.' Well, who are we to argue? By the way, that 1882 contest was decided by the magnificent bowling of Frederick Spofforth (see **Demon Bowler**), who took 14 for 90 and carried Australia to a dramatic 7-run victory.

Aunty

Popular nickname for the ABC (the Australian Broadcasting Corporation).

Aunty arms

With many women, when they get to a certain age their upper arms (their triceps) get to be …. well … there's no other way to say this: flabby. These flabby upper arms in older women can be called 'aunty arms' (because everyone's aunty has got them); or 'nanas' (because your nana has probably got arms like this); or 'tuckshop lady arms' (because those nice ladies in the school tuckshop all have them); or 'bingo wings' (because when they leap up to shout 'Bingo!' this is the bit that flaps); or 'goodbye muscles' (because this is the bit that flaps around when they wave goodbye); or 'piano arms' (because when they're belting out a tune on the piano this is the bit that flaps around like mad) – or (and this is my favourite) they can be called 'reverse biceps' (because instead of standing up, as biceps normally do, they hang down). All of which is a salute to Aussie verbal inventiveness. And to how much we love our dear old aunties.

Aussie

The word Aussie was born in World War I. Australians have long been inventors of verbal diminutives (indeed, Professor Roly Sussex has collected several thousand distinctively Australian diminutives). And what we've done to other words, we've done to our nation's name as well. The earliest citation for the shortened word 'Aussie' in *The Australian National Dictionary* is from 1915, and refers to the country, not the person. There was even a magazine called *Aussie* – printed 'in the field' says the front cover, 'by the AIF' as the *Australian Soldiers' Magazine* from 1918. Then from 1920 a civilian (commercial) version appeared as *Aussie*: 'The Cheerful Monthly' (it survived until 1931). By then the word Aussie had been firmly cemented into our national life – and we've been Aussies ever since.

Aussie for food

There are a number of distinctively Aussie expressions for food. Most people will have heard of a 'brown sandwich' – that's a bottle of beer. But what about a 'seven-course meal' – that's a six-pack of beer and a meat pie. On the subject of which, there are all those delightful expressions for 'meat pie' in Aussie English – such as a 'rat coffin' or a 'maggot bag'. With the same display of exquisite good taste, Aussie English has nicknamed the vanilla slice either a 'snot block' or else a 'phlegm sandwich'. By the way, in both Perth and Brisbane sandwich shops you should order a 'round' of sandwiches (a 'round' being one sandwich), while in Tasmania that same sandwich would be called a 'four-pointer'. And Aussie English has a nice description of someone who is a little too fond of their 'tucker', or food: a fatty is called a 'salad dodger'.

Aussie philosophy

Said to be summed up by pioneering bush balladist Adam Lindsay Gordon (1833–1870) in his famous lines:

Life is mostly froth and bubble,
Two things stand like stone:
Kindness in another's trouble,
Courage in your own.

These words are engraved at the foot of the statue of Gordon that stands in central Melbourne. Sadly, on 24 June 1870, the day after the publication of his book *Bush Ballads and Galloping Rhymes*, Gordon committed suicide on Brighton Beach, Melbourne.

Monty Python, however, had a different view of Aussie philosophy in their famous sketch in which every member of the Philosophy Department at the (non-existent) University of Woolloomooloo is called 'Bruce'. The sketch ends with a rousing rendition of the 'Philosophers Song' (including the line 'I drink therefore I am').

Aussie Rules

Shortened form of 'Australian Rules' – the code of football invented in Australia (in Victoria, to be precise, in the mid-19th century). Nowadays most often referred to as AFL, from the initials of the Australian Football League. The formal and official name of the game is Australian National Football.

Australaise, The

In 1910 the **Bulletin** ran a national song competition. The only entry that survives is the song by C. J. Dennis (1876–1938) entitled 'The Australaise'. The name was based on France's 'La Marseillaise', and it was intended to be sung to the tune of 'Onward Christian Soldiers'. It appeared in the *Bulletin* on 12 November 1908, and then in Dennis's first book *Backblock Ballads and Later Verses* in 1913. He later slightly revised it for use by **diggers** in World War I:

Fellers of Australier,
Blokes an' coves an' coots,

Shift yer — carcases,
Move yer — boots.
Gird yer — loins up,
Get yer — gun,
Set the — enermy
An' watch the blighters run.

CHORUS:
Get a — move on,
Have some — sense.
Learn the — art of
Self de- — -fence.

And so on for another six verses! He called it 'a marching song' and if you sang all the verses and choruses you would have covered a lot of territory before you ran out of words. And, as a footnote to the World War I version had it, 'Where a dash (—) replaces a missing word, the adjective "blessed" may be interpolated. In cases demanding great emphasis, the use of the word "blooming" is permissible. However, any other word may be used that suggests itself as suitable.'

Australasia

When I was a schoolboy I was taught that the word Australasia meant 'Australia and New Zealand'. Now I discover that the word is far more complex (and uncertain!) than that. It was first coined by a French geographer Charles de Brosses in 1756. In carving up the globe he labelled the bit where Australia stands as 'southern Asia' – Australasia ('austral' being Latin for 'south'). So he made us part of Asia long before Paul Keating did. Since de Brosses's time the word 'Australasia' has been re-imagined (if you like) as if it were a combination of 'Australia and Polynesia' (that's to say, our bit plus the nearby Pacific islands), while botanists use Australasia to mean 'Australia, New Zealand and Papua New Guinea'. But how did my school teacher get just 'Australia and New Zealand' out of Australasia?

A clue can be found in a pioneering book on Australian English called *A Dictionary of Austral English* by Edward E. Morris. It was published in 1898 when Morris was professor of English, French and German Languages and Literature at the University of Melbourne. The book's title again uses 'Austral' to mean 'southern' because Professor Morris covers both Australian and New Zealand words in his book. The 'running head' (as printers call it) at the top of each page identifies the book with just two words: 'Australasian Dictionary'. And the full title on the original title page (in typical Victorian fashion) reads: 'Austral English, A Dictionary of Australasian Words, Phrases and Usages'. So the idea that Australasia means 'Australia and New Zealand' lumped together is an old one. But that doesn't make it any more logical!

Australia

Australia wasn't always Australia. At first the continent had two names: New Holland for the western side (discovered by the Dutch in the 17th century) and New South Wales for the eastern side (discovered by Captain Cook in 1770). Matthew Flinders circumnavigated the place in 1803 and discovered that western and eastern bits met in the middle and, hence, the place deserved a single name. He suggested Australia – apparently his own adaption of the expression *Terra Australis Incognita* ('unknown south land') that had been marked on old maps (rather than just leaving the bottom half of the map blank). In 1817 Governor Lachlan Macquarie promoted Matthew Flinders' idea, and by the late 1820s it had caught on, and the place became generally known as Australia.

Australia Day

On 26 January 1788 the First Fleet landed at Sydney Cove and proclaimed the place a British colony. From 1818 the date was celebrated annually as Anniversary Day. Later the name was changed to Foundation Day, and (following Federation in 1901) to Australia Day. Some Aboriginal leaders refer to this date as 'Invasion Day' and say that a more appropriate date for a national celebration should be found. (See also **First Fleet**.)

Aurora Australis

The illumination in the night sky generated around the southern magnetic pole. The name means 'southern lights' and it is the southern hemisphere equivalent of the aurora borealis or 'northern lights'. The expression has occasionally been borrowed: for example, the first Sydney–Melbourne single-gauge express train was called the 'Southern Aurora'.

'Ave a go, ya mug!

This is what you shout at your favourite sports team (or one particular player on that team) when they're not doing as well as you reckon they should. This is what, in Aussie English, counts as encouragement. It probably began life in England in such expressions as 'Well played, that man!' – ''ave a go ya mug' being the Australian translation of all such expressions. If you're a fan shouting this at your favourite club team (or at an Aussie national team) that makes you a dinky di supporter (see **Dinky di**). But if you're a parent shouting this at your son's under-sevens team, that makes you a dill (see **Dill**).

Away

Where people who are not born in Broken Hill come from. Also used in the same way on King Island. You're either from 'here' or from 'away'.

Babbler

Drovers' rhyming slang for a cook ('babbling brook'). (See also **Poisoner**.)

Backblock

A rural property in remote and sparsely populated country. C. J. Dennis called his first book of verse *Backblock Ballads and Later Verses*.

Back o' Bourke

Way, way out in the outback, beyond even the back of beyond. Bourke is a town on the banks of the Darling River, more than 700 kilometres by road north-west of Sydney on the Mitchell Highway. It's often called 'The Gateway to the Real Outback'.

Backpacker

An elderly person occupying a room in an aged care hostel on a respite-care basis.

Backyard

The *Macquarie Dictionary* says: 'an area, often of some size, with gardens and lawn, at the back of a building, usually a house'. In fact, this is the important bit of any suburban house: it's where Mum gardens and hangs the clothes out to dry on the **Hills hoist**; where Dad mows the lawn and burns everything to a crisp on the **barbie**; and where the kids learn to play cricket. Before sewerage was laid on, backyards included a **dunny** down the back, and up until the 1950s many (perhaps most) backyards included a chook yard.

Badger box

If you had a holiday cottage or shack would you call it a badger box? Probably not. This is historical Australian slang that has now disappeared into the mists of time. It comes from the 19th century, and even then it was a distinctive piece of Tasmanian slang, not found widely across the rest of Australia. A badger box was a shack or poorly built house. The term was used by workers (called 'piners') felling Huon pine trees on the west coast of Tasmania in the 19th century for the small, temporary huts they built. Conditions in these huts were poor – they were prone to flooding and constantly leaking due to the metres of annual rainfall in the area. The name came from the fact that in Tasmania, and only in Tasmania, wombats were once called 'badgers'. Hence the number of Tasmanian place names that include the word 'badger' – and hence this nickname for a shack not fit for human habitation: badger box.

Bag of death

A cask of cheap wine, usually red.

Bag of doughnuts, a

A fat person.

Bags

Bags is recorded in June Factor's wonderful book *Kidspeak*, where it's said to mean 'to reserve an object or position' – as in 'I bags the back of the bus'. June Factor says this can be strengthened by saying 'double bags' or 'triple bags'. She also notes it can be used negatively, as in 'bags I don't' or 'bags not me'. What none of these explain is where the expression comes from. However, it probably arises from the idea that something is mine because 'it's in my bag'. In effect, when I claim something, I as good as bag it – I bags it.

Bags, rough as

Uncouth; of unpleasing outward appearance; lacking in refinement; not entirely civilised. A bit of slang from the Anzac diggers of World War I. Probably from the rough texture of hessian bags.

Baggy Green, the

The caps worn by cricketers chosen to represent Australia at the level of Test cricket. The tradition is reported to go back to 1877, and to the first Australian test cricketer to score a century: Charles Bannerman (1851–1930), who played three tests for Australia between 1877 and 1879. (See also **Akubra** and **Slouch hat**.)

Bagman's Gazette

A mythical newspaper that was (supposedly) published for the benefit of swagmen (see **Swaggie**); a mythical source of rumours in the bush: 'Gotta be true, mate – I read it in the *Bagman's Gazette*.'

Bailed up

Bailed up is used in Australia to mean being held up. People say, 'He bailed me up in the corridor to talk about today's meeting.' In Britain, folk would be more likely to say 'He button-holed me ...' Here in Australia, bailed up meaning 'trapped' or 'cornered' was originally used to describe the 'stand and deliver' tactics of Ben Hall, Ned Kelly and their professional colleagues – 19th-century Australian bushrangers. Before that, bailed up was used to describe a confined animal, a bail being a wooden bar or frame that held an animal in a stall. Dairy farmers still talk about putting a cow into a 'milking bail'. Used in this sense, the word 'bail' comes from the same source as the bails in cricket – apparently from an Old French word meaning 'a horizontal piece of wood fixed upon two stakes'.

Bald Archies

Annual parody of the **Archibald Prize** for portraiture, featuring satirical caricatures of people in the news.

Ball of muscle, a

Full of dynamic energy; physically fit; can be applied to a person, or to a horse or other animal.

Banana

One strongly opposed to development of any kind. From 'Build Absolutely Nothing Anywhere Near Anybody'. An extreme case of the 'Nimby' ('Not in My Backyard').

Banana bender

Someone from Queensland.

Bandicoot

A marsupial mammal. Most bandicoots weigh less than 1 kilogram. Their coarse fur is chiefly brown or grey, and they have a long, narrow head and sharp teeth. However, while the animal is a native, the word is not. The name comes from India, being a corruption of a Telegu word *pandi-kokku*, translating loosely to 'pig-rat', which is applied on the sub-continent to a large rat. The Indian animal is very different from the Australian one, so how the transfer of the Anglo-Indian name occurred is a bit of a puzzle. There must, I guess, be some resemblance, even though the Indian version is a large, destructive rat, and the Aussie animal is an insect-eating marsupial. (In case you've forgotten, a marsupial is an animal with a pouch for carrying the young.)

However it happened, once bandicoot had arrived it became widely used as part of the Aussie vernacular in a number of expressions: 'as bald as a bandicoot' means remarkably bald; 'as bandy as a bandicoot' means, as you might expect, remarkably bandy-legged; 'like a bandicoot on a burnt ridge' means all alone; lonely and forlorn; 'as miserable (or as poor) as a bandicoot' means excessively miserable (or poor); 'as barmy as a bandicoot' means mad; loony; completely insane; subclinically neurotic.

You get the feeling that Aussie English rather likes the sound of the word, don't you?

Banjo, a

A nickname for a frying pan, a shovel or a shoulder of mutton (from the shape of the things so named).

Banjo

The pen name used by A. B. Paterson (1864–1941), who wrote 'Waltzing Matilda', 'The Man from Snowy River' and heaps of other bush ballads:

And where around the Overflow the reed-beds sweep and
sway
To the breezes and the rolling plains are wide,
The man from Snowy River is a household word today,
And the stockmen tell the story of his ride.

Paterson was a top horseman, and he took the penname 'Banjo'
from the name of one his favourite horses.

Banksia

An Australian shrub named after Sir Joseph Banks, the botanist
on board Captain Cook's ship the *Endeavour*. The open seed pods
have a prickly appearance, and these entered the nightmares of
Aussie kids when artist and writer May Gibbs used them in her
children's classic *Snugglepot and Cuddlepie*. The Big Bad Banksia
Men are villains, the cruel enemies of the cute little gumnut babies.

Barbecue stopper

The fourth edition of the *Macquarie Dictionary* includes the
expression 'barbecue stopper' with the definition: 'a topic of
conversation or issue for discussion which is of general concern,
especially one of political significance'. And the dictionary says
that 'barbecue stopper' was coined by Prime Minister John Howard
in 2002. Well, either by him or one of his staff, but certainly the first
recorded usage is by John Howard when Prime Minister.

Barbie

The Aussie abbreviation for 'barbecue'.

Barbie, a snag short of a

A way of saying that someone is 'not all there', that 'the lights are
on but nobody's home': 'He's a sausage short of a barbecue – a
snag short of a barbie.'

Barcoo rot

Sick; unwell; come down with a mysterious illness; if you have the barcoo rot for long enough you get the 'barcoo spews'!

Bare-bellied joe

This expression turns up in the old Australian folk song 'Click Go the Shears', where it has, undoubtedly, puzzled many:

> The ringer looks around and is beaten by a blow
> And curses the old snagger with the bare-bellied joe.

A 'bare-belly' was a sheep with a defective wool growth caused by a break in the fibre structure. This causes the wool to fall off the belly and legs. So a sheep that has lost its belly wool was called a 'bare-bellied yoe'. And that last bit (the 'yoe') is supposed to be from the Irish pronunciation of 'ewe'. Because that was such an unfamiliar word, as the folk song was transmitted orally, the word 'yoe' was changed into the more familiar 'joe' and so the last line of the chorus referred to a 'bare-bellied joe'. This type of sheep was also, sometimes, called a 'blue-bellied joe'. In the song, the point is that the **ringer** (the fastest shearer in the shed) is annoyed that an old-timer gets a bare-bellied (or blue-bellied) sheep that (obviously) has less wool and (hence) is quicker to shear, and (thus) the old bloke beats the ringer's tally for the day (the 'tally' being the number of sheep shorn).

Bark hut

A simple hut with walls and roof made from sheets of bark. Often the first dwelling on a Selection (see **Selection/selector**).

Barker's eggs

Dog poo on the footpath. (Careful where you put your foot! Don't step in it!)

Barmaid's blush

A drink of rum and raspberry cordial. Remarkably, this seems to have once been a popular drink with old-time bushmen.

Barrack

According to *The Dictionary of Cricket* 'to barrack' means 'to shout sarcastic or abusive comments about the performance of a team or player'. But this word appears to be an 'auto-antonym' – that is, it can also have the opposite meaning of shouting support or encouragement. There are a couple of suggestions as to the source. One is that it comes from an Aboriginal word *borak*, meaning 'to poke fun at'. However, *The Australian National Dictionary* disputes this idea and suggests that 'barrack' is more likely to come from an English dialect word that originally meant 'to brag or boast'. Is it possible that both are true? Could it be that barracking for a team (shouting encouragement) comes from the old dialect word for bragging, while barracking in the sense of 'shouting abuse and ridicule' comes from *borak*? It is, I suppose, possible – and it would explain the two opposite meanings of barracking.

Oh, and there's an urban myth that needs to be disposed of here. I heard a cricket commentator on ABC radio repeat the old story that 'barrack' comes from the proximity of Melbourne's Victoria Barracks to playing fields, and the cheering and jeering soldiers were called 'barrackers', from which the verb 'to barrack' developed. This is almost certainly untrue. If this story were correct then the term 'barrackers' would have to be recorded before the verb 'to barrack' – and it's not. 'Barrackers' is first recorded in 1889 and the verb in 1878. And the tale about the nearness of the Victoria Barracks being the source does not appear until 1944 – so it's almost certainly yet another urban myth; a bit of folk etymology.

Barramundi

An Aboriginal name given to a number of different fish caught in rivers and coastal waters.

Barrier rise

The start of a horse race. Today, races begin with the horses in starting boxes, but before the 1960s the horses stood behind a wire barrier that was raised on a spring mechanism to start the race. And the word 'barrier' has long survived the change. Race callers still talk about horses 'walking up to the barrier' and the expression 'barrier rise' was still appearing in newspaper reports of race meetings in the first decade of the 21st century, some 50 years after the old wire barrier had disappeared from race tracks.

Barrier to box, from

An expression used by race callers to describe a horse that has led from the start to the finish of the race: from barrier to box. The 'barrier' here is the starting line (referring to the old wire barrier starting mechanism in place before the 1960s), while the 'box' is the trainer's horse box, to which the horse will return at the end of the day's racing. It's been suggested the expression was coined by legendary race caller Ken Howard in the 1950s. (See also London to a brick on.)

Barry

A real shocker (rhyming slang, from the Australian singer Barry Crocker).

Barwell's bull

A type of rail car introduced on South Australian country lines in the 1920s. From the name of the premier at the time, Hon. Sir Henry Barwell, KCMG (premier of South Australia 1920–24), and the horn of these railcars, described as being 'a loud and not very melodious bellow'. (One is preserved and still operates on the Pichi Richi Railway.) The last of these 75 class railcars was retired in 1971.

Bastard

Of illegitimate birth. A very old English word (recorded from the 13th century) employed in extremely flexible ways in Australia. It is an expression of friendship to greet a mate by saying, 'G'day, you old bastard!' But if you describe your boss as 'a real bastard' you are not speaking of him in a kindly manner. So it's important to distinguish between friendly and unfriendly bastards. Then there are those for whom the word indicates their level of suffering ('the poor old bastard') or their level of incompetence ('a useless bastard'). Care should be exercised in the employment of such a subtle and flexible word when speaking Aussie English.

Batavia, the wreck of the

One of Australia's most famous shipwrecks. In 1629 the *Batavia* was one of a fleet of 11 vessels sailing to the Dutch East Indies (now Indonesia). A storm in the Indian Ocean separated the Batavia from the rest of the fleet. The Batavia ran aground on Morning Reef, off the coast of Geraldton, Western Australia, before dawn on 4 June 1629, shaking the 316 people on board from their bunks. Most of the passengers and crew survived the original shipwreck – but worse was to come, as the crew had been close to mutiny before the storm struck. The merchant in charge of the expedition and the ship's skipper set sail in small boats, with a few crew members, to the mainland in an attempt to find water, fresh water being scarce on the rocky islands where the survivors were camped out. They failed to find water on the barren Western Australian coast, so they sailed north to Batavia (modern Jakarta) to report the shipwreck, and then returned with a large rescue vessel. Meanwhile, on the survivor's island, a violent mutiny erupted with the mutineers eventually killing 125 men, women and children. When the rescue ship arrived, the mutineers were overwhelmed, and they were later tried and executed. The story has been retold often: in novels by Ernest Favenc (*Marooned on Australia*, 1905) and Henrietta Drake-Brockman (*The Wicked and the Fair*, 1957); in Douglas Stewart's play *Shipwreck* (1947); and in numerous non-fiction books.

Bathing box

A small privately owned structure erected on a beach, particularly those of Port Phillip, to provide shelter for those enjoying beach activities. Those that still survive are now regarded as a valuable asset.

Battered sav

The battered sav was one of the savoury delights of my childhood, which I now realise must have been almost pure cholesterol on a stick. It consisted of a cooked, seasoned sausage with a red skin, called a saveloy, fried in centimetre-thick greasy batter and sold on a stick after being dipped in tomato sauce. You could always buy them at the Royal Easter Show, and I loved them. (How could you not love anything that unhealthy?) They went by at least three other names: 'dagwood dogs' or 'pluto pups' or (chiefly in South Australia) 'dippy dogs'.

Battler

The word 'battler' has an entirely positive meaning these days, especially in the phrase 'little Aussie battler'. But battler once had several negative meanings. For instance, up to the 1950s 'battler' was a nickname for a prostitute – as in someone who has to 'battle' for a living. Earlier, 'battler' was used to describe an unemployed person. And in 1914 Banjo Paterson wrote: 'A battler is a turf hanger-on who has not enough capital to be a backer, not personal magnetism enough to be a whisperer and not sense enough to get work.' But the positive meaning of 'battler' (someone who's always prepared to have a go, regardless of the odds) seemed to develop at the same time as the negative ones. Now the negative has been forgotten and 'battler' has turned into a class term – a polite way for media commentators to say 'lower-class'.

Beg pardon

The Australian National Dictionary thinks this is an informal form of apology, but I've only ever heard it as an indication of having missed a remark: 'Beg pardon?' means 'What was that? I didn't quite catch what you said.'

Behind

A near miss in Aussie Rules that still scores one point (the kick has missed the goal but crossed the behind line).

Bellbird

A native Australian bird, the *Manorina melanophrys*. It has a distinctively musical and ringing call, and was immortalised by Henry Kendall (1839–82) in his poem 'Bell-Birds':

And, softer than slumber, and sweeter than singing,
The notes of the bell-birds are running and ringing.

Berrimah line

An imaginary line separating Darwin from the rest of the Northern Territory. From Berrimah, a suburb on the southern edge of Darwin, on the Stuart Highway (supposedly the limit of Territorian politicians' interests).

Berrima's headless ghost

Lucretia Dunkley was hanged at Berrima Jail, in the southern highlands of NSW, on 22 October 1843. She'd been found guilty of the murder of a wealthy farmer and of stealing 500 gold sovereigns from his corpse. After the hanging the head was removed from the corpse for scientific examination. For decades afterwards eyewitnesses claimed to have seen her headless spectre, late at night, roaming through the pine trees in front of the jail. However, when the pine trees were cut down the apparition ceased its appearances.

Berko

Berserk; really, really, really, really angry.

Berley

Fish bait that you scatter in the water, or hang over the side of the boat in a bag, to attract fish before you start fishing.

Bernborough

A Queensland racehorse (1939–60) who dominated many racing events in the 1941–46 period and was famous for making a late run from the back of the field to finish first. Hence in any sporting event when someone makes a late run from behind and wins they can be said to have made 'a Bernborough finish'.

Bewdy

Excellent; really good; a way of saying 'I approve' – it's how Aussies like to say 'beauty' when they're giving you the thumbs up.

Bible basher

'Bible basher' is an expression coined in Australia to label anyone who spouts religion – specifically someone who's a Christian and who won't keep quiet about their Christianity. It's first recorded in the *Bulletin* in 1904 in a reference to the 'rich store of opprobrious appellations from irreverent Australians'. Once invented, 'Bible basher' never quite disappeared as an Aussie expression. Gough Whitlam, in a fit of petulance, used the expression of Sir Joh Bjelke Peterson. And it turns up in Xavier Herbert's epic novel *Poor Fellow My Country*. It was, obviously, intended as a slight, an insult, but (as so often happens) has been cheerfully taken up as a badge, with the result that it's now employed by Christians of themselves – especially on university campuses. (Christian students invite their sceptical friends to a conversation over coffee where they can 'bash a Bible basher'.)

Big ask

A big ask is 'an expectation which it would be extremely difficult to meet' (*Macquarie Dictionary*). Kate Burridge says that 'ask' is one of those verbs Aussie English has turned into a noun. And 'big' is a much-used adjective in Australia: we speak of the big boss, the big wet, Jack Lang was 'the Big Fella', Malcolm Fraser was 'Big Mal' – and so on. When US presidential candidate John Kerry used the expression in a speech ('I'm asking you to trust our nation, our history, the world, your families, in my hands. I understand that it's a big ask.') he provoked a linguistic furore. American wordies clucked their tongues and suggested this was a regrettable usage. Perhaps John Kerry had an Aussie speech writer!

Big bickies

A lot of money.

Big Brother

In Australia, neither George Orwell's spying government nor a reality TV show, but the name of an organisation that fostered young migrants (the Big Brother Movement).

Big ditch, the

The old-time riverboat men's name for the Murray River.

Big note yourself

To boast (as in 'Just listen to that bloke big noting himself!'). (See also **Blow** and **Skite**.)

Big smoke

A town or city – an expression of Aboriginal coinage, first recorded in 1848.

Bikie

A leather-jacketed member of a motorbike gang. Some are harmless old duffers who now wear their greying hair in ponytails. Others are the ground soldiers of organised crime. Depending on which type you run into, if you annoy a bikie he'll either knife you or spit his dentures at you.

Bill Lawry

A bottle opener. Bill Lawry was one of the best opening batsmen Aussie cricket ever had – he was an 'opener', you see!

Billabong

A waterhole in an anabranch (a branch of a river which leaves the main stream and enters it again further on), replenished only in flood time – first recorded in English in 1836. There are a number of linguistic myths surrounding 'billabong'. One is that the last syllable (bong) comes from the Yagara word 'bung', meaning 'dead'. According to this theory, billabong either comes from an expression meaning 'dead river' (where 'billa' means 'river' and bong 'dead') or from an empty or polluted waterhole that leaves the disappointed traveller with a 'dead' (meaning 'empty') billy can, or billy – hence 'billabong'. The truth seems be that 'billabong' comes from a Wiradjuri word that originally meant 'a watercourse that runs only after rain'.

Billy

The *Macquarie ABC Dictionary* defines a billy as 'a cylindrical container for liquids, sometimes enamelled, usually having a close-fitting lid' or 'any container (even a make-shift one) for boiling water and making tea'. The word is first recorded in this sense from the 1840s in Australia, although there is a suggestion that it might have been used with this meaning in the 1830s in New Zealand. Sue Butler explains that there are several different stories that claim to explain the origin of the term 'billy'. One claim is that it comes from the French expression *boeuf bouilli,* making *bouilli* tin (with *bouilli* anglicised as billy) the tin in which the beef was boiled. Another theory is that it comes from the Aboriginal word billabong, 'billa' being the word for water. A third theory is that it comes from the contraction of the name William – the notion being that itinerant bush workers gave affectionate personal names to their cooking utensils. However, none of those (very common) theories is the truth. It seems most likely, says Butler, that 'billy' is a variation on the Scottish dialect word 'bally', which appears in the term 'bally-cog' meaning 'milk pail'. And given the number of Scottish settlers in New Zealand, that, I suppose, must increase the likelihood that the word 'billy' first appeared in New Zealand. In the old days, of course, every Aussie swaggie used to carry one:

> With a swag all on my shoulder,
> Black billy in my hand,
> I'll travel the bush of Australia,
> Like a true-born native man.

Billy Barlow

A fictional character whose misadventures are recounted in a number of early bush ballads, including 'Billy Barlow in Australia', 'Billy Barlow's Wedding' and 'The Death of Billy Barlow'. He was usually portrayed as a gullible migrant who suffered every conceivable misfortune that might strike a new settler. The words were composed to fit existing English or Irish folk tunes:

> O! When I was born, says old Mother Goose,
> He is a fine boy, but he'll be of no use;
> My father he said that to church I should go,
> And there they christened me Billy Barlow.

Billy cart

A small, home-made cart used as a downhill racer (propelled by gravity, and stopped, as a rule, by crashing into the nearest large object). At one time the standard billy cart consisted of a fruit box on old pram wheels (although ball-bearings made a better noise and were, possibly, faster). The name billy cart (sometimes as one word, billycart) was coined to describe a small hard-cart drawn by a goat (a 'billy' you see). This name was then transferred to home-made downhill racing carts.

Bindi-eye

Sharp prickles that grow in the grass and stick in your feet. The name comes from a word found in the Kamilaroi and Yuwaalaraay Aboriginal languages: *bindayaa*.

Binjour bear

A legendary creature living in the Binjour Plateau area in Queensland. It might be a type of yowie, or possibly an ape or bear escaped from a circus. Or, perhaps, a mutant bunyip? The possibilities are endless.

Bishop of Botany Bay, the

A jocular title given by William Wilberforce (the legendary opponent of slavery) to Rev. Richard Johnson (1755–1827) the colonial chaplain who arrived on the First Fleet and conducted the first Christian worship in Australia on Sunday, 3 February 1788. It was the influence of prominent London evangelicals Wilberforce and John Newton that saw Johnson appointed as chaplain to the convicts (and their military guards).

Bishop's Palace ghost, the

The first man appointed as Anglican bishop of North West Australia was Gerard Trower. Holding the post from 1910–27, he lived in a modest bungalow in Broome jokingly known as 'the Bishop's Palace.' One still, moonlit night Bishop Trower awoke to find a ghostly figure walking through the French windows into his bedroom. Dressed in the robes of a Jewish rabbi, the figure lingered for a moment and then vanished. From the description, locals identified the spectre as the ghost of a Jewish pearl buyer named Davis who died in 1912 when his ship, the *Koombana*, sank in a storm. Davis had previously lived in the bungalow occupied by the bishop, and locals believed his ghost had returned to search for pearls he had hidden in the house.

Blackbird

A Pacific Islander brought to Australia as a labourer, especially in the Queensland sugarcane fields. The traders who kidnapped and transported them were called blackbirders. Some 57 000 Pacific Islanders were brought to Queensland and northern New South Wales between 1863 and 1904, when the practice was finally stamped out by the federal government.

Black Bobs

This is a slightly mysterious Tasmanian expression and, according to one report, Black Bobs originally referred to 'rather seriously inbred descendants of runaway convicts who lived a secluded life in isolated areas'. There is certainly a small town called Black Bobs in Tasmania, but there's very little evidence for the extended use of the expression. Clearly it was never meant to be a compliment, and its use may have died out. But just exactly how this expression arose in the first place, and what insult it was intended to convey, remains unclear.

Black Horse of Sutton, the

A riderless ghost horse said to haunt the Monaro district of New South Wales. According to legend, the spectre appears when bad news or danger is on the way. It is said to have appeared twice to the same woman in the district, the first time just before she heard that her eldest son had died in the Boer War, and the second time just before the news arrived that her youngest son had died in an accident.

Black Saturday

Saturday 7 February 2009, when bushfires raged across Victoria, taking 173 lives and destroying thousands of homes – the worst natural disaster in Australia's history.

Black snake it, to

To go to bed in your work clothes, without the benefit of a bath or shower. (See **King cobra**, which is one step worse.)

Black snow

The burnt trash from sugar cane fires drifting through the air (and settling on the washing you've just hung out to dry).

Black stump

Somewhere over the horizon is the charcoal-black remnant of a long-dead, burned-out tree. This is the black stump. It's a boundary marker, said by the *Oxford English Dictionary* to mark the last outpost of civilisation. But more importantly, in Aussie English, the black stump is the marker against which everything is measured. When you want to describe something, you can label it as the biggest, the best, the smallest, the worst, the silliest, the meanest, or the ugliest 'this side of the black stump'. (And, of course, what's on the other side of the black stump doesn't matter – it's so far away – and, anyway, all that lies beyond the black stump is an infinity of sand hills.)

> Out beyond the Black Stump,
> The dust goes whistling by,
> And the crows out there fly backwards,
> To keep the dust out of their eyes.

The expression 'the black stump' was first recorded in an article in the *Bulletin* in 1900.

Bligh under the bed

British navel officer William Bligh (1754–1817) had an unfortunate career. In 1789, when he was captain of H.M.S. *Bounty*, his crew mutinied against him, under the leadership of Fletcher Christian. Then in 1808, when he was governor of the Colony of New South Wales, he was the target of the **Rum Rebellion**, led by John Macarthur. The story quickly spread that when the soldiers from the rebellious New South Wales Corps came looking for Bligh they found him in a back room of Government House, hiding under a bed. A widely circulated print showed Bligh being dragged out from under the bed by an armed soldier, with two other soldiers looking on. Bligh vigorous denied the story, insisting that he was in the back room destroying official papers he didn't want the rebels to get their hands on.

Blind Freddy

The Australian National Dictionary says that Blind Freddy is 'a most unperceptive person'. Gerry Wilkes says that Blind Freddy is 'an imaginary figure representing the highest degree of disability or incompetence, and so used as a standard of comparison', as in the expression of disgust 'Blind Freddy could see it!' The earliest citation is from Dal Stivens's 1944 collection of short stories *The Courtship of Uncle Henry*: 'He doesn't want to go on with tonight. Blind Freddy could see that.' The great Sid Baker suggested the expression might derive from a blind hawker well known in Sydney in the 1920s. However, I want to suggest that the title Blind Freddy existed for some time before it was applied to any hawker in the 1920s.

I believe the original Blind Freddy was an English baronet by the name of Sir Frederick Pottinger. He was the man put in charge of catching the 'noblest bushranger of them all', Ben Hall. As a new chum who knew nothing of the bush Pottinger regularly failed in his attempts to trap Ben Hall and his gang – and Ben Hall's organising ability and knowledge of the bush meant that he ran rings around the Englishman. The sheer incompetence and clumsiness of Sir Frederick, I suggest, made him the original Blind Freddy. I propose that the expression remained part of the oral culture over the succeeding decades (occasionally being applied to particular persons – including a blind hawker in Sydney in the 1920s) until Dal Stivens finally captured it in print in 1944.

Blinky Bill

Much loved character in a series of children's books written and illustrated by Dorothy Wall (1894–1942). The first book featuring the adventures of the dungaree-wearing larrikin little koala was published in 1933.

Bloke

An Aussie male. No one knows for sure the origin of 'bloke', but the best guess is that it comes from the language of gipsies and tinkers. Presumably it was brought to Australia by convicts. Its earliest recorded usage here is from 1841, from Van Diemen's Land, where it referred to the man in charge, the proprietor or boss. And if you wanted to be treated decently and fairly then you had to find a boss (or bloke) to work for who was a 'good bloke'. As a result, qualities of fairness and decency came to be attached to this word 'bloke' as it became a generalised term in Aussie English for an adult male. The word has developed again in more recent times, to be associated with what is called 'blokeyness' – for instance, in the hearty, noisy behaviour of football players or fans. But the word 'bloke' retains its association with good intentions, good heartedness and decency.

Bloody

This is a general, all-purpose swear word that is certainly not limited to Australia – nevertheless, Aussies have (somehow) claimed it as their own. There was a time when bloody was labelled 'the Great Australian Adjective'. Where does its use as a swear word come from? Well, it's not certain, but it seems to have started as a reference to the 'bloods' or aristocratic rowdies of the 17th and 18th centuries. The phrase 'bloody drunk' originally meant 'as drunk as a blood' (that is 'as drunk as a lord'). From this it was extended, first to related expressions, and then more broadly. Its (apparent) associations with bloodshed and murder may have recommended it to the rough classes as a word that appealed to their imagination. At the time (the 17th century) there was something of a craving for impressive or graphic intensifiers such as jolly, awfully, terribly, devilish, deuced, damned, ripping, rattling, thumping, stunning, thundering, and so on. There's no ground for the notion that 'bloody', offensive as it now is to polite ears, contains any profane allusion or has any connection with the old oath 'God's blood!'

The distinctive use of 'bloody' in Aussie English has been captured by John O'Grady in his verse 'The Integrated Adjective'. He demonstrates the conversational employment of the adjective in such lines as:

> And the other bloke said, 'Seen 'im. Owed 'im 'alf a bloody
> quid.

Forgot ter give ut back to 'im; but now I bloody did.
Coulda used the thing me-bloody-self; been orf the bloody
booze,
Up at Tumba-bloody-rumba shootin' kanga-bloody-roos.

Blouse

The word 'blouse' first appeared in English in 1828 with the meaning of a loose upper garment of linen or cotton. These days we generally use blouse to mean a woman's shirt. However, in Aussie sporting slang to 'blouse' an opponent is to defeat them by a very narrow margin (recorded from the 1980s). For example, there are sports reports of one racehorse blousing another in the final stride. Or you could read about England blousing Australia in a test match. The experts seem to think this usage began in horse racing and probably comes from the silks the jockey wears, the upper garment of which is called a blouse. So a horse could win a race by a length, by a head, by a nose, by half a nostril, or just by the merest flap of the jockey's blouse.

Blow

To boast – apparently only in Australia was the expression 'to blow your own trumpet' shortened to this one word condemnation: blow. Anthony Trollope recorded this Aussie use of the word in his 1873 book about his travels in Australia and New Zealand. And, following on from this, a blower is a boaster. This vernacular use of blow is capture by Banjo Paterson in 'Mulga Bill's Bicycle':

'See here, young man,' said Mulga Bill, 'From Walgett to the
sea,
From Conroy's Gap to Castlereagh, there's none can ride like
me.
I'm good all round at everything, as everybody knows,
Although I'm not the one to talk—I hate a man that blows.'

(See also **Big note yourself** and **Skite**.)

Blowie

A blowfly (sometimes spelled 'blowy'). According to *The Australian National Dictionary* the word applies especially to the *Lucilia cuprina* (those big, blue-black blowflies) introduced into Australia early in the 20th century. 'Blowie' is first recorded from 1916.

Blowhole

Most commonly a wave-and-wind-worn hole in a rocky coastal cliff face through which the wind and sea spray is pushed by the action of the waves (for example, the Kiama blowhole south of Sydney). More rarely it refers to an inland phenomenon where wind whistles out of a vent in the ground rock from an underground cavern when the temperature changes.

Blow-in

A new person; a late arrival; someone who's just turned up (perhaps uninvited).

Bludger

A lazy person. 'Bludger' began life as London criminal slang for a prostitute's pimp. The word comes from 'bludgeoner' (recorded 1856), meaning a pimp who bludgeons (beats with a stick) troublesome clients, or just any of the prostitute's clients in order to rob them. 'Bludger' faded out of use in London, but made its way to the Australian colonies, where it's recorded in 1882. By 1900 it was being used as a general term of abuse, especially for a lazy loafer. About the same time the back formation 'bludge' arose, meaning 'to evade one's own responsibilities and impose on others'. Interestingly, as evidence of Australia's impact on American English, 'bludger' appears in the latest (the 11th) edition of *Webster's Collegiate Dictionary*, which defines bludging as 'goofing off'. However, most of the citations in the *Oxford English Dictionary* come from Australia. For better or for worse, this is our word!

Blue

1. A fight, dispute or argument.
2. A mistake.
3. A summons to appear in court.
4. Describing a vulgar joke (in bad taste).
5. A feeling of depression.
6. A nickname for someone with red hair (alternatively Bluey).
7. To 'blue your dough' is to spend your money carelessly (and, thus, lose your money quickly).

Blue Hills

The longest-running radio serial in Australia. It dealt with the lives of ordinary country folk living in a fictional outback district. It began in 1949 as *The Lawsons*, changing its name to *Blue Hills* in the early 1950s. The final episode was broadcast in September, 1976. Gwen Meredith wrote all 5795 episodes. This gave rise to the (now dated) response to a long, boring anecdote: 'This is going longer than Blue Hills!'

Blue-tongue

1. Short for blue-tongue lizard (genus *Tiliqua*) – a large Australian lizard with a bluish tongue. They often live in our backyards, where they eat spiders. (Given how poisonous many Australian spiders are, this is a good thing.)
2. A nickname given to small children, toddlers, who are down around your ankles at about the height of blue-tongues. (See also **Ankle biters.**)

Bluey

1. Aussies like to call anyone with red hair 'Bluey'.
2. A swaggie would call his swag (the pack he carried on his back) his bluey, because of the blue-grey colour of the blanket that was the usual outer wrapping.

3. A durable woollen jacket or full-length coat, both warm and waterproof, designed by an early pioneer of Tasmania's Derwent Valley, Robert Marriott. The slogan used to sell it was: 'Put your bluey on if you're going out in this weather.'

Bluey and Curley

Comic strip characters created by Alex Gurney in 1939. They began in uniform as typical Aussie diggers, and when World War II ended they were demobbed and became knock-about tradies.

Bodgie

'Bodgie' is an Australian word that is most commonly used to describe anything that's worthless – either because it's a fake, or because it's broken. So 'bodgie number plates' are fakes, and a job that's 'a bit bodgie' is one that's not done well. Bodgie appears to come from an older word, 'bodger', meaning something unreliable or dodgy, and this, in turn, comes from a very old English word, 'bodge', meaning 'a botched piece of work' (in fact, 'bodge' and 'botch' seem to have originally been the same word). However, in the 1950s 'bodgie' briefly had another meaning. Then, a bodgie was a young Australian male who conformed to certain fashions in dress and loutish or rowdy behaviour. His female counterpart was a widgie. The bodgie's trademarks were greasy hair and tight jeans. This use of the word seems to go back to the notion of bodgie as 'fake' – in this case, they were seen as being fake Americans, or 'half-baked Yanks', or bodgies.

Bodgie's blood

A fairly hideous concoction served in milk bars back in the 1950s – the heyday of the Aussie bodgie. To make bodgie's blood, you put some thick red cordial into a glass, and then, instead of adding water, you fill the glass with cola soft drink and add a scoop of ice-cream. It would probably result in a sugar surge of hyperactivity, and even with my sweet tooth I'm not sure I could face it. And I reckon after drinking a tall glass of bodgie's blood you'd bodge anything!

Bodyline

A form of bowling attack in cricket during the 1932–33 Ashes Test series in Australia that was designed to combat the brilliance of Don Bradman (see **Bradman**). England's captain Douglas Jardine instructed fast bowler Harold Larwood to intimidate the batsmen, and a number of Australians suffered injuries, including wicketkeeper Bert Oldfield, who had his skull fractured by a ball from Larwood. It provoked intense debate, in political as well as sporting circles, and (for a time) cooled relations between Australia and Britain.

Body surf

To ride a breaking wave towards the beach without the help of a surfboard by streamlining the body and holding it rigid to catch the wave.

Bog a duck in boots

Heavy mud: 'Just look at that paddock, mate – it'd bog a duck in boots.'

Bogan

Originally a young man so desperately unfashionable (and so unaware) as to think it cool to dress in black jeans and black T-shirt with checked, flannelette shirt over the top and either (a) moccasins, (b) ugg boots, or (c) desert boots. This entire ensemble is often completed by a mullet haircut, a taste for heavy metal music, and an old bomb car with a noisy muffler. Now the expression has been extended to cover anyone regarded as being part of 'the great unwashed'. There are regional variations: in some parts of

Australia a bogan can be known as a 'bevan', a 'bog', a 'chigger', a 'booner', a 'boonie', a 'feral', or a 'westie'. Essentially, it's a term that allows the user to feel smug and rather superior to the people being spoken of. (Incidentally, the experts remain baffled as to the origin of the word.)

Bogof

'Buy One Get One Free' – the enticing offer made by enterprising retailers.

Bogong Jack

Legendary bushman, said to have lived in eastern Victoria in the 1850s. A horse and cattle thief, the legend says he blazed trails across Victoria's Great Divide, from Omeo to Bright, through some of the densest bushland in Australia.

Bogong moths

Every spring there is a mass migration of Bogong moths from their lowland breeding grounds to the high country of the Snowy Mountains. They hide in crevices during the day and fly by night, in such large numbers, and such tightly packed formations, as to be a nuisance. In 1865, Bogong moths invaded a church in Sydney in such numbers the service had to be abandoned. In 1988 vast numbers of moths caused havoc at the newly completed Parliament House on Capital Hill and engineers had to reduce the lighting and redesign the air intakes. Winds have been known to carry bogongs out to sea, on rare occasions as far as New Zealand. In earlier times Aboriginal tribes in southern NSW treated the migrating moths as fast food, roasting them over a slow fire and snacking on them. The Bogong moth has even been celebrated in an Aussie kids' nursery rhyme:

> The Bogong moth was passing through,
> And as he passed he said, 'Hey you!

I'd like to linger longer,
In the city of Wodonga,
But the lady moth for whom I long,
Is far away on Mount Bogong.'
And with these words he flapped his wings,
And sang the song the Bogong sings,
Then flew to the one who'd waited long,
Upon the peak of Mount Bogong.

Bogey

Having a wash, or a bath, or a swim. It seems to have been a very early borrowing from the Aboriginal language spoken in the Sydney area, but unlike most other borrowings it's a verb, not a noun. First recorded in Alexander Harris's 1847 book *Settlers and Convicts*. Rock pools used for swimming were often known as bogey holes, and near Newcastle there is a place officially named Bogey Hole.

Boilover

A surprise result. When the wrong team wins a game that looked like a dead cert, it's as much of a surprise as that time when the saucepan boiled over while you were on the phone and deposited its contents all over the stove.

Boil the billy

Make a cup of tea. This can be used even if you're using tea bags and an electric jug in the kitchen rather than boiling the billy on a campfire.

Bombora

A word from Australia's surfing subculture. A bombora is a wave generated by a submerged reef, loved by surfers as it gives them a chance to catch a wave in deep water. *The Australian National*

Dictionary says the word (probably) came from a New South Wales Aboriginal language.

Bondi beach

The most famous beach in the world takes its name from an Aboriginal word for a heavy war club. Probably a Kamilaroi word.

Bondi chest

A skinny chest. Bondi Beach is a long way from Manly Beach – so a Bondi chest is 'far from manly'.

Bondi tram

The trams haven't run to Bondi for years, but there was a time when if someone left hurriedly they were said to 'shoot through like a Bondi tram'.

Boned

Sacked. Made famous by Eddie McGuire during his brief reign as head of the Nine Network, when he was reported using this word to describe the planned sacking of presenter Jessica Rowe.

Bonzer

'Bonzer' is (or was) a general term of approval. If anything was pretty good, you could say, 'Hey, that's bonzer, mate!' As for its origin: its starting point ('perhaps' says *The Australian National Dictionary*) is the French word for 'good', bon. By the late 19th century it was made more emphatic by being turned into the colloquial word 'bonster'. And this, in turn, developed into the rather easier-to-say 'bonzer' – perhaps influenced by the Mexican–American word 'bonanza'. Sue Butler says that until Word War II, 'bonzer' was a powerful word in Aussie English, but after that we were internationalised. Michael Quinion (on his World

Wide Words website) has described 'bonzer' as 'an archetypal Australianism, typical of the lively and expressive slang of that country'. So I hope we're not losing this rather beaut Aussie word!

In 1928, distinguished Australian essayist Sir Walter Murdoch was asked to judge 300 odes submitted in an 'Ode to Western Australia' competition to mark the centenary of that state. In a later essay Murdoch complained that the vast majority of the entries began with 'Hail' or 'All hail' and then threw in an extra 'hail' when the author's feelings got the better of them. After slogging patiently through 300 of these things he offered his readers this:

Hail beauteous land!
Hail bonzer West Australia;
Compared with you,
All others are a failure.

This probably makes it the only ode in the world to contain the word 'bonzer'. (See what the rest of them are missing out on!)

Boobook

Australia's smallest and most common owl, with a distinctive two-note call which its name attempts to capture.

Boofhead

'Boofhead' is Australian slang for a stupid person, a fool, a blockhead, a fat head. It probably derives from an old English dialect word, 'bufflehead', dating back to at least 1659. However, the distinctive Australian variation, and its wide currency, is due to a comic strip called 'Boofhead', written and drawn by R. B. Clark from 1939. It appeared in the Sydney *Daily Mirror* from May 1941 until Clark's death in 1970. Several collections of the comic strip were published as comic books in the 1950s. Boofhead's name was a description of his character. For instance, when his doctor asked: 'Did my medicine do you any good?' Boofhead replied: 'It was a wonderful remedy, doctor. I took three spoonfuls and my cough went. I rubbed four spoonfuls into my knee and it cured my rheumatism and I just left my mother at home using the rest of it to clean the silver.'

Booligal

A New South Wales outback town on the banks of the Lachlan River. The name comes from an Aboriginal word meaning 'windy place'. It once had a reputation as the hottest, driest, most unpleasant place to live in the world – a reputation celebrated by Banjo Paterson in his ballad 'Hay, Hell and Booligal':

> Of course, there's heat—no one denies—
> And sand and dust and stacks of files,
> And rabbits, too, at Booligal.

The old joke said that if you owned Hell and Booligal you'd rent out Booligal and live in Hell.

Boomer

A large, adult male kangaroo. (In the early days it was sometimes spelled 'boomah'.) The word is recorded with this meaning from 1830. It seems to derive from the early English dialect word 'boomer', meaning 'anything which is a very large example of its kind' – although its adoption here may have been influenced by the giant strides made by a large kangaroo in full flight. This Aussie meaning of 'boomer' is used by Rolf Harris in his popular children's Christmas song, 'Six White Boomers':

> Six white boomers, snow white boomers,
> Racing Santa Claus through the blazing sun,
> Six white boomers, snow white boomers,
> On his Australian run.

Boomerang

An Aboriginal invention used both in combat and in sport. There are two types of boomerangs: returning and non-returning. Both are carefully carved flat, curved sticks. The non-returning boomerang was used as a weapon in hunting or tribal battles – it was, in effect, a flying missile or club. But the better known is the remarkable returning boomerang that employs highly sophisticated aerodynamics so that, when thrown correctly, it will curve up in flight, catch the breeze and return to the thrower. They seem to stop and hang in the air before they glide back down. Returning boomerangs are used mainly for the sport of boomerang throwing. Because of their glide path they can be dangerous – inexperienced throwers can be clobbered by their returning boomerang. As a metaphor, 'boomerang' has travelled around the world. Anything which returns to (or impacts upon) its originator can be said to boomerang (turning the word simultaneously into both a metaphor and a verb).

And these metaphorical meanings keep growing. According to the Word Spy website, someone who's called 'a boomerang' is either (a) an employee who quits a company and later returns to that same company, or (b) an employee who's laid off and then re-hired as a consultant or contractor. For instance, one company boasted of having 'a 12 per cent boomerang rate', meaning they were such great employers 12 per cent of workers who quit came back. An ancient word with a growing set of meanings.

Boots and all

Absolutely, completely, and with no reservations. This is an Australian expression (not found elsewhere – or, if it now is, they got it from us), and it seems to date back to the 1940s. Beyond that, nothing is known. We can only assume it paints a picture of a worker who throws himself into a situation where he would normally remove his boots without bothering to do so: perhaps into bed out of sheer exhaustion; or into a billabong at the end of a long, hot day on the track.

Booze

Not, of course, an Aussie word, but one which has a particular currency here as the most common nickname for an alcoholic drink (or a drinking bout or spree). Booze first turns up in English back in the 14th century as a verb – 'to booze' meaning 'to drink deeply, to guzzle'. It comes from a Middle English term 'bouse' or 'bousen', which meant 'to drink to excess'. A very similar word is found in Middle Dutch and early Modern Dutch. The origin, says the Oxford English Dictionary, is 'not quite clear' but the Dutch word seems to be directly related to a large drinking vessel called a *buise*. Both the verb and the noun seem to have become generally known in the 16th century as thieves' or beggars' cant (or slang). In the 18th century, 'booze' turned up in the expression 'a peck and a booze' – meaning 'meat and drink'. And from the 19th century, 'booze' in America has tended to mean specifically spirits, rather than any other kind of alcoholic drink. In Australia 'a boozer' can refer to a pub or to a bloke who's drinking (especially if he's drinking heavily), and 'booze' here probably refers more often to beer than any other beverage.

Boree

An Aboriginal word that white settlers applied to a type of acacia tree, having the reputation of making good firewood. The word itself comes from the Wiradjuri and Kamilaroi languages. Boree was made famous by the title of a book of bush ballads, *Around the Boree Log* (1921) by 'John O'Brien' – pen name of Roman Catholic priest Patrick Hartigan (1878–1952). His delightful bush ballads celebrate everyday life in an outback Irish Catholic community. The most famous of John O'Brien's bush ballads is 'Said Hanrahan', in which the gloomy central character predicts droughts and bushfires when it's dry and floods when it's wet, and concludes every prediction with the famous words 'We'll all be rooned.'(See also **Said Hanrahan** and **Rooned**.)

Boronia

A sweet-scented shrub. The name is recorded from 1798. It was English botanist Sir James Smith who gave the plant its name – a specimen had been sent to him from Australia. He had just heard that his friend and colleague Francesco Borone, the Italian botanist, had died, falling from a window while suffering the after-effects of a fever. So the name of the Italian (who had never been to Australia, or even seen the specimen from Australia) was commemorated in the botanical name of the Australian shrub. Mind you, plants often commemorate names. For instance, 'Sturt's desert pea' and 'Sturt's desert rose' both contain the name of explorer Charles Sturt (1795– 1869). (See also **Macadamia**.)

Borroloola sandwich

A goanna between two sheets of bark: 'I'm so hungry, mate, I could eat a Borroloola sandwich!' Borroloola is a tiny, remote town in the Northern Territory. Also known as a **Murrumbidgee sandwich**.

Boss of the board

The man in charge of a shearing shed. He's another of those characters celebrated in the folk song 'Click Go the Shears':

In the middle of the floor in his cane-bottomed chair,
Sits the boss of the board with his eyes everywhere;
Notes well each fleece as it comes to the screen,
Paying strict attention that it's taken off clean.

Boss

This word 'boss' is American in origin, and until the 19th century, was largely confined to the US. It seems to come from a Dutch word – which makes sense when we remember that the Dutch settled parts of the east coast very early in the piece, and New York was New Amsterdam before it was ever New York. The Dutch source word was *baas*, meaning 'master', and from this source it may have become common on the slave plantations. By the late 19th century it was used in a political sense in the US: a boss was a man who controlled the party machinery in a ward or district. In Australia it was adapted into a nickname for a squatter: namely, a 'boss cocky'.

Botany Bay

A large bay, not far south of Sydney, with a gently sloping shoreline. This is the place where Captain Cook anchored on his 1770 voyage of exploration on the ship Endeavour. He first named the place 'Stingray Bay' but changed it to Botany Bay after the ship's scientist, Sir Joseph Banks, discovered a wealth of botanical specimens in the area. This was the destination of the First Fleet of white settlers (convicts and their guards) under Captain Arthur Phillip. However, because of the shallow, sloping shoreline Phillip decided the site was unsuitable, explored a little further north, and discovered Sydney Cove with its deep-water shoreline ('here a Thousand Sail of the Line may ride in the most perfect Security', Phillip wrote). Despite this move, Botany Bay remained the popular short-hand label for the convict colony throughout its early years – hence, the frequent appearance of Botany Bay in early folk songs:

> Farewell to old England forever,
> Farewell to me rum culls as well,
> Farewell to the well known Old Bailey,
> Where I once used to cut such a swell.
> Singing toorali-oorali-addity,
> Singing toorali-oorali-ay,
> Singing toorali-oorali-addity,
> For we're bound for Botany Bay.

Bottler

Excellent; really good; a way of saying 'I approve'. It comes from the expression 'His blood's worth bottling!'

Boundary rider

A stockman who rides the boundary fences on a sheep or cattle station, checking for breaks or damage.

Bowser

We owe this word for a petrol pump to an American – Sylvanus Bowser, of Fort Wayne, Indiana. At the start of the 20th century he invented what he called 'the self-measuring gasoline storage pump'. The device consisted of a measuring pump attached to a tank. Bowser's firm was in the business of making these things early on, though it only trademarked the name in 1921. And it was those trade-marked petrol pumps that found their place in every petrol station in Australia and New Zealand – which is why in Australia and New Zealand (but only here) petrol pumps are called bowsers. Like 'Hoover' it's one of those trade names that became a generic word.

Bowyang

A bowyang is an old bush word for a cord, or a bit of leather or string, that swaggies and other bush workers would tie around each trouser leg just below the knee. According to some accounts they did this so the belt and braces did not have to take the whole weight of the moleskins, while according to other accounts it was to keep the trousers from dragging over the knee when doing stooping work. Of course, that's not what the old bushies told kids who asked. They used say, 'It's to stop the snakes getting up the trousers'. Bowyangs is a distinctively Australian piece of slang, although it probably has its source in an old English regional dialect word – bow-yanks (recorded in the *English Dialect Dictionary*). The word 'bowyangs' came to be so closely associated with bushies that C. J. Dennis used it as the name of a fictional character: Ben Bowyang from Gunn's Gully, a farmer and philosopher. During the 1920s and 30s, when Dennis was on the staff of the Melbourne *Herald*, Ben Bowyang often turned up in his daily humour column, sometimes in verse and sometimes in prose, quite often writing (comically misspelled) letters to the editor complaining about the strange happenings in the big city. After the death of C. J. Dennis, Ben Bowyang of Gunn's Gully became a character in a long-running comic strip. Over the years the comic strip was written and drawn by Alex Gurney, Mick Armstrong, Keith Martin, Sir Lionel Lindsay, Alex McRae and Peter Russell-Clarke.

Box of budgies, a

Very bright and lively, as in the expression 'As bright as a box of budgies'.

Bradman

Sir Donald Bradman (1908–2001), the greatest batsman the game of cricket has ever seen. Known to most Australians simply as 'The Don'. So famous is his batting average of 99.94 that those numbers were chosen as the post office box number for the ABC. His name is surrounded by legends: the way he developed his uncanny eye as a boy by hitting a golf ball against a tank stand with a cricket stump; the notorious **Bodyline** series; the unbeaten tour of England by 'The Invincibles' in 1948; his highest ever first-class score of 452 not out; and his Blackheath innings, playing for an Invitation XI against Lithgow Pottery, when he compiled 100 runs in just three eight-ball overs. So complete was his dominance of the game that any outstanding person in any arena might be nicknamed 'the Bradman of ...', as Walter Lindrum was called 'the Bradman of billiards' and Banjo Paterson was 'the Bradman of the bush ballad'.

Brasco

Men's public toilet. The origin is obscure, but there is a story claiming that many gentlemen's conveniences used while standing up were plumbed by the Sydney Brass Company. Fellows availing themselves of these installations would not be able to see the top half of the company's plaque, attached under the rim of the porcelain, and could see only the second line, which read 'Brass Co.' It's a good story (and it might even be true).

Brass razoo

The word 'razoo' first appeared in Aussie English in World War I as soldiers' slang. The *Oxford English Dictionary* defines it as 'a non-existent coin of trivial value', adding 'origin unknown'. Some suggest the name might have been based on an Egyptian coin, and others an Indian coin, the word being brought by the British Army from India. Another idea is that 'razoo' is a playful variation on the expression 'not a sou', which dates back to the late 18th century. Brass has long been a slang word for money, so it's hardly surprising the two words came together to give us a brass razoo. Enterprising folk have attempted to plug the gap by manufacturing novelty coins with inscriptions along the lines of 'the one and only authentic brass razoo'. But there never was a real razoo – brass or otherwise.

Breaker, the

Pen name of Harry Harbord Morant (1864?–1902), bushman, horse-breaker and writer of bush ballads. Court-martialled during the Boer War for shooting Boer prisoners. He was executed by firing squad on 27 February 1902. The story is told in Bruce Beresford's 1980 movie *Breaker Morant*.

Brekkie

Short for breakfast – yet another of those many words Aussies like to shorten.

Brickie

A bricklayer. This slang abbreviation is now used around the world, but it was coined in Australia, where it's first recorded in 1900.

Brindabella

A drink of rum followed by a beer chaser. Recorded from 1959 as a term that had long been part of the spoken language. Brindabella is the name of a range of mountains, and, before that, of a legendary sheep station in southern New South Wales, not far from Canberra. Miles Franklin (author of *My Brilliant Career*) spent her childhood on Brindabella Station. Calling a rum and beer chaser a brindabella seems to come from the drinking habits of shearers, who had a reputation for drinking one or two bottles of beer, or a brace of rums, between knock-off and tea time, with the last drink of the day being called the 'rum run'. And 'run' was also the name given to sheep stations, so, perhaps, if Brindabella Station had a reputation as a large run, or as a 'rum' (meaning 'unusual') run, that might explain the 'rum run' being called a brindabella.

Broggie

A tight, high-speed turn in a car – sometimes called a 'wheelie' or a 'donut' or a 'spin'. 'Broggie' appears to be a regional word for this manoeuvre in parts of South Australia and Western Australia, but it may be known elsewhere as well. The earliest citation is from 1992. Broggie is probably an abbreviation of 'broadside'. It may have originally existed as the word 'broadie', which in turn became 'broggie'. 'Broadside' goes back to the 1930s and seems to have originated in the world of dirt-track motorbike racing as the word for a deliberate sliding manoeuvre when the bike rider is hugging a corner. Then, over time, and only in Australia, it turned into broggie. But how did this happen? One suggestion is that this variation began in the 1960s with kids skidding their pushbikes on the grass so that 'broadsiding on grass' became 'broggie', which was later extended to cars and their wheelies in the gravel.

Brumby

A wild bush horse, descended from runaway stock. The word first appears in 1880 and there are several theories as to its origin. One is that it's from the name of a person (possibly a Lieutenant or Major Brumby) whose horses escaped and started the breed. Another is that it's a corruption of Baramba Station in Queensland, a cattle station whose stud horses ran wild when the station went broke. Banjo Paterson, in an 1896 poem, repeats the theory that 'brumby' is based on an Aboriginal word. In response to a judge who, hearing about 'brumby horses' asked 'Who is Brumby, and where is his run?', Paterson wrote:

> It lies beyond the Western Pines
> Beneath the sinking sun,
> And not a survey mark defines
> The bounds of 'Brumby's Run'.
>
> On odds and ends of mountain land,
> On tracks of range and rock,
> Where no one else can make a stand,
> Old Brumby rears his stock.

Buckley's chance

No chance at all; a snowball's chance in hell: 'You've got two chances, mate – yours and Buckley's!' (Meaning: 'Give up – you haven't got a chance!') There are various suggestions as to the source of the expression 'Buckley's chance', including the notion that it came from one William Buckley (1780–1856) who lived for 32 years with Aborigines in southern Victoria. However, here is the true story behind the phrase.

In 1851, a certain Mr Mars Buckley, in partnership with one Crumpton Nunn, set up a store in a small shack in Melbourne. The business of Buckley & Nunn flourished. Then in 1893 a depression hit Melbourne and there was a run on the banks. Wily old Mars Buckley, accompanied by four assistants carrying four leather suitcases, pushed through the crowds around the bank who were demanding their money and withdrew 10 000 gold sovereigns, which he then locked away in a safe in his shop – leaving no chance that the bank might fritter away his fortune among other anxious depositors'. Two years later, in 1895, the expression 'Buckley's chance' first appeared in print, leading to the expression that you have two chances: Buckley's or none – both a play on the name of the shop, and a reference to Mars Buckley being the only winner on the day he withdrew all the cash from the bank.

When first coined, the expression must have meant that to have Buckley's chance was to have a good chance. But the meaning appears to have rapidly reversed to the bleak moan we know it as today.

Budgie

Short for budgerigar — an Australian green and yellow coloured parrot often kept as a pet.

Budgie-smugglers

When it became profitable for criminals to smuggle Australian exotic birds overseas, where they would fetch high prices from collectors, someone dreamed up this witty description of men's snug-fitting swimmers. (See **Speedos®** for a list of 33 different nicknames for these swimmers.)

Buggerlugs

The Speaker of the Northern Territory Parliament ruled that buggerlugs was 'unparliamentary language'. It strikes me as odd that this mild word was found to be so offensive. Its history appears to be this: it began in the Royal Navy some time in the 19th century where, says Jonathan Green, an expert on the history of slang, it was a casual and affectionate form of address, usually among men. Now 'buggerlugs' seems to have died out in much of the rest of the world and survived only in Australia, where it has two uses: either to refer to a specific but unnamed person ('As buggerlugs at the post office was saying to me the other day …'), or as an affectionate form of address to a child ('Come on, buggerlugs, it's time for bed …'). Which of these meanings the Speaker of the Northern Territory Parliament took offence at is unclear.

Build-up

In northern tropical Australia there are only two seasons: 'the dry' and 'the wet'. When the wet is getting closer and is about to begin, the air gets very hot and humid and drives people nuts – this is called 'the build-up'.

Bulldust

Fine, powdery dust or dirt – for instance, the sort of finely powdered dirt you'll find in a stockyard.

Bulletin, the

A weekly publication founded in Sydney in 1880 by John Haynes and John Feltham Archibald (who later, as he became a more bohemian and artistic character, changed his Christian names to 'Jules François'). Within a decade it was selling some 80 000 copies per week and its popularity gave it the nickname of 'the Bushman's Bible'. It published contributions from readers scattered across

Australia, had a fiercely nationalistic tone, and encouraged the careers of many Australian writers and cartoonists of the period. In the 1960s it became a less distinctively Australian weekly newsmagazine. It ceased publication in 2008.

Bullswool

A colloquial name for the inner portion of the covering of the stringy-bark tree. It's a dry, fibrous material, easily disintegrated by rubbing between the hands. Bullswool was (and is) used as kindling when lighting a campfire in the bush. By extension, bullswool is a polite way of saying 'Nonsense!' or 'What a load of old rope that is!' It's an exclamation of disbelief or disgust.

Bundaberged

Slang for 'immunised' – as in 'Have you had your kids Bundaberged yet?' Probably now dated, and (going by its absence in the Australian National Dictionary Centre database) also most likely only a regional expression. Apparently the story is that it comes from an incident in 1928 when a local doctor in the Queensland city of Bundaberg inoculated children with a vaccine against diphtheria. Unfortunately, it was bad batch of vaccine and 12 children died.

Bundaberg snow

The ash that rises from the sugar cane fires common along the Queensland coast and settles on the landscape – and on any wet washing you've left on the **Hills hoist**. Also used, with suitable place name adjustment, in other cane-growing areas of Queensland. (See, for example, **Burdekin words**.)

Bundaberg suitcase

An old sugar bag used by a swagman or itinerant bush worker to carry his belongings.

Bundy

Proprietary name for a time-clock recording the time when employees start and finish work, usually by punching a card into the clock, which stamps a time on it. Recorded in Australia from 1912 in such expressions as 'to bundy on/off' and 'to beat the bundy'. Now used as a generic name for any staff time-registering clocks in Australia.

Also the abbreviation of the proprietary name of Bundaberg rum, hence 'drown your sorrows in a bundy' and the drink known as a 'bundy and Coke', the second ingredient being, of course, the well-known American proprietary brand name.

Bung

1. Broken, damaged, or impaired, as in 'This computer's gone bung.' But originally bung meant 'dead' and 'to go bung' meant 'to die'. It's recorded in this sense from the 1840s, and it seems to come from an Aboriginal word (from the Yagara language): *boang* or *boung*. From this, 'bung' was extended metaphorically to mean 'to go bankrupt; financial ruin' or 'to become incapacitated; exhausted; broken'. This wider usage of 'bung' is recorded from 1885. All of which seems quite reasonable. However, further extensions of 'bung' in Aussie English are more baffling.
2. To put or place without much care, as in 'Ah, just bung it over there.'
3. 'To bung it on' means to complain and whinge very loudly; to chuck a temper tantrum.
4. 'To bung on an act' means 'to stage something; to put on airs and graces; to behave in an exaggerated or affected fashion'. The intention might be to either gain attention or to deceive. Related to this is the expression 'to bung on side', meaning 'to behave in a pompous, self-important fashion'.
5. To organise or to arrange something, especially at short notice, as in 'Just hang about and I'll bung on a bit of tucker for you'.

... And all of this from a word that originally just meant 'dead'!

Bungarribee House Ghost

Bungarribee House was built in 1827–28 for Colonel John Campbell, Secretary to the Governor of NSW, in the outer Sydney suburb of Doonside. It was demolished in 1957. While it stood, so the legend says, it was the scene of hauntings by a murdered convict.

Bunyip

An imaginary monster in Aboriginal legends who hangs around billabongs and swamps. Robert Holden's book *Bunyips: Australia's Folklore of Fear* tells the story of these bizarre and imaginary creatures and the legends and folklore surrounding them. The word 'bunyip' comes from the Wemba-wemba people of north-western Victoria, and is first recorded in 1845. That reference is to a large fossilised bone that had been discovered, quite possibly a bone from a diprotodon – a very large marsupial that once inhabited the swamps and waterways of Australia, and that became extinct some thousands of years ago. In fact, the diprotodon may be the source of the whole bunyip legend. Early settlers may have used the legend of the bunyip to frighten their children into not wandering away from lonely bush settlements. But once the word entered Aussie English it took on a life of its own – for instance, Norman Lindsay named one of the characters in *The Magic Pudding* 'Bunyip Bluegum'.

Burdekin words

The Burdekin River in Queensland is one of the major east coast river systems, draining a vast catchment area. And, for some reason, the Burdekin has lent its name to a wide range of things. For instance, the expression 'Burdekin duck' is applied to two things: a real duck (scientific name *Tadorna radjah*) and also (perhaps sarcastically) to corned beef fritters – slices of corned beef deep-fried in batter. Then there's Burdekin mud, a nickname for chocolate blancmange; Burdekin snow, meaning the ash that rises from the sugar cane fires common along the Queensland coast; the Burdekin plum, a native Queensland tree which yields both timber and a dark, plum-like fruit; Burdekin vine, a native vine that is a source of bush tucker – but of course if you eat too much you could end up with an attack of Burdekin vomit. The Burdekin has even given its name to an Australian naval frigate – HMAS *Burdekin* was launched in 1943. As for the river that set all these names flowing, it was named in 1845 by Ludwig Leichhardt in honour of a certain Mrs Burdekin, a Sydney widow who had partly financed his exploratory expedition into northern Australia.

Burgoo

In her book *Australia's Alps* Elyne Mitchell calls both porridge and porridge-like snow 'burgoo'. According to the *Oxford English Dictionary* burgoo is 'a thick oatmeal gruel or porridge used chiefly by seamen'. It's also known as 'loblolly'. The earliest citation is from 1750. The English language is notorious for borrowing words from every other language on earth, and this one appears to be a Turkish loan-word originally meaning a dish of cooked and crushed wheat – so, in a way, not unlike porridge. In America 'burgoo' came to mean 'a soup or stew made with a variety of meat and vegetables, used especially at outdoor feasts'. A quote from 1966 says that 'Burgoo is traditionally served at a barbecue for thousands of Kentucky colonels during the weekend of the Kentucky Derby.' And from Elyne Mitchell we also know that it's a word that was adapted and survived in the high country of Australia.

Burke's ghost

According to tradition the ghost of the explorer Robert O'Hara Burke walks at Innamincka Crossing in Central Australia. According to the legend, it whines with the wind around the old pub at Innamincka, and groans like an old iron gate near where he died.

Burl

To give something a burl is to give it try, give it a go. Used in this way 'burl' is distinctively part of Australian and New Zealand English, where it's first recorded in 1917. In 1981 expat Clive James used 'give it a burl' in a poem he wrote about Prince Charles. 'Burl' seems to derive from an earlier Scottish word meaning 'the sound of something revolving rapidly'. As such, it is, like 'whirl' and 'twirl', basically onomatopoeic. Once the word 'burl' referred to something turning or spinning the meaning was transferred to the spinning of a coin, so originally 'to give it a burl' meant to bet on the turn of a coin. And before you know it, it had extended from two-up to a wider (metaphorical) usage. It may, or may not, work out, but, hey, mate, you might as well give it a burl.

Bush

The inland of Australia; country areas; anything that's not city or suburbs – that still has gum trees and grass – can be called the bush. In *The Australian National Dictionary* there are 12 pages of entries incorporating the word 'bush'. That's 36 columns of entries – here's a selection to give the flavour of how 'bush' has been used in Aussie English over the years:

bush Baptist – person of vague but strong religious beliefs

bush bed – a bed made at a camp site from light branches and long grass

bush biscuit – a thin cake of flour and water baked on the hot embers of a campfire

bush blow – clearing one's nose without the use of a handkerchief

bush bread – damper, made from a simple flour and water dough, cooked in the coals or in a camp oven

Bush Brotherhood – an Anglican missionary organisation founded to provide an itinerant ministry in remote areas

bush carpenter – a rough amateur carpenter

bush constable – an ex-convict, or ticket-of-leave man, or a local

Aborigine, sworn in as a constable to help maintain law and order

bush cook – a rough-and-ready cook of limited skill (the nickname for such cooks was **poisoner** – which will give you some idea of their skills)

bush fashion – an indifferent, slapdash style; something thrown together any old how has been put together 'bush fashion'

bush feed – a big meal; can refer to abundant feed for stock or the size of meal a hungry stockman can knock over

bush fence – a rough enclosure for animals made by piling up cut scrub

bush fever – a longing to return to the bush

bush foal – a child born out of wedlock

bush honey – honey from the nests of wild bees

bush hospitality – generous, open-handed hospitality

bush hut – very modest accommodation; often (in the early years) nothing more than slab walls, dirt floor and bark roof

bush knife – a large knife with many uses; the sort of impressive blade flashed by Crocodile Dundee on the streets of New York

bush lawyer – 1. an argumentative person, especially one who attempts complicated and often specious arguments to prove a point 2. a person who pretends to a knowledge of the law

bush madness – a common affliction in the early years, caused by living alone with only sheep and kangaroos to talk to – when they start talking back you have 'bush madness'

bush mile – longer than a mile in town ... or, at least, it feels that way

bush missionary – one who, in the early years, travelled up the country to teach the Bible to shepherds and other remote bush workers

bush parson – a minister who builds a church and cares for a congregation in a remote area

bush poet – the writers of bush ballads and their modern imitators

bush races – an informal race meeting, organised by the local community and held in a paddock (often a paddock not too far from a pub)

bush road – one where the bushes have been cleared, banks of rivers and gullies levelled, trees notched on the route, and cuts made on the tops or faces of hills where necessary, the remainder being left in a natural state

bush school – a one-room, one-teacher school located in the backblocks

bush shower – a tin with holes punched in the bottom hanging from a gum tree, under which it is possible to shower as the water runs out

bush tea – strong, black tea boiled in a billy over a campfire and sweetened with coarse, dark sugar

bush yard – stakes of wood driven into the ground with tree branches in between, used as a temporary holding yard for animals

bushed – lost in the bush; or just lost, in a general sense (either literally or metaphorically)

bushfire – a wildfire that burns out of control through bush land (often threatening farm land, buildings, towns or suburbs)

bushy (also spelled 'bushie') – countrified; lacking the supposed refinements of urban life

take to the bush – to run away; to escape from custody (originally of convicts); to leave the town for the country

to go bush – to escape; to disappear from one's usual haunts; to leave the beaten track and travel cross-country; to leave the urban life for that of the country.

Bush ballad

A poem in a ballad metre dealing with aspects of life in the Australian bush, either sentimental or comic. A ballad is basically a short story in verse. So a story about life in the outback, beyond the city limits, told in ballad metre is a bush ballad. The masters of the bush ballad were Banjo Paterson, Henry Lawson and C. J. Dennis.

Bush bashing

There's two types of bush bashing – the good and the bad.

1. Bad bush bashing happens when city yahoos without any sense run their four-wheel drives over bush roads and remote tracks (or worse, through national parks) not bothering to shut farm gates they drive through, and reckless of any damage they may do to the environment.

2. Good bush bashing also involves city types taking their four-wheel drives to the bush, but doing so responsibly: if they're in remote parts of the outback they travel in convoy, carry plenty of supplies and spare parts, and behave responsibly, shutting every farmer's gate they drive through.

Bush chook

An emu: next to the ostrich, the largest of all birds, flightless but swift-footed – able to run at up to 50 kilometres an hour. (As John Williamson says in his song, he can 'run the pants off a kangaroo').

Bush telegraph

1. The informal network of communication in remote areas.
2. Any gossip ('I heard it on the bush telegraph').
3. Someone who informs a bushranger about the movements of the police (in Rolf Boldrewood's *Robbery Under Arms*, the boy who keeps Captain Starlight's gang informed is called 'a bush telegraph').

Bush tucker

1. Simple fare, as eaten by one living in or off the bush.
2. Food from Australian indigenous plants and trees.

Bush week

Bush week refers to a fictitious festival when bushies come to town in droves. The bushies, of course, are supposed to be a bit slow on the uptake (and perhaps as thick as a brick) so lots of greasy larrikins and city slickers try to rip them off. Thus the expression 'bush week' is used ironically by someone who suspects they're being made the victim of a scam or prank, as in the question 'What do you think this is, bush week?' To which the proper response is, 'Yes, and you're the sap!' The first recorded instance of the term 'bush week' is from 1919, when it was used to describe a serious attempt to organise a Bush Festival in the City of Sydney. Within a few years it was being used ironically, and entered Aussie English as a standard conversational ploy, recorded as such by Sid Baker in 1949.

Bushfire

The rest of the world calls these events 'wildfires', meaning widespread fire in an uncleared, wild area. But since all such areas in Australia are called 'the bush', that makes them bushfires here.

Bushman

One who has knowledge of the bush, and is skilled at surviving in the bush. An early settler in an area who survived would earn the title of 'a good bushman'. In *While the Billy Boils* Henry Lawson wrote: 'He was a typical bushman … and of the old bush school; one of those slight, active little fellows whom we used to see in cabbage-tree hats, Crimean shirts, strapped trousers, and elastic-sided boots.' Today the title of 'good bushman' is more likely to be applied to someone who plays a leading role in a **bushwalking** club, who has wide experience of bushwalking and good survival skills. In that way, even a city-dwelling Aussie can become 'a good bushman'.

Bushranger

A thief, a thug, a robber, especially one who held up coaches to rob the passengers and steal gold during the gold rushes. Today we associate the word 'bushranger' with those 'stand and deliver' gangs who bailed up **Cobb & Co** coaches: **Ned Kelly**, Ben Hall, Captain Thunderbolt, **Captain Moonlite**, and the rest. But originally, at least in Australia, a bushranger was an escaped convict who took to living in the bush, and supported himself by raiding the stores of outlying settlements. However, the earliest evidence for the term 'bushranger' is in the United States, where it appears to be a translation of the Dutch word *boschloper* – literally 'woods runner'. The word 'bushranger' is first recorded in the United States in 1758, referring to a frontiersman, or a woodsman. Governor Macquarie used 'bushranger' in the Australian sense in 1814. Escaped convicts were often desperate, and they often had little option but to turn to a life of crime such as stock theft and (as in the title of Rolf Boldrewood's classic novel) *Robbery Under Arms*.

Bushwhacker

Someone who lives in the country (in 'the bush') and not in a city, town or suburb. From this comes the verb 'to bushwhack', meaning to work in the bush – usually as an unskilled labourer, clearing scrub and felling trees.

Bushwalking

What is called 'hiking' in America, 'tramping' in New Zealand or 'rambling' in Britain is called bushwalking in Australia. The *Macquarie Dictionary* defines this as: 'the sport of making one's way on foot through the bush, often on tracks designed for this [purpose] but sometimes for longer periods through virgin terrain'. There are bushwalking clubs in every major city, and shops that sell outdoor and bushwalking gear dot the city centres. One of the icons of Australian bushwalking, Paddy Pallin, once wrote: 'If you have not rested at dusk and cooked a meal over a scented fire of gum-sticks and yarned and sung songs around the fire – if you have not done these things, you have not entered into your heritage as a true Australian.'

Cactus

1. Broken, ruined, finished, useless: 'This TV is cactus.'
2. 'In the cactus': in great difficulty.

Call, the

A ghostly sound resembling the sound of a man in agony that tradition says is heard in the Cooper's Creek country of western Queensland.

Calendar house

'Mona Vale', a country mansion in Tasmania, was nicknamed 'the calendar house' because it (reputedly) had 365 windows, 52 rooms, 12 chimneys and seven entrances. It was completed in 1868 at the then phenomenal cost of £40 000.

Callithumpian

An imaginary religion; a fictional protestant denomination. It's sometimes used as the equivalent of a generic 'religious belief of any kind', as in: 'It doesn't matter if he's Catholic, Congregationalist or Callithumpian.' It's first recorded in the notorious John Norton's orthodoxy-rattling Sydney *Truth* newspaper in 1892 with this meaning. From the 1970s it broadened to mean any kind of beliefs (or no beliefs at all), as when a newspaper referred to the range of political beliefs that cover 'Labor, Liberal, National Party and Callithumpian'. I had always thought the word had been formed as a joking variation on Presbyterian, but it turns out that behind the Australian usage was an American phrase, 'callithumpian band', meaning 'a band of discordant instruments'. This is recorded from 1836. And behind this American coinage seems to lie an older English dialect word, 'gallithumpians', meaning 'people who disturb the public order at parliamentary elections'. But it was only in Australia that 'Callithumpian' became the name of a fictional Protestant denomination, and (later) a name for any sort of vague belief.

Canberra

Australia's national capital. Brian Kennedy, in his book on Australian place names, says 'Canberra' comes from an Aboriginal word said to mean 'meeting place'. But Shane Mortimer, an Aboriginal elder of the Ngambri people, says the place and the people (the earliest inhabitants) shared the same name. Hence the area where Canberra now stands was originally called 'Ngambri'. But the new settlers in the 1820s found this hard to pronounce so they anglicised it into 'Kamberri'. And that's the name that appears on documents from 1832. Then in 1913 the wife of the then Governor, Lady Denman, declared the new capital of Australia to be called Canberra. From 'Ngambri' to 'Kamberri' to Canberra – that's the journey. As for meaning, 'Ngambri' meant the cleavage between a woman's breasts because the land lies between what are now called Mount Ainslie and Black Mountain. (For another example of people and place sharing the same name see **Kakadu**.)

Cane toad

Officially the *Bufo marinus* or giant neotropical toad. The cane toad has poison glands and its tadpoles are toxic to most animals if ingested. They were introduced into Australia from Hawaii in 1935 to control the native cane beetle. The cane toads proceeded to eat the beetles and anything else that stood still for long enough. The exploding population of cane toads has now spread well beyond Queensland, with toads being discovered well into northern New South Wales, in the Northern Territory and even the top end of Western Australia. In 1988 Mark Lewis made a documentary film called *Cane Toads: An Unnatural History* which elevated them beyond mere pests and made them part of the lexicon of Australia's legendary weird animals.

Cameron Corner

The remote spot where the borders of three Australian states meet: New South Wales, Queensland and South Australia. Named after a New South Wales Lands Department surveyor, John Brewer Cameron. The nearest town is Tibooburra, while the corner territory itself is occupied by Sturt National Park, named for pioneering explorer Charles Sturt (1795–1869).

Captain Cook

Look (rhyming slang) – from James Cook (1728–79), the Yorkshire-born sea captain and navigator who discovered and mapped part of the east coast of Australia. It was Cook's discoveries that led to the British settlement of Australia.

Captain Moonlite

Name chosen by Andrew George Scott (1842–80) for his career as a **bushranger** and bank robber. The erratic spelling is his own invention. He was captured after a gun battle with troopers at Wagga Wagga and died on the gallows in Sydney on 20 January 1880. Until he was caught, he managed to combine his criminal career with being a pillar of the Anglican Church at Mount Egerton in Victoria.

Captain Thunderbolt

The name chosen by Frederick Ward (1835–70) when he embarked on a career as a bushranger. He adopted his nickname when he took to crime in February 1863, assisted by his wife and various (mainly juvenile) gang members. They began around Bourke but later operated largely in the New England and Upper Hunter region. Ward was shot by a constable in 1870 and is buried in the Uralla cemetery. The puzzling thing is why men such as Moonlite and Thunderbolt felt it necessary to give themselves military titles. Since the troopers were their sworn enemies, it seems an odd thing to do. Perhaps they saw it as part of the romance of bushranging.

Cardie

Aussie abbreviation of 'cardigan' – what the Americans would call a sweater. In its unabbreviated form, the name of the garment comes from James Brudenell, the 7th Earl of Cardigan, a British military commander in the Crimean War (who, I gather, was never known to his troops as 'Lord Cardie').

Cark (or Kark)

To die. This can be used of people or of things, as in 'My computer has carked it.' It appears not to be an old word, the earliest recorded usage being 1977. But where does it come from? Well, *The Australian National Dictionary* suggests from the mournful cry of the crow – a carrion bird. This usage is recorded from a little earlier: from 1936 there are descriptions of crows carking (or cawing) as they feed on a dead carcase. However, there is a much older English word 'cark' which, from the 14th century onwards, appears to have meant load or burden. (In origin it's related to the word 'charge', in the sense of 'a burden of responsibility'.) To be carked, then, was to be burdened with care, burdened with worries and troubles. Now, if we see death as the ultimate burden that crushes the life out of a bloke, that could be the source of our word 'cark', rather than the cry of the crow. It's a possibility, anyway.

Cascade Country

Tasmania is a divided state – the dividing line being which of the state's two major beers you drink. Southern Tasmania is Cascade Country. In the north of the island state they drink Boag's, but this seems not to have a territorial title attached to it. Perhaps it's time to coin the phrase 'the Boag Border'– above which Boag is preferred to Cascade. (Cascade is brewed in Hobart; Boag in Launceston.)

Cat head

The *Emex australis* is a low-growing plant producing small, hard fruit with three spines of about three millimetres in length, which always have one spine pointing upwards when they fall to the ground. And if you ever step on one of these things you're sure to know it – as will everyone else within earshot! I first came across them in New South Wales, where they're called 'cat heads' or 'cat's eyes'. However, in Victoria and South Australia they're called 'prickly jack'; in Queensland 'three-corner jack' or 'bullhead' or 'caltrop' or 'California puncture weed'; while in West Australia this razor-like vegetation is known as a 'double-gee'. Originally a native of South Africa, this prickly pest was introduced to Australia in the 19th century and since then has been busy acquiring all those different names in different states.

Cattle duffer

Cattle thief. What Americans calling 'rustling' is calling 'duffing' in Australia.

Cattle ticks

Aussie kids' nickname for Catholics, possibly mocking the Irish pronunciation of the word 'catholic'. (See also **Rock choppers.**)

Cattle grid

If you've driven to a farm you'll know one of the most important things to remember is to close every gate you open as soon as you drive through so that the animals don't start wandering. On some properties in rural Australia the necessity for this constant opening and closing of gates is avoided by the installation of a grid set into the road or track at the point where it passes through a paddock fence. Hoofed animals won't walk over the grid, so it works as well as a gate. But these things have different names in different parts of Australia. 'Cattle grid' is probably the most common name, but sometimes it'll just be called a 'grid', sometimes 'cattle ramp' or just a 'ramp' and sometimes a 'cattle grate'. In New Zealand they're called a 'cattle stop'.

Catchya

An Aussie way of saying 'goodbye', short for 'catch ya later'. (See also **Hooroo.**)

Cazaly

Roy Cazaly (1893–1963) was a legendary Aussie Rules player for South Melbourne (1921–24, 1926–27). The cry of 'Up there, Cazaly' was originally an encouragement to take a high mark, but is now often a shout of general encouragement, approval or endorsement.

Channel country

A region of inland flood plains marked by twisting gullies and (often dry) creeks, fed by three rivers: the Cooper, the Diamantina and the Georgina.

Charlie's Trousers

Rhyming slang for the inland Queensland city of Charters Towers. This does open up all kinds of possibilities for misunderstandings, depending on the context in which it's employed. For instance, if you were asked where your wedding was held, and the answer was 'Charters Towers' it might be unwise to reply 'I got married in Charlie's Trousers'. (Well, I suppose … something borrowed …)

Chateau de cardboard

Cheap cask wine.

Cheesed off

Irritated or annoyed. This began life as thieves' slang. The earliest citation is from 1812, and comes from the very first dictionary ever produced in Australia, *A Vocabulary of the Flash Language*, compiled by convict author James Hardy Vaux. In it he defines 'cheese it' as meaning 'stow it' or 'put it away'. More broadly, thieves used 'cheese it' to mean 'To stop, give up, leave off … have done! run away!' This steadily came to mean, more or less, 'leave or depart'. So in *The Inimitable Jeeves*, P. G. Wodehouse writes: 'Jeeves had been clearing away the breakfast things, but at the sound of the young master's voice he cheesed it courteously.' It's not a big step from that meaning to the current one of annoyance – one is cheesed off because the delights of life have 'cheesed it'.

Chesty Bond

Character created in 1938 to advertise singlets made by the Bonds Company. In all the cartoon-like drawings of him, Chesty Bond displayed rippling muscles, a square jaw and a big smile. This appearance put his name into the language as a way of describing any young Aussie male with similar solid build and good looks. Hence, a sportsman or a lifesaver on a beach might be described as being 'a Chesty Bond type'. His name was also invoked to describe anything that was beyond mere human muscle to achieve: 'Even Chesty Bond couldn't lift that, mate.'

Chew someone's ear, to

1. To complain loudly.
2. To try to cadge money.

Chiack

Chiacking is used in Australia to mean 'taking the mickey out of someone; teasing or ridiculing'. However, the older meaning of chiacking tends to be a bit more cheerful and less teasing. Gerry Wilkes says that chiacking used to mean 'cheerful banter'. In this older sense it was a variation of another expression, 'chi-yike' (or 'chi-hike'), which was 'a noisy cheer, a jeering salute, or friendly banter'. 'Chi-yike' is British in origin and began life as a street cry used by costermongers – the 'barrow boys' of London. For them it seems that 'chi-yike' was a cheer or cry of commendation. It made its way to the colonies (possibly with convicts), was corrupted in 'chiack' and became the word we know today. By the way, it seems to be fading from common use. Fairly savage teasing is less likely to be called chiacking now than it used to be.

chinaman

The word Chinaman spelled with a capital 'C' is an archaic (and now derogatory) name for a Chinese male. But spelled with a lower case 'c', 'chinaman' means 'a left-hand bowler's off-break or googly to a right-handed batsman'. The earliest citation in the *Oxford English Dictionary* for 'chinaman' is from 1937. It's commonly supposed to have been named after Ellis Achong, a Trinidadian left-arm bowler of Chinese descent who played six tests for the West Indies between 1930 and 1935. However, there is no contemporary evidence of the term so arising. Michael Rundell, in his *Dictionary of Cricket*, suggests it arose in the late 1920s or early 1930s, based on the widespread view that the Chinese, as a race, were inscrutable, and devious, and impossible to predict. You can see how a ball that was inscrutable (unreadable by the batsman) could come to be called a chinaman.

Chloe

Perhaps Australia's best known nude. She was painted in Paris in 1875 by Jules Lefebvre (1836–1911) and brought to Melbourne for the Great Exhibition of 1880. Since 1908 she has hung in the bar of Young and Jackson's hotel on the corner of Swanston and Flinders Streets in Melbourne. She's still there, so she must like the place.

Chook

'Chook' is now the common Australian expression for a chicken, a domestic fowl. The only citations in the *Oxford English Dictionary* come from Australia and New Zealand and start from the 19th century. Although we spell the word with a double-O today, it used to be spelled with a U. The earliest citations in *The Australian National Dictionary* have the 'chuck' spelling. But because it began life as a north of England dialect word, it may still have been pronounced as we pronounce 'chook'. Dr Johnson, in his dictionary, says that 'chuck' or 'chook' was a familiar term of endearment applied to husbands, wives, children and close companions. This makes sense, since it would be the equivalent of calling a child 'my little chicken'. (Or, as W. C. Fields would have said, 'my little chickadee'.) Dr Johnson also says that 'chuck' or 'chook' was a dialectal corruption of 'chick' (the abbreviation of chicken). The word 'chuck' is used this way by Shakespeare in *Love's Labour's Lost*. It seems never to have caught on in the south of England, and to have largely died out by the late 19th century. But by that time the word had been carried to Australian and New Zealand, where we have kept the word alive, by calling our chickens not 'chicks' but 'chooks'. In Australia, 'chook' is also likely to be the nickname of anyone with the family name of Fowler (since a 'chook' is a fowl).

Chook run

1. A fenced-off area where domestic poultry are kept, behind 'chicken wire' – what else? Also called a chook yard or chook house.
2. A social competition, most commonly in bowls or golf, with a frozen chicken as the prize.

Chop picnic

What a barbecue was called before the word 'barbecue' was imported from America. ('Barbecue' was being used in the US by the 1700s but only reached Australia in the 20th century.) As the name implies, a chop picnic featured lamb chops, rather than the burnt steaks and charcoal sausages that later became the stars of Aussie barbies.

Christmas

Writing for a largely English readership in *A Dictionary of Austral English*, in 1898, Edward E. Morris felt he had to explain what was distinctive about the Australian Christmas. Here's his explanation: 'As Christmas falls in Australasia at Midsummer, it has different characteristics from those in England, and the word has therefore a different connotation.' More than a century later, we can say that Christmas is still distinctive in Australia, with traditional roast turkey often replaced by seafood, barbecues and salads.

Donald Horne has remarked that Australia has three culturally significant annual events: Anzac Day (which he describes as, in his view, a celebration of mateship); Melbourne Cup Day (the annual national celebration, says Horne, of luck); and Christmas Day (which, he says, in Australia is a celebration of family). In other words, Christmas Day, on Donald Horne's reading, now plays much the same social and cultural role in Australia that Thanksgiving Day plays in the United States – a day centred on a meal with the gathered family.

Christmas beetle

A scarab beetle (genus *Anoplognathus*) that emerges in summer.

Christmas bells

A flowering grass-like plant, *Blandfordia nobilis*.

Christmas bush

A small, green bush, with deep pink flowers that appear in early summer.

Chuck

A news report about a crocodile caught in suburban Perth by a local dog catcher included his statement that he couldn't 'chuck the croc in the dog pound, because it would eat its neighbours'. A very Australian statement, containing what appears to be (at first glance) a distinctively Australian use of the word chuck – meaning 'to throw'. But as Australian as this sounds, the word 'chuck' meaning 'to throw' has been part of the English language since the late 16th century. It was probably first used of throwing or tossing money or anything light, and from this the meaning extended over time.

However, there are two distinctively Australian meanings for the word 'chuck': when you mock someone by 'chucking off' at them, that's an Australianism; and so is chuck meaning 'to vomit'. *The Australian National Dictionary* does not record this second usage earlier than 1957, but it was undoubtedly part of the oral culture long before that. Aussie English may be blunt, but at least it's colourful.

Chuck a wobbly

To blow your top, to go **crook** on someone, to **arc up**.

Chunder

'Chunder' is yet another Aussie expression meaning 'to vomit'. Does it come (as has been suggested) from a contraction of 'Watch under'? Barry Humphries – who popularised the word through his 'Barry McKenzie' comic strip and movies – says it does. It's an old nautical expression, he suggests; a courtesy shout from the upper decks to those below. That might well be so, but there is an alternative suggestion: namely that it's rhyming slang – chunder being short for 'Chunder Loo', which rhymes with 'spew'. 'Chunder Loo of Akin Foo' was a cartoon figure in a long-running series of advertisements for Cobra boot polish that appeared in the *Bulletin* in the early years of the 20th century. It's another of those cases where 'ya takes ya pick' of the explanation you prefer. By the way, it's considered more polite these days to use Barry Humphries's other delightful expression for a vomit: a 'Technicolor yawn'.

Chutney

A chutney is 'a grumpy old bloke'. This is a bit of Aussie kids' slang, and it's another piece of evidence that Aussie English is in good hands, and its future is assured. Kids who are inventive enough to call a grumpy old bloke a chutney will clearly treat our language with the respect it deserves!

Clancy of the Overflow

Legendary character created by Banjo Paterson. The bush ballad 'Clancy of the Overflow' first appeared in the *Bulletin* on 21 December 1889. In 1895 it was included in his first book, *The Man from Snow River and Other Verse*. Paterson himself later wrote: 'I got the idea for ... "Clancy of the Overflow" through writing a business letter to a man named Clancy and getting the reply, 'We don't know where he are.' I made that into a verse, as I thought that most of us had a bit of a craving for the free life, the air, and the sunshine, and to be done with the boss and the balance sheet.'

> In my wild erratic fancy visions come to me of Clancy
> Gone a-droving 'Down the Cooper' where the Western
> drovers go;
> As the stock are slowly stringing, Clancy rides behind them
> singing,
> For the drover's life has pleasures that the townsfolk never
> know.

In the 1950s, 'Clancy of the Overflow' became the eponymous hero of a daily afternoon radio serial with Howard Craven playing the lead role. (See also **Man from Snowy River** and **Saltbush Bill**.)

Clappers

To 'go like the clappers' is to go very fast. It's a bit of slang I've used, and heard used, for many years. And yet I can't find the clappers listed in any dictionary of slang, not even in the excellent *Macquarie Book of Slang*, which has brief definitions of most current slang words. So it's not surprising that none of the textbooks explain the origin of clappers, since none of the textbooks appear to have heard of it! However, there is a possible source: the tongue of bell is a called a clapper, and to ring the bell the clapper has to be banged back and forth rapidly – hence, moving quickly is 'going like the clappers'. Plus, in the UK, before sirens, emergency vehicles (fire engines and ambulances) had bells. This might have supported the notion that to 'go like the clappers' is to go very fast. That's certainly as good an explanation as any.

Clayton's

Clayton's is a product name that has entered the language. Originally it was a soft drink called Clayton's Tonic, famously advertised by Jack Thompson with the slogan: 'It's the drink I have when I'm not having a drink'. The line was coined by Noel Delbridge, creative director of the advertising agency D'Arcy, MacManus and Masius. 'Clayton's' became part of Aussie English to mean 'a substitute for the real thing'. Originally this was spelled out in full, as in the case of a politician who says that his opponent has 'a Clayton's policy: the policy you have when you don't have a policy'. But the full explanation was soon dropped, and labelling something a 'Clayton's' whatever was enough. The original advertising campaign ran in 1980. It's now fading, and like previous advertising slogans (such as 'It's moments like these you need **Minties**' and '**Gone to Gowings**') is perhaps being forgotten.

Cleanskin

In a little over a century this word passed from agriculture to people to wine. 'Cleanskin' is first recorded (by *The Australian National Dictionary*) from 1881 to mean 'an unbranded animal'. So, in its first incarnation cleanskin had an almost literal meaning. Then from 1907 it was applied to people. A cleanskin could be either a bloke with no criminal record, or someone who was new to the job with no experience (and no skills). Nowadays, 'cleanskin' refers to unlabelled bottles of wine sold in bulk by a winery to a retailer. The retailer sticks their own label on the unlabelled (hence cleanskin) bottles and flogs them off as their own brand.

Clean Up Australia Day

Australia's largest annual community-based environmental event, in which community groups gather up rubbish left in public areas, and clean up the natural environment. It began in 1989 as the idea of Sydney born yachtsman Ian Kiernan for cleaning up Sydney Harbour, and has since spread around the nation, and around the world, and to every type of natural environment.

Click go the words

Click go the shears boys, click, click, click,
Wide is his blow and his hands move quick,
The ringer looks around and is beaten by a blow,
And curses the old snagger with the bare-bellied joe.

'Click Go the Shears', celebrating the days of blade shearing, is probably one of the best-known Australian folk songs, and yet it includes many terms perhaps unfamiliar today. There's the **bare belly joe** – a sheep with defective wool growth, hence no wool on its belly and legs, hence, quicker to shear. This enables the old snagger to beat the ringer – the fastest shearer in the shed, by a blow – one clip of the shears. There's **boss of the board**, the man in charge of the shearing (the 'board' being that area of the shed where the sheep are shorn); the **new chum**, someone new to the bush or new to shearing; and:

The colonial-experience man, he is there, of course,
With his shiny leggin's, just got off his horse.

This is the over-paid self-important younger son of a British family sent out to get some 'experience in the colonies', often because it was thought to be character-building.

Cliner

Girlfriend. This now-vanished bit of Aussie slang is perhaps best known from C. J. Dennis's *The Songs of a Sentimental Bloke* (1915), where he writes:

Gorstrooth! I seemed to lose me pow'r o' speech.
But, 'er! Oh, strike me pink! She is a peach!
The sweetest in the barrer! Spare me days,
I can't describe that cliner's winnin' ways.

But the word was recorded long before C. J. Dennis, in W. T. Goodge's comic ballad 'The Great Australian Slanguage' (1897), where he writes:

And a bosom friend's a 'cobber'
And a horse a 'prad' or 'moke',
While a casual acquaintance
Is a 'joker' or a 'bloke'.
And his lady-love's his 'donah'
Or his 'clinah' or his 'tart' …

In these slang terms for a girlfriend, 'tart' is British rhyming slang ('jam tart' = 'sweetheart') but 'cliner' (or 'clinah', choose your own spelling) seems to be a bit of Aussie slang from an immigrant language: German. There was a significant German speaking population in South Australia in the 19th century, from whom the word *kleine* was borrowed. *Kleine* (pronounced 'cliner') is the feminine form of the German word for 'small' or 'little', and comes from the period when a man would refer to his wife as 'the little woman'.

Coat hanger

Nickname for the Sydney Harbour Bridge. This is another of those terms first coined as a sneering put-down but enthusiastically embraced and employed by those being sneered at. It's Sydneysiders more than anyone else who are likely to call 'the Bridge' the old coat hanger these days.

Coat, to put (someone) on the

To ostracise someone, to socially shun a person; sometimes uttered as a threat: 'I've put you on the coat, mate!' To 'coat' someone originally (early 20th century) meant to threaten or reprimand them, as by grabbing someone by the lapels of their coat. Later, by the 1940s, the expression had come to mean ostracism rather than reprimand. Vaudeville and radio station Roy 'Mo' Rene (real name Harry van der Sluys, 1891–1954) as part of his stage act used to finger his lapels to indicate that he had 'put someone on the coat'.

Cobb and Co.

Legendary outback coach line, founded by American Freeman Cobb, along with John Peck, James Swanton and John Lamber, in 1853. The success of the line, especially in its early years, was based on its use of a type of American coach called a Concord – a light, hickory-framed vehicle with leather springs and thin-spoked wheels. At its peak, Cobb and Co. had a network of lines across most of eastern Australia. The last Cobb and Co. coach ran in 1924. Henry Lawson celebrated the legend in his bush ballad 'The Lights of Cobb and Co.':

> Past haunted half-way houses—where convicts made the bricks—
> Scrub-yards and new bark shanties, we dash with five and six;
> Through stringy-bark and blue-gum, and box and pine we go—
> A hundred miles shall see tonight the lights of Cobb and Co.!

Cobber

The news story was about the uniforms to be worn by Australian Olympians and the headline said: 'Nice clobber for a cobber at the Games'. This is one of the rare recent appearances of the word 'cobber' in print, and it's always nice to see it again. 'Cobber' is first recorded from 1893. In his *Dictionary of Australian Colloquialisms* Gerry Wilkes – after giving the definition of cobber as 'friend' or 'mate' – adds the statement 'obsolete'. And that I find sad. I can remember 'cobber' still being an active part of Aussie English when I was a small boy, and to me it's as distinctively Australian as the smell gum leaves on a hot day. Mind you, as Tasmanians keep reminding me, 'cobber' is still part of the living language in Tasmania.

Jonathon Green, who's a hot-shot on slang, thinks that 'cobber' comes from a Hebrew/Yiddish word 'chaver', or 'khaver', meaning 'a pal', 'a chum'. And there is another suggestion: that 'cobber' is one of those English dialect words that survived here in

Australia after it died out in England. There is an old British dialect word 'cob', meaning 'to take a liking to'. All the citations in the dictionaries for 'cobber' are from Australia and New Zealand, and the earliest is from Sydney in 1893.

Sadly, 'cobber', like that other great Australian word 'bonzer', is now nearly defunct. So may I draw your attention to a very modest, very low-key campaign I'm running – namely, a quiet campaign to revive the word 'cobber' as part of our spoken language. If the idea of reviving a **dinki-di** word appeals to you, all you need to do to join the campaign is to occasionally greet a friend with the words 'G'day, cobber'.

By way of encouragement there is some evidence that Aussie kids are now using 'cobber' to mean 'a very cool person'. So perhaps the word is not quite dead yet.

Cockatoo

The word cockatoo refers to those gregarious Australian parrots that gather in large flocks and make their presence felt with their loud, screeching cries. The word itself comes from a Malay word *kakatúa*, and is recorded in English from 1616 (because these birds also turn up in the East Indies, and that's where they were first named). Cockatoo has since been transferred to a variety of other meanings. A lookout, especially a lookout posted at a two-up game, is called a cockatoo. And because early small holding farmers struggled to make a living, trying to raise crops and keep away large flocks of these birds, they were jokingly called cockatoo farmers – meaning that they appeared to be raising more cockatoos than anything else. This was later shortened to 'cocky', so that we still talk about small farmers as cow cockies.

Cocky's joy

This is an old nickname for golden syrup, which the *Macquarie Dictionary* defines as 'a supersaturated solution of sucrose and invert sugars, derived from sugar processing; used in cookery and as a sauce for porridge, desserts, etc.' The nickname came from the idea that golden syrup on damper was one of the few pleasures a poor cockatoo farmer could afford. In *On the Wool Track* (1909), C. E. W. Bean describes cocky's joy as 'golden syrup in two pound tins, then costing seven pence – four times as cheap as jam and six times as portable.'

COD gate

A 'carry or drag' gate on a rural property: either a rough home-made timber gate or a commercial gate that's stopped making any real effort and has sagged despondently across the track. (Pronounced 'see-oh-dee gate'.)

Codswallop

'Codswallop' is not an exclusively Australian word, but it's used a lot here so it's well worth a look at. The *Macquarie* defines codswallop as a colloquial expression meaning 'rubbish' or 'nonsense'. It is of more recent origin than you might think, the earliest citation in the *Oxford English Dictionary* being from 1963. Officially the origin is unknown. However, perhaps we can do better than that by taking the word apart and looking at its bits. The first bit ('cod') has many meanings in English, but one of them is: 'a joke, a hoax, a leg-pull, a parody'. There's a related verb: to 'cod' someone was to hoax them in some way. As for 'wallop' it, too, has many meanings, mostly connected with hitting people, or the noise made when you do so. But 'wallop' was also once a nickname for beer. So, something that wasn't real beer would be codswallop. Well, it's one possible origin.

Colour

During the gold rush era traces or particles of gold in dirt being washed was called colour. Also used in opal mining for the presence of opal in rock.

Convict words

The first European settlers in Australia were hand-picked by the best judges in England. And these convicts brought with them their own strange way of talking – the thieves' cant (or argot) usually called 'the flash language' but sometimes known as St Giles' Greek, or Billingsgate or Newgate slang. In fact, the first Australian dictionary was something called *A Dictionary of the Flash Language* by James Hardy Vaux, himself a convict. And Dr Amanda Laugsen has produced a comprehensive survey of these words of early Australia in a book called *Convict Words*. It explains the origins of **swag** – originally the booty stolen by a thief, and in the Australian bush transformed into the bed-roll carried by an itinerant bush worker. Among the many words convicts contributed to Aussie English are **cove, lag, trap** and **duffer**, as in **cattle duffer**.

Cooee

When two things are far apart, why do we say they're 'not within cooee of each other'? 'Cooee' was originally a call used to attract attention in the bush. The first part of the word is long and the second part has a rising tone ('coooooo—*whee!*'). It's of Aboriginal origin, coming from the Dharuk people who lived in the west of what is now Sydney. It's first recorded in 1790 in Governor Hunter's journal. Because of the peculiar carrying quality of this call it was adopted by white settlers for the same purpose – attracting attention in the bush, sometimes over considerable distances. And because 'cooee' works, as a call, over distance it became a reference to distance, as in the expression 'not within cooee', meaning not within hailing distance.

In Queensland there's a place called Cooee Bay (near Yeppoon) where they have an annual Cooee Calling Contest, with winners judged on the loudness and length of their cooee. The record is in excess of 20 seconds. It was set by Mrs Clarice Sanderson, of Bauhinia, in 1987. And the year she set the record her feat was celebrated in a bush ballad called 'The Terribly Long Cooee':

We cooeed from the outback,
To the suburb of Balmain,
We cooeed down to Mudgee,
And we cooeed back again.
We cooeed in the paddock,
And up the garden path,
We cooeed in the shower,
And also in the bath.
We cooeed up to Townsville,
And down to Wollongong,
We must have got our cooee right,
Cause we didn't get it wrong.
We cooeed loud to Raeleen,
And John and Ruth and Stanley,
We cooeed on the ferry,
As we sailed across to Manly.
We cooeed up on top of hills,
We cooeed underneath,
We cooeed in the bathroom,
After taking out our teeth.
We cooeed, oh we cooeed,
With all the cooee in us,
And now we're in the records
Of the book put out by Guinness.

Coolgardie safe

A cabinet used to store perishable foods in the days before
refrigeration. The sides were either wire or lattice, and a damp
cloth was draped over the cabinet so that air blowing through the
damp cloth would keep the contents cool. Coolgardie is the name
of a hot, dry town, and shire, in the south of Western Australia.

Cookies and biscuits

What we call a biscuit is a cookie in America – a word that first appeared in print in the 18th century. Back then cookie was the word used in Scotland for a baker's plain bun. It comes from the Dutch word for cake, *koek*. Dutch cooks used to test oven temperature by first baking a little cake before putting the big cake tin into the oven. Biscuit (on the other hand) comes from a source that originally meant 'twice baked' (that's where the 'bi-' in biscuit comes from) – that being the original mode of preparation. Over time, the cooking technique was forgotten and biscuit was applied to various crisp, brown, baked items. Meanwhile, the Yanks had picked up the Scottish word 'cookie' and applied it to the same brown, crisp items. Confusingly, the Americans still use the word 'biscuit' but they use it for what we'd call scones. Confusing, isn't it? Safer to just point and say 'I'll have one of those'.

Coolibah

A common type of gum tree found in the bush, often around billabongs, as anyone who's ever sung 'Waltzing Matilda' knows. It's a species of eucalypt – the *Eucalyptus microtheca* (you wanted to know that, didn't you?) – and is said by the *Macquarie Dictionary* to be 'common in the Australian inland and usually associated with areas subject to occasional inundation'. It's sometimes spelled coolabah. The name comes from the Yuwaalaraay language.

Cornstalk

A person from New South Wales – an old nickname, no longer used. From the early 19th century the free white settlers were divided into two groups: the English and the cornstalks, this nickname being coined 'from the way they shoot up' (according to a quote from 1827). They were frequently the sons and daughters of convicts, and the 'English' constantly expressed surprise that these young people were taller, fairer and (utter amazement) more honest than their parents! (See also **Currency**.)

Corroboree

An Aboriginal gathering for a festival of dancing and singing. The word comes from the Dharuk language, and was recorded as early as 1790. It seems to have been fairly quickly extended, metaphorically, from Aboriginal ritual gatherings to almost any sort of assembly, especially a festive one. Today any large or noisy gathering can be nicknamed a corroboree.

Corroboree Rock Ghost, the

One of those rare apparitions that is prepared to pose for a photograph. The snapshot in question was taken in May 1956 by a Presbyterian minister, Rev. R. S. Blance, at Corroboree Rock west of Alice Springs. The developed photograph showed 'the ghostly figure of a man wearing a night-shirt and a balaclava with his hands clasped in prayer'. Sadly, the ghost has declined to appear in any further photographs since his one and only appearance in 1956.

Could eat a pineapple through a tennis racket

This means 'has big front teeth that stick out'. Another colourful (and offensive) expression coined, as far as I can discover, by young Aussies – who are clearly doing their bit to keep Aussie English as polite and considerate as ever!

Could talk under wet cement

A motormouth; someone who'll still be talking as the coffin lid's being nailed down. The earlier version of this expression was 'Could talk underwater' – but Aussie English found that a bit feeble, and beefed it up to 'Could talk under wet cement'.

Country

Journalist Robert Murray has pointed out that the good, solid old Australian word 'country' has been replaced (by politicians and city-bred journalists) with the phrase 'regional and rural Australia' – an extraordinarily bloodless term, he calls it, for the Australian countryside. When Dorothea Mackellar wrote: 'I love a sunburnt country ...' should she have written instead 'I love a sunburnt rural and regional Australia ...'? Spare me! It's a clumsy city-ism, which I'm sure country people can't abide. And while we're at it: any place too small for a pub, or with only one pub, is a township, while a place with two or more pubs is a town. (There are no such things as villages or hamlets in Australia.) But if the population is 30 000 or more, it's no longer a town – it's a city. Let's see if we can train our politicians to give up this ugly expression – 'regional and rural Australia' – and show some respect by calling the country the country.

Cove

It's probably been some time since an Aussie has been called a cove, but it used to be common. A bloke, a chap, a fellow, could be called a cove. From as late as 1969, from the Adelaide *Advertiser*, comes this citation: 'You Aussie coves are just a bunch of drongos.' It's earliest recorded use here is from the convict James Hardy Vaux who (in his *Dictionary of the Flash Language*) says that a cove is a 'boss' – the man in charge. Which is why a shearer, or swaggie, would go 'seeking a job off the cove', meaning the station owner or manager. Later, 'cove' came to apply to any bloke. C. J. Dennis wrote about Aussies as 'blokes and coves and coots' but that was when the diggers were marching off to World War I, and, sad to relate, 'cove' seems to be going the way of 'cobber' and slowly fading into the linguistic sunset. (See also **Cobber.**)

Cranky

We employ 'cranky' in Australia to mean 'ill-tempered' or 'cross', while in the UK and the US 'cranky' seems to mean 'eccentric' or 'foolish' or 'obsessive'. It seems to me that both of these uses of 'cranky' may (ultimately) trace back to the same source. 'Cranky' was coined in the 19th century and, says the *Oxford English Dictionary*, it consists of a group of meanings that hang together only loosely. Where it comes from, none of the experts seems to know, but the *Oxford* people suggest that it may be associated with the far older noun 'crank'. This seems to come from an Old English source word that means 'bent'. That's why a 'crank handle' is so named, and if you think of someone who's eccentric or ill-tempered as 'bent' out of shape, then it would make sense to call them cranky.

Crawler

A simpering sycophant who sucks up to the boss.

Creek

In Australia a creek is a small stream or rivulet, but (originally) in British English 'creek' meant a narrow inlet in a coastline: the tidal estuary of a river could be called a creek, and the word could also be applied to a small port or harbour. But in Australia, 'creek' came to mean a tributary, a brook or a small stream. This Australian variation on the British original is recorded from 1805.

Cricket lingo

Like all sports commentators, the ABC's cricket commentary team have their own particular lingo. Some of it is rhyming slang, as in 'Bunsen burner' for 'turner' – a pitch that'll help the spin bowlers. Some of it is typical Aussie irony, as in 'He's not a mug with the bat!', said of the bloke who's just scored a ton. But some is simply peculiar. A term that Kerry O'Keeffe uses (and takes responsibility for have coined) is 'pongo', as in the expression 'He's giving him some serious pongo!' It seems that 'pongo' is a form of punishment inflicted on a struggling bowler. Mind you, it might be the bowler's fault – he might be bowling 'pies': sitters that get splattered all over the ground.

Crikey

Amazing! Really surprising: 'Crikey! Did ya see what that bloke did?' The late Steve Irwin ('the Crocodile Hunter') has linked this term in American minds with the way Aussies talk through his hugely popular documentaries on the Discovery Channel. It's actually first recorded in England in 1838, and it appears to be an attempt at avoiding blasphemy by substituting the alliterative 'crikey' for the blasphemous use of 'Christ' as a swear word. Since avoiding blasphemy is always to be encouraged, this is a good move.

Cripple

Surfers' slang for a knee-boarder. Surfing has, of course, generated a whole language of its own, and a great deal of that linguistic invention has happened here in Australia. Once again we see the DNA of Aussie English showing its strength and adaptability as it passes from generation to generation.

Crocodile Dundee

A movie from 1986 starring Paul Hogan in the title role. Now sometimes used by journalists to identify someone as a stereotypical outback Aussie male – macho, laconic and quintessentially Australian: a genuine 'Crocodile Dundee type.' Territorian Rod Ansell was known to many as 'the original Crocodile Dundee'. His legendary outback survival skills preceded, and may have partly suggested, the fictional movie character.

Crook

This is a flexible and useful word in Aussie English.

1. If you're feeling a bit sick then you might say 'I'm feelin' real crook' (sometimes by using the rhyming slang 'butcher's', short for 'butcher's hook').
2. If you blow your top and shout at someone you might explain that 'I went crook on 'im'.
3. If you got diddled when you bought a second-hand car you might explain 'I got a crook deal'.
4. If there's someone you don't trust, and suspect of being dishonest, you might say 'I think that bloke's a bit of a crook'.
5. If something is broken, damaged or inferior you might say, 'Don't bother fiddling with the dial – that TV's crook'.
6. If you're annoyed with someone you might say 'I'm really crook on that bloke'.

   One small word with a rich world of uses!

Crooked Mick

Mythical bushman. The hero of many tall tales and bush yarns. Mick was bigger, better, faster, stronger, smarter, etc. than anybody else. Crooked Mick was a station hand on the legendary Speewah Station. (See **Speewah**.)

Crook in Tallarook

One bit of OBV (Old Bush Vernacular) that's almost died out is 'Things is crook in Tallarook' – a general form of complaint in response to bad news. At one time it was so common that Jack O'Hagan wrote a song with those words as the title.

But this, it turns out, is only one of many such place name rhyming phrases once common in Aussie English. Many are listed in the great Sid Baker's pioneering book *The Australian Language*. Examples include: the girls are bandy at Urandangie; there's not much work at Bourke; I got a feed at the Tweed; there's no lucre at Echuca; everything's wrong at Wollongong; might find a berth at Perth; there's bugger all at Blackall; and there's nothin' doin' at Araluen.

Crow-eater

Why are South Australians called crow-eaters? The earliest citation is from 1881, when someone called J. C. F. Johnson, in a book entitled *To Mount Browne and Back,* wrote: 'I was met with the startling information that all Adelaide men were croweaters ... because it was asserted that the early settlers ... when short of mutton, made a meal of the unwary crow'. And this, it appears, is literal truth, not mere myth. There are also stories of early settlers eating cockatoo and parrot. Dorothy Jauncey, in her dictionary of South Australian words, quotes one pioneer as saying that the breast of a cockatoo was thought very good eating, and parrots were particularly good in a pudding or pie. So I guess South Australians might have been nicknamed 'parrot-eaters' or 'cocky-eaters', but it was crow-eater that stuck.

Cultural cringe

This term, coined by literary critic A. A. Phillips in 1950, sought to capture the sense of inferiority that Aussies felt at that time when confronted by the ancient culture of the English, or the popular world-conquering culture of the US. In the more than half-a-century since the term was coined it seems to have become a ghost, an echo from a distant past. Today Australian culture is brash, confident, and seems not to give a toss what a bunch of people on the other side of the globe might think. The period of the cultural cringe now looks to be a lull, a temporary dip in confidence, between today's energy and the pragmatic confidence of the early settlers and nation builders of 150 years ago.

Curly

Aussie nickname for a bald-headed bloke.

Currency

From early in the 19th century locally born white settlers were often nicknamed 'currency'. You see, the English settlers were known as 'sterling', while the locals were not as valuable (or as genuine, perhaps) as British coins or treasury bills – they were only 'local currency'. In particular, those with convict parents were referred as currency lads and lasses.

Cut and come again

See Magic Pudding.

Cut lunch and a waterbag

A long way: 'Is it far, mate?' 'Yeah, it's a cut lunch and a waterbag away.' This is another of those ways of indicating distance that are imprecise, and yet create the right impression. In that sense, this expression works in the same way as 'within cooee' or 'not within cooee' – we know at once what is meant, even if we couldn't put a number on it. And when we're told that we'll need a cut lunch and a waterbag to get to Oodnagalahby, we get exactly the right impression: it's a long way off. (See also Cooee.)

Cut out

To separate an animal (sheep or cattle) from a mob.

Cyclone

While the United States is sometimes hit by 'hurricanes', Australia is struck by cyclones. These appear to be two different words for the same weather phenomenon: huge, destructive whirlwinds that rotate around a centre of low barometric pressure. The American choice ('hurricane') came into English, via Spanish, from a West Indian word and is therefore sometimes said to apply only to such wind storms when they arise in the West Indies. Our preferred word, 'cyclone', is a meteorologist's word from a Greek source word meaning 'circular'. Australia's most notorious cyclone was undoubtedly Cyclone Tracy, which devastated Darwin on Christmas Eve, 1974 (although some reports say that Cyclone Yasi, which struck north Queensland in 2011, was more powerful).

Dad and Dave

Typical blokes from the bush, not very sophisticated and not too smart – what Americans might call 'hayseeds'. They began life in a series of stories by Steele Rudd (1868–1935), starting with the book *On Our Selection* (1899). Rudd portrayed Dad and Dave (who were father and son) sympathetically in his stories, showing them, and all their family, battling to survive on a small selection on the Queensland Darling Downs. That first book became a popular stage play, then a movie, directed by Ken Hall for Cinesound, and then a long-running radio serial under the name of 'Dad and Dave from Snake Gully', produced by George Edwards, who himself played the lead role of 'Dad'. In the 1960s there was a short-lived weekly TV comedy series based on the characters, with Gordon Chater as 'Dad'. Their names can sometimes still be invoked today, for example by environmentalists who will accuse the 'Dad and Daves' of chopping down native trees and burning off bushland on their farms. (See also **Selection**.)

Daggy

If something (or someone) is daggy then it (or he or she) is out of date; ugly; useless; something you don't want and don't want to know about. ('What a daggy haircut!', 'What a daggy sheila!', etc.). A person or thing can be 'a dag'. Originally dags were the locks of wool clotted with dirt around the hinder parts of a sheep. The word is recorded with this meaning from 1731, and may have originally come from the English county of Kent. This wool on a sheep's rear quarters was often dirty with mud and excreta that attracted flies. To protect sheep from the resulting 'fly strike', the animals would be 'crutched', the daggy wool being shorn away from their private parts. Because of its unpleasant associations, 'daggy' was gleefully taken up by Aussie English as a way of saying the sorts of colourful things noted above. And there have been lots of variations in its usage. For instance, a 'daggy person' might simply mean a slovenly person, and a 'daggy room' an untidy room – though just like 'bastard', 'dag' can also (strangely) be used as a term of affection for an old friend (but don't try it on someone you've never met before). Also, according to the *Macquarie Dictionary* 'rattle your dags' is a colloquial expression meaning 'hurry up'.

Dak

The verb 'to dak' means to pull down, or remove, someone's trousers, usually as a joke, but possibly as a form of tribal punishment. (Sometimes spelled 'dack'.) The Australian National Dictionary Centre says that dakking 'often occurs in association with footballers, but it's clear its origin lies with schoolchildren'. In other words, the notion that it's hilarious to embarrass someone by pulling down their trousers in one swift move comes from children or from big, boofy footballers who think like children. The earliest citation seems to be from 2001, but it was probably part of the oral culture long before that. And this Aussie verb is based on a noun that's part of British slang. Trousers have been 'daks' since 1933; it began life as a proprietary name. Daks was the label, or brand, given to trousers manufactured by a company called S. Simpson Limited, of Stoke Newington Road, London. And 1933 is the year in which the label 'Daks' was registered as a trade mark. In the decades that followed, the word 'daks' travelled down the path previously trodden by 'Hoover' (and a number of other proprietary brand names) and entered the language as an ordinary word. And that's why what the English call 'debagging' is called dakking in Australia.

Damper

Bread cooked in a campfire, and usually round and doughy – another of Australia's national foods. Traditionally it's unleavened and baked in the ashes of an outdoor fire. It's first recorded in this sense in 1825 by Baron Field in his memoirs (in 1817 he had become judge of the Supreme Court of New South Wales). Before that, back in England, damper was used to mean 'something that takes the edge off the appetite' (because it 'damped' the appetite!). There are lots of recipes for modern (cooked in an oven) damper, such as this one:

Ingredients:
2 cups of self-raising flour
½ teaspoon of salt
1 teaspoon of sugar
1 teaspoon of butter
1½ cups of milk

Method:
Sift the flour, sugar and salt into a bowl. Add the butter and enough milk to make a manageable dough. Shape into a flat ball and place on a greased and floured oven tray. Bake at 220°C for 25 to 30 minutes.

Damper hole

In Baz Lurhmann's epic movie *Australia* the character 'Drover', played by Hugh Jackman says to another character, 'Shut your damper hole!' This is, clearly a variation on the earlier expression 'Shut your cake hole!' meaning 'Shut your mouth!' The problem is that 'cake hole' for 'mouth' seems to be not Australian but British RAF slang and is not recorded any earlier than 1943. Hence, 'Shut

your damper hole!' may (just possibly) be earlier Aussie slang –
but this seems unlikely. Much more likely is that it's an attempt
by Baz Lurhmann's scriptwriters to coin a bit of 'Aussie slang' that
would sound authentic. They failed.

Dampier's ghost

Captain William ('Black Bill') Dampier (1652–1715) was an English
buccaneer and adventurer. On 26 July 1699 Dampier reached Dirk
Hartog Island at the mouth of what he called Shark Bay in Western
Australia. According to a legend popular in the pearling port of
Broome, on misty nights the ghost of his ship the *Roebuck* (with
Dampier himself on the poop deck) can be seen driving before a
south-easterly breeze into Roebuck Bay, with its milky white sails
almost transparent in the moonlight. If you ask the locals about the
legend the usual reply is, 'I haven't seen it myself, but I once met a
bloke who had.' Good luck finding the bloke!

Dangle the Dunlops

To lower the wheels of an aircraft when it's coming in to land –
Royal Australian Air Force slang. The expression was made famous
by legendary Sydney broadcaster Gary O'Callaghan – but whether
he got it from the RAAF or they got it from him is unclear.

Darwin rig

Informal dress. Also known as 'Territory rig'. It originally
referred to the acceptability of less formal clothing in the heat of
the Northern Territory. At one stage Darwin rig consisted of, for
gentlemen, 'neat casual trousers with an open-neck shirt', and
for women, 'neat casual wear'. Mind you, a Darwinian recently
told me that getting dressed up in the Top End meant 'wearing
the T-shirt without the writing'. And Darwin rig has, and can be,
used in a more jocular way to mean pyjamas (the most informal of
informal wear).

Dead

Very – so you can be dead keen, or dead tired, or dead lucky, or dead anything else.

Dead horse

Sauce (rhyming slang). Usually restricted to tomato sauce, and its liberal application to meat pies.

Dead set

1. For certain; guaranteed; an expression of confidence, as in 'That horse is a dead set winner'.
2. True; honest; you can trust me on this, as in 'It's a dead set fact – would I lie to you?'

Dead spit

In his 1953 novel *Murder Must Wait* Arthur W. Upfield writes: 'The son's the dead spit of the old man.' This may be a conflation of 'dead ringer' and 'spitting image', or an abbreviated version of 'spitting image' with 'dead' used as an intensifier, or it may have arisen separately. It seems the oldest form of 'spitting image' was 'the spit and image of'. The great Eric Partridge said that he had traced the idea behind all these expressions back to 1440, in such statements as 'He's as like thee as if thou had spit him.' This is the source of the notion that 'He's the very spit of his father'. These expressions may mean something like: 'He's as like his father as if he'd been spat out of his mouth' – intended to convey that he had his father's character, his father's spirit. This is intensified if you say that he is the 'spit and image' of his father – has both his father's spirit and his appearance. (And, of course 'spit and image' was corrupted into 'spitting image'.) It strikes us as an odd thing to say, but I guess they thought (and talked) like that in the 15th century. And in one of those odd linguistic quirks, 'dead spit' remains part of the spoken language in the Aussie outback.

Deadly

Aboriginal slang word for 'fantastic', 'great' or 'awesome' (in the same way that wicked is used by many young English speakers). The 'Deadlys', established in 1983, are awarded annually for outstanding achievement by Aboriginal and Torres Strait Island people. This usage is not exclusive to Aborigines – 'deadly' is also Irish slang for 'excellent'. Although there are no early written citations, Aboriginal community leaders say this use of 'deadly' goes back many generations. It has been suggested that Aborigines may have picked it up from Irish arrivals, either settlers or convicts, as both communities were thrown together by their experience of repression. (See also **Didgeridoo** for another Aboriginal–Irish connection.)

Deadly treadly

A pushbike; a two-wheeler.

Death adder

A venomous Australian snake, scientifically the genus *Acanthophis*.

Dekko

To take a dekko means to take a look. If you'd asked me, I'd have guessed that this was an Aussie coinage. And I would have been wrong, although it's used more commonly in Australia than elsewhere. In fact, it comes from a Hindi word, *dekho*, being the imperative (or commanding) form of the word, meaning: 'Look!' The earliest citation is from 1894, from a London daily newspaper. There was a related expression earlier in the 19th century – to 'have a deck' at something. This came from another part of the same Hindi verb: *dekha*, 'sight', or *dekhna*, 'to see or look at'. This form ('have a deck' at something) appeared in the middle of the 19th century, mainly in publications about India. It seems to have died out once 'dekko' turned up and displaced it later in the century.

Demon bowler, the

Fred Spofforth (1853–1926). The first of the great overarm bowlers, who is said to have done more than any other player to put Australian cricket on the map. Playing for Sydney University in the 1873/74 season he took nine wickets for ten runs in an innings, seven of the batsmen being clean bowled. (The one batsman he failed to get out that day was Edmund Barton, who went on to become Australia's first Prime Minster in 1901.) Spofforth represented Australia on the 1878 tour of England, and on four subsequent tours. It was the English who gave Spofforth his nickname of the demon bowler. He once bowled the greatest batsman of his era, W. G. Grace, for a duck.

Der

A grunt of disapproval; a bit of oral punctuation that means, 'You've just said something really, really obvious. Like, so obvious that I'm embarrassed for you.' (Apparently a stronger version of the same expression is 'nah-der'.)

Derro

Short for 'derelict' – meaning those blokes who sleep rough on the streets and drink cheap wine (or even cheaper metholated spirits) out of a bottle wrapped in a brown paper bag.

Devlin's ghost

According to legend, Devlin's Pound in South Australia is named after an enormous Irishman who lived there in the 19th century. He was, so the story goes, a rogue who ran a wine shanty and stole cattle and sheep from local properties. For many years after his death, it's claimed, Devlin's ghost, mounted on a white horse, continued to haunt the area, supposedly seeking revenge on the police troopers who harried him throughout his life.

Didgeridoo

The Australian National Dictionary says that 'didgeridoo' is an Aboriginal word, originating in Arnhem Land. But now a researcher at Flinders University, Dymphna Lonergan, has suggested that this most Australian sounding of all words may, in fact, be Irish in origin. (No, that's not an Irish joke.) Lonergan argues that Aboriginal languages have names for this musical instrument such as *bambi, bombo, illpera* and *yidali* – none of which resemble 'didgeridoo'. Further, she argues that it can't be 'imitative' since the word 'didgeridoo' does not resemble the humming, droning sound it makes. However, both Irish and Scots Gaelic have a word meaning both a pipe and a crooning or droning sound. This word is pronounced (roughly) 'dooderreh' or 'doodjerreh'. When added to the Gaelic word for native, this becomes 'doodjerreh doo'. This theory would explain the failure of linguists to find 'didgeridoo' in any Aboriginal language.

Digger

Another slang way to speak to an Aussie male; if you forget a bloke's name you can always say either 'G'day, mate' or 'G'day, digger' and that'll cover up the fact that you forgot. Originally, a digger was a goldminer during the gold rushes; then a digger was an Aussie soldier in World War I (an **Anzac**); and now digger applies to any Aussie male. Can be shortened to 'dig'.

Digger dialects

Any major war produces a new rush of slang words. World War I was no exception, and the Aussie diggers were among the most inventive. For instance, they came up with 'a duck's breakfast' – meaning 'a drink of water and a wash' (a common breakfast on the front line); 'FFF', meaning 'completely miserable' (literally 'forlorn, famished and far from home' … although there were sometimes less polite words attached some of those Fs); 'nail scissors', for the crossed sword and baton worn as a badge of rank by a general; and 'nosebleeds', for the red tabs worn by staff officers. Someone who was always hard to please would be asked 'Do you want port holes in your coffin?'; a tall tale or unbelievable story was greeted with the response 'kangaroo feathers'; and wine (from the French *vin blanc*) was called 'plonk' – a bit of World War I slang that survives to this day.

Words and expressions such as 'Aussie' and 'furphy' and 'possie' and 'your blood's worth bottling' (later shortened to 'bottler') all came into our language for the first time on the battlefield. When you get a bunch of Aussie blokes together to fight in a big stoush suddenly, for some reason, language invention simply explodes. One oddity does emerge: it appears that World War I produced far more lasting verbal inventions than any of the others. Perhaps that was because of the role that the 1914–18 conflict played in shaping Australia's national consciousness. (See also **Plonk, Aussie, Furphy, Bottler,** and **Stoush.**)

Dill

The question is, which came first? The word dill meaning 'dimwit', 'drongo', 'dope', 'boofhead'? Or dill meaning 'a herb'? Well, the herb came first, by about a thousand years. The botanical name existed by around AD700. And I'm sure you'll want to know that botanically, dill is 'an umbelliferous annual plant with yellow flowers'. The 'nitwit' (or 'dumbo' or 'drongo') meaning of 'dill' came as an abbreviation of 'dilly', and that came from 'daffodil'. Hence, anyone who was 'daft' or 'daffy' (as in that well-known little black duck) was then called dilly, and then, simply, a dill. (See also **Drongo** and **Boofhead.**)

Dilly bag

Any small bag such as a handbag or a carry bag can be called a dilly bag. Dilly comes from a Yagara Aboriginal word for a bag or basket made from woven grass or fibre, and is first recorded from 1830. The compound expression 'dilly bag' is recorded from 1867, and from early in the 20th century the meaning was extended to cover a bag of any sort.

Diminutives

Every language on earth has abbreviations – however, Aussie English seems fonder of diminutives than most. Professor Roly Sussex and his team have been studying the role of diminutives in Australia, and have compiled a list of no fewer than 4000 of them to date! That's a lot of word shrinking we've been doing! There are several common forms of Aussie abbreviation. One is the 'O' ending found in 'arvo', 'wino', 'derro', 'Salvo', 'yobbo' and a host of others. Then there's the 'IE' or 'Y' ending – 'cardie', 'brekkie', 'footy' and the rest. Sometimes 'A' is added – as when Barry becomes 'Bazza' and 'Warren' becomes 'Wazza.' Sometimes it's just a straight-out shortening – as when Woolloomooloo becomes 'the Loo', Mount Isa becomes 'the Isa' and Woolloongabba become 'the Gabba'. Roly says we do this sort of thing out of (a) verbal playfulness, (b) informality, and (c) as an expression of group solidarity. (See also **Arvo, Wino, Derro, Salvo, Yobbo, Cardie** and **Brekkie**.)

Dingo

The Australian wild dog; often yellow in colour, it has pointed ears and instead of barking or yelping it howls, a bit like a wolf. 'Dingo' was first recorded by Watkin Tench in 1789 as the word for the native dog. Then came the metaphorical extension to human beings. If you call someone a dingo, you're not being polite. And, of course, there is also the verb 'to dingo', meaning to behave in a cowardly manner, especially in the sense of backing out or retreating. This verb is first recorded in the 1930s. When the then leader of the Queensland Liberal Party, Bob Quinn, criticised the then Queensland Premier, Peter Beattie, he ended his criticism with a challenge: 'Don't dingo out any longer.'

Dink

When you were a kid and gave someone a ride behind you on the back of your pushbike, what did you call it? The answer will probably depend on where you grew up. In much of Queensland and New South Wales, you'd be giving your friend a 'double'. In Victoria, Tasmania and Western Australia, it would be a 'dink' or a 'double-dink'. In South Australia it would be a 'dinky'; in southern Queensland and the north coast of New South Wales you'd be giving your friend a 'bar' on your bike; and elsewhere it's a 'barie'. However, in the ACT and close-by parts of New South Wales, it would be a 'doubler' or a 'dub'. The word 'dink', by the way, probably comes originally from a British dialect word for dandling a baby on your knee.

Dinkum

See Fair dinkum.

Dinky di

Genuine; real; reliable; true: 'Just trust me – what I'm saying's dinky di.' This is an abbreviation of the 'dinkum' part of 'fair dinkum', with a sort of rhythmic, alliterative final syllable added as an intensifier. It's first recorded from 1918, and that makes it another of those World War I coinages. (See also Fair dinkum.)

Dinner

For many years, and for many Australians, lunch was called 'dinner', while the main meal of the day, eaten in the evening, was called 'tea'.

Dishlicker

A greyhound. The popularity of these racing dogs among working class Australians led 'Rampaging' Roy Slaven and H. G. Nelson to coin this nickname for the slender speedsters.

Dob in/on

To tell on; if you tell the authorities about someone, you are dobbing on them: 'Ah, come on, ya don't dob in a mate!' The earliest recorded citation is from 1955 – but it's obviously older than that. It seems to come from a 19th-century English dialect word meaning 'to put down' or 'throw down', as in 'he dobbed it down the well'. (This 'dob' is a variation on 'dab', which came into English around 1300 from a Dutch source word.) The development of the word in the Australian climate is clear: if you inform on someone you are 'putting or doing him down' and, hence, 'dobbing' on him. The word embodies an Australian national value, perhaps one that goes all the way back to our convict forebears – you don't tell the authorities more than they need to know.

Dodgy Brothers

The Dodgy Brothers have made it into the dictionary. Among the seven and a half thousand terms added to the fourth edition of the *Macquarie Dictionary* was the expression 'Dodgy Brothers'. The definition for 'Dodgy Brothers' runs as follows: 'a company, operation, etc., which is unreliable and possibly underhand'. The expression comes from the ABC television series *Australia – You're Standing In It* (1983–84). From that show only the Dodgy Brothers made it into the dictionary, possibly because they are such a useful label for useless tradesmen. Dickens's Mr Micawber makes it, as does Shakespeare's Hamlet, but very few fictional characters overall make it into the hallowed pages of a dictionary. And this select few now includes the Dodgy Brothers.

Dog fence

The dog fence was built to keep dingoes out of areas where sheep were being run; it's the longest man-made structure on Earth, even longer than the Great Wall of China – 5400 kilometres of wood and wire that begins on a beach in Western Australia and ends in the Bunya Mountains in Queensland. It's sometimes called 'the dingo fence'.

Dog on the tuckerbox

See **Tucker**.

Dog-whistle politics

Aussie Lynton Crosby (who ran four election campaigns for John Howard) was hired by the British Conservative party to help in one of their elections. And as a result of his involvement, British newspapers picked up the Aussie expression 'dog-whistle politics'. This refers to a campaign message that will not cause general offence, but which contains a coded message to which sympathetic voters will respond, in the same way that a dog will hear a supersonic whistle inaudible to the humans around it. Both the *Observer* and the *Independent on Sunday* newspapers in London accused the Tories of dog-whistle campaigning through using language that sent subtle messages designed to appeal to prejudice and bigotry. Both papers are very PC and only ever spoke of dog-whistle politics in a very snooty tone. But it is nice when language from the colonies infects the British press!

Dole, the

Unemployment benefits.

Don, the

See **Bradman**.

Donah

Girlfriend. Now no longer used. Originally this comes from the Spanish word for 'woman', *dona*, and found its way to Australia via British slang.

Donga

A gully or channel formed by water erosion.

Donkey vote

Under Australia's compulsory voting preferential system a voter who simply numbers the candidates down the card (in the order in which they appear) is said to have cast a donkey vote – they've fulfilled their legal requirement to cast a vote, but have done so unthinkingly.

Dooverlackie

'Dooverlackie', or 'doover', is one of those words (like 'thingummyjig') that is used when you can't remember (or don't know) the proper name for something. 'Doover' was also Aussie military slang in World War II for a dugout or foxhole. And, according to one yarn, 'doover' was also slang for the bedpans used in military hospitals, and the bloke who had to empty the bedpans was the 'dooverlackie' – 'lackey' being a very old word for a servant. It's a good story ... it might even be true.

Dorothy Dix

Although the real Dorothy Dix was an American, the phrase used as a political expression is an Australian invention. When a minister in an Australian parliament is asked a question by a backbench member of his own party, a real 'sitter' of a question that gives him a chance to promote himself, his work, and his party, it's called a Dorothy Dixer. The assumption behind the expression is that the minister has written the question himself, and instructed the lowly backbencher to ask it. Dorothy Dix was the pen name of American journalist Elizabeth Meriwether Gilmer (1870–1951), who wrote a popular question-and-answer advice column (advice to the lovelorn – that sort of thing). And it was widely believed that 'Dorothy Dix' wrote the questions, as well as the answers, for her own column. Her syndicated advice column appeared in newspapers around the world for some 50 years. Hence her fame in Australia. Hence, also, the adoption of her name in the late 1950s or early 1960s for this parliamentary practice. The earliest recorded citation is from 1963.

Dough-banger

A cook; might also be known as a **babbler** or a **poisoner**.

Dough-whacker

Those who are lethargic and a bit slow on the uptake, as in 'you bunch of dough whackers'. This seems to be derived from two earlier Australian slang terms. 'Dough-banger' has been Aussie slang for a cook since at least the 1890s. 'And bushwhacker' is an expression from around the same period for someone who lives in the country – a bushie. When dough-banger and bushwhacker came together, they gave us dough-whacker, with perhaps the implication that a dough-whacker is someone who's not too bright and needs facts pummelled into them in the way that a cook pounds dough.

Down under

The nickname given to Australia, originally by the British. Recorded from 1886 as a colloquial rendition of the earlier expression 'the antipodes', from a Greek word meaning 'the other side of the globe' – literally, 'those having their feet opposite'.

Dreamtime (or The Dreaming)

The word English-speakers use for the Aboriginal creation legend: a 'golden age' in which the first ancestors were created; the source of stories, songs and rituals; the source of a sense of spiritual identification with a place or plant or animal. The English word 'Dreamtime' was coined as an approximate translation of the Aboriginal word *alcheringa* (from the Aranda language).

Dress circle

'Dress circle' is an expression that originated in the world of the theatre. The dress circle was one level above the ground floor, or the stalls. It was usually a semicircular gallery and the 'dress' was because those who sat there were (originally, at least) expected to wear 'dress' or evening clothes. So the dress circle captured something of the class structure, with the well-dressed families looking down on the great unwashed in the stalls below them. In Australia, and only in Australia, this theatrical expression has taken on a meaning in real estate. Those housing developments in elevated locations, with good views and large quality houses (the bricks and mortar equivalent of 'dress' or evening clothes) came to be called dress circle locations in the jargon of real estate agents. So the dress circle became a place to live with a nice view – if, that is, you can afford the house prices in a dress circle suburb.

Drip

An idiot; a real, brainless dropkick. The *Macquarie Dictionary* suggests that it can also be used to mean 'an insipid or colourless person'.

Dripping

The melted fat that drips from roasting meat, usually beef. In days gone by it was possible to buy a container of dripping from your local corner butcher's shop. The butcher had made the dripping by rendering down animal fat. You took home this container of pure saturated fat and when it was time for the Sunday roast you melted it in a pan in the oven in which you then cooked your rolled roast beef. And in poor families, especially during the Depression, school lunch consisted of sandwiches made of bread spread with dripping. Now, that would definitely not get the Heart Foundation's tick of approval!

Drongo

Drongo is yet another of those Aussie expressions meaning 'an idiot'. The story goes that there was a racehorse named Drongo that ran between 1923 and 1925. This horse supposedly always ran last, or near to last. Cartoonist Sammy Wells, then of the Melbourne *Herald*, apparently adopted Drongo as a character in his political and sporting cartoons. In these cartoons Drongo was the no-hoper in every situation. That's the story that's told. In fact, the earliest citation for the word 'drongo' is from the Melbourne *Argus* of 1924, and says: 'Drongo is sure to be a very hard horse to beat. He is improving with every run.' But, hang on, that doesn't sound like a horse that consistently ran last (or near to last)! Furthermore, there was a bird called a drongo and, just possibly, the insult 'You drongo' originally meant 'You bird brain'. Or perhaps both the bird and the racehorse played a part in the adoption of 'drongo' into Aussie English.

Drop bear

A drop bear is a savage marsupial that drops from gum trees onto unsuspecting travellers and tourists, uttering a wild and terrifying cry as it does so. Although its teeth and claws can cause considerable injury, no one has as yet actually died from a drop bear attack. (However, one elderly Canadian suffered from severe heart palpitations as a result of such an attack and needed medical attention.) Chameleon-like, they can disguise themselves as koalas sleepily eating gum leaves until a tourist has drawn near enough to leap upon. Their sensitive hearing can detect the sound of cameras clicking hundreds of metres away. Scientists say the breeding habits of the drop bear resemble those of the **hoop snake**, the **bunyip** and the **yowie**. Kenneth Cook once wrote a book about the habits and habitat of the drop bear.

Drover

A stockman who drives a herd of cattle, or a flock of sheep, over a long distance. (Today they've been replaced by big semi-trailers called 'road trains'.) This is an English word that can be traced back to at least 1425. But it remains especially relevant to Australia because of the legendary role the drover has played in building the modern nation. The great drovers of the late 19th century walked huge mobs of cattle from Queensland, or northern New South Wales, as far as the Northern Territory, to stock new stations in the Top End. (See also **Overlander**.)

Drover's breakfast

A **leak** and a look around.

Drover's dog

1. Something or someone that is unimportant.
2. Someone who works hard for very little reward: 'Is that all I get? After working all morning like a drover's dog?'

Drover's Guide

A mythical publication, said to be the source of all the rumours circulating in the bush. ('It must be true mate, I read it in the *Drover's Guide*'.) Sometimes called the **Bagman's Gazette**.

Drum

1. In Australian slang to be 'given the drum' means to be given a reliable piece of inside information. The word 'drum' turns up in the 16th century, with the meaning of a percussion instrument. It came into English from Middle Dutch, and there are related words in Middle High German, Danish and Swedish. By the late 16th century the expression 'by the drum' mean 'a public announcement' (a kind of forerunner of the town crier with his bell and his 'Hear ye, hear ye'). And if you were 'beating the drum' over something, you were making a loud, ostentatious noise on the subject. So there always was (almost from the beginning) an association between the beating of a drum and an announcement of news of some kind. But it's only in Australia that 'the drum' took on this meaning of inside information – sound, reliable information. The earliest citation is from 1915, from an early sporting newspaper called *The Grafter*. The citation reads: 'It beats me how the punters get the drum' (and I suspect the awful pun was intended).
2. A drum was also another name for a swag – a backpack consisting of all a bloke needs when tramping through the bush, wrapped up in a blanket – probably because of the drum-like shape of the blanket roll.

Ducks on the pond

A shout of warning, used in shearing sheds to announce the arrival of a lady – the shearers would then stop swearing until she left the shed. (Feminism brought a swift end to that sort of consideration being shown to women.)

Duck shoving

The *Macquarie Dictionary* records several meanings for the expression 'duckshoving', including: 'using unfair methods'; 'being unscrupulous or dishonest'; 'evading your responsibilities by passing them to someone else'; or (in the case of taxi drivers) 'soliciting passengers along the roadside, rather than waiting in turn at a rank'. And that last definition seems to be the original. 'Duckshove' is first recorded in *The Australian National Dictionary* from 1870 to describe the pushy behaviour of Melbourne cab drivers. It seems to have grown out of observations of ducklings, waddling in an orderly queue behind mother duck. The idea is that there's always one little duck that is pushy, and elbows the others aside to get what it wants. If that is correct, then it means that the original duckshoving was actually done by ducks – from where it extended to human behaviour that involves 'elbowing others'.

Duck's nuts

Excellent! A kind of squeal of pleasure.

Duffer

This word 'duffer' is part of a large family of words that were originally very negative and became softer and less pejorative over time. In the 18th century, duffing was 'passing off a worthless article as valuable'. From this it's clear that a 'duffer' was a criminal of sorts, specifically one who sold trashy goods. Thus, 'duff' goods were goods that were not what they appeared to be, or were not the real thing, or were not up to scratch. In 19th-century Australia a cattle thief was not a rustler (that's an American expression) but a **cattle duffer**. From all this came a further spin: a person who was a bit useless, without practical ability, inefficient, incapable, was called a duffer. By the mid 20th century this had been softened into 'silly duffer'.

Dumper

A wave which crashes downwards as it breaks, pounding the poor surfer it catches into the sand and half drowning them.

Dunny

Dunny seems to have descended from the 18th century word 'dunneken'. The last syllable ('ken') probably comes from a source meaning 'house', while the first syllable is probably related in some way to 'dung'. The *Oxford English Dictionary* defines a dunny as 'an earth closet, or an outside privy'. In Aussie English, 'dunny' has a wider application, and can be used to name any toilet or lavatory, inside the house as well as outside. However, the older, free-standing, outdoor dunny is preserved in some well-known Australian expressions such as 'As lonely as a country dunny' and 'I hope your chooks turn into emus and kick your dunny down.'

Dunny budgie

Blowflies have their own part in Australian culture and in the Aussie language – perhaps because there are so many of them (especially those big, blue-black bush flies) and because they're such a pest. Given the inclination Aussie English has for abbreviations, blowflies inevitably become 'blowies.' Waving them away as they buzz around you over the barbecue becomes 'the great Australian salute'. And blowflies are also known as 'dunny budgies' because of their prevalence around old-fashioned unsewered backyard dunnies. The 'budgie' part suggests that these giant blowies grow as big as budgerigars ('budgies' for short). 'Budgie' is recorded from 1935 and 'dunny' from 1933, but the earliest citation for the combination 'dunny budgie' is only from 1989. Hence outback dunnies are famous for both the redbacks that hide under the toilet seat, and for the dunny budgies that buzz around them. (See also **Blowie**, **Budgie**, **Dunny** and **Redback**.)

Dunny bunny

A person with a dirty mind, or a dirty mouth (or both).

Durry

'Durry' is an Australian slang word for a cigarette, especially a roll-your-own cigarette. It's first recorded with this meaning in Sid Baker's 1941 *Dictionary of Australian Slang*. There Sid says that 'durry' doesn't so much mean a cigarette as a cigarette butt. This was confirmed when I was doing talkback on ABC local radio and a caller said that back in the Depression if you didn't have time to finish a cigarette you didn't throw it away, but tamped it out and put it in your pocket to finish later. These half-smoked cigarettes, he said, were called durries. He added that the homeless (and desperate) used to look for discarded cigarette butts on the footpath, and smoked the durries they found.

But where does the word come from? I used to think it might have been soldiers' slang, but if so it certainly doesn't come from World War I, because it's not listed in W. H. Downing's comprehensive little book, *Digger Dialects*. The *Macquarie* suggests 'durry' may have come from a brand of roll-your-own tobacco called 'Bull Durham' – the 'Durham' part being shortened to 'durry'. The other possible source is a Hindi word, *dhurrie*, meaning 'a kind of cotton carpet of Indian manufacture, usually made in rectangular pieces with fringes at the ends, and used for soft covers, curtains and similar purposes'. If a bad cigarette (or a stale butt) tasted like smoking a bit of carpet, it might have been nicknamed a dhurrie. Well, it's a possibility.

Dynevor Bunyip, the

A monster that occupies the Dynevor Lakes in the Thargomindah district of south-western Queensland. A distant relative of the Loch Ness monster.

Earbasher

A person who won't stop talking; they just keep on thumping your ear with words; someone who drones on, and on, and on, and on, and on ….

Echidna

Why in some parts of Australia, such as rural Queensland and New South Wales, are echidnas commonly referred to as 'porcupines'? If echidna is correct, how did 'porcupine' become adopted as their name in some places? Or are these different names all correct? Well, there is only one correct name for these spine-covered, insect-eating monotremes and that is 'echidna' – a name given to them by a visiting French naturalist as long ago as 1798. A monotreme (just to remind you) is a mammal that lays eggs. True porcupines, on the other hand, are rodents, and grow much bigger – up to a metre in length. But early settlers called echidnas 'porcupines' because of the spiny resemblance. In much that same way, early settlers in Tasmania called wombats 'badgers'. And, that old (incorrect) name for the echidna survives even to this day in some areas.

Eh

1. An expression of inquiry or surprise.

2. An expression that invites agreement.
3. A verbal 'tag' with the meaning of 'Isn't that so? (cf. the French *N'est-ce pas?*). Often no question is implied and the expression is little more than a verbal tic or spoken punctuation mark. 'So, you're a north Queenslander, eh? I was born up that way, meself, eh. But ya'd never know from the way I talk, eh?' Sometimes expanded into 'waddayareckon, eh?' In some parts of Australia 'but' is added to the end of utterances in the same role ('It's a hot day, but') and sometimes the two are combined, as in, 'I reckon we'll get some rain, eh, but.'

Eight, ten, two, and a quarter

In the early colonial days this was a week's ration for a station hand on a sheep or cattle station: eight pounds of flour, ten pounds of meat, two pounds of sugar and a quarter of a pound of tea. (That's what once counted as a balanced diet!)

Ekka

1. Abbreviation for the Brisbane Exhibition Ground.
2. More commonly, the Brisbane Royal Agricultural Show held at that ground.

Emu

Australia's large, flightless bird. It stands around one and half metres tall, weighs around 45 kilos and has brownish-black, thick feathers. Only Africa's ostrich is a larger bird. The name seems to come not from any Aboriginal language (as you might expect) but from a Portuguese word, *ema* – originally denoting a type of crane, but later applied to ostriches, and ostrich-type birds. Emu eggs (as you might expect) are very large, and, in the colonial era, were often collected and decorated. The emu has been known to hit almost 50 kilometres per hour when running at full tilt. Aussie icon John Williamson coined the expression 'Old Man Emu' and focused on this high speed performance in his famous song:

While the eagle's flyin' round and round,
I keep my two feet firmly on the ground;
Now I can't fly, but I'm tellin' you
I can run the pants off a kangaroo!

(See also **Bush chook.**)

Emu words

The large flightless Aussie bird the emu has made a number of contributions to Australian English. It turns up in expressions such as 'emu bob', 'emu walk' and 'emu stalk', all with much the same meaning. They all refer to picking up litter from an area, usually by an organised group of people, often on school grounds as a punishment. The same activity occurs in the army, where it's usually called an 'emu parade' or 'emu patrol'. 'Emu bobs' are now sometimes organised by community groups as part of **Clean Up Australia Day.** And emu eggs have long been used in Aussie English as an expression of size, as in 'That cricket ball gave me a lump as big as an emu's egg, mate.'

Enough bends to break a snake's back

Standard Aussie description of a bending, twisting, winding road.

Enzed

Aussie nickname for New Zealand. (Pronounced 'en-zed'.)

Ern Malley hoax

A literary hoax perpetrated by two Sydney poets, James McAuley and Harold Stewart, in 1944. They wrote a number of unintelligible or semi-coherent poems and submitted them to the literary journal *Angry Penguins* as the work of a deceased mechanic and insurance salesman named Ern Malley. The poems were accepted, published and praised by Max Harris and John Reed, both in *Angry Penguins* and in a booklet called *The Darkening Ecliptic*. After publication, McAuley and Stewart revealed the hoax, describing their work as 'consciously and deliberately concocted nonsense'.

Esky

This is a registered trade mark that has become part of the Australian language. Malleys began marketing these small, portable coolers called Eskies (from 'Eskimo') in the early 1950s – and given the universal need that Aussies have to keep the beer (and soft drink, and salad) cool when they go to the beach or a barbecue, they quickly became a universal household item.

Eternity

'Eternity' was the one-word message of one of Australia's most colourful characters: Arthur Stace, known as 'Mr Eternity'. It's estimated that between the 1930s and the 1950s he wrote the word 'Eternity' some half a million times on Sydney's footpaths, in beautiful copperplate handwriting in yellow wax crayon (so that rain would not wash his message away). And Australia shared Arthur's one-word message with the world in giant, illuminated letters across the Sydney Harbour Bridge on New Year's Eve, 2000. So what did his message mean? Leo Schofield wrote: 'Stace's goal was to help us consider our mortality.' Exactly right. Arthur was asking everyone who saw his message a question: 'Where will you spend eternity?'

Ettamogah pub

The Ettamogah pub is the fictional locale of a long-running series of cartoons by Ken Maynard (1928–98). His series of cartoons featuring the distinctive lean-to pub began appearing in the *Australasian Post* in 1958. There are now at least four pubs in different parts of

Australia erected in the style of Maynard's cartoon building, all bearing the name of the Ettamogah Pub.

Eureka rebellion

An armed conflict between diggers and government authorities on the Ballarat goldfields in Victoria in 1854. The diggers were protesting against excessive taxation (in the form of a gold digger's licence) imposed by a government for which they had no vote, and which, therefore, did not need to respond to their protests. That makes it a 'no-taxation-without-representation' battle for democracy. The actual battle, early on Sunday morning, 3 December 1854, was quickly won by the troopers. But at the trials that followed, juries refused to convict those charged over the rebellion, and a subsequent Royal Commission granted the diggers the rights they had battled for. Out of the rebellion came the Eureka flag, based on the Southern Cross: a white cross with five white stars on a blue background.

Fair crack of the whip

Being given a fair opportunity, or a reasonable chance. First recorded in 1924 in the Sydney *Truth* newspaper, where it appears with the explanation 'just treatment' – and if an explanation was needed, then the expression must have been fairly new at the time. Five years later 'fair crack of the whip' can appear without explanation in Katharine Susannah Prichard's novel *Coonardoo*. None of the experts offers any suggestion as to the origin of the expression, except to say that it's one of a group of sayings, all of which capture the Australian principle of a fair go. Since the idea here is fairness, 'fair crack of the whip' may have come from the notion of a horse-drawn wagon or coach, with the idea of treating all the horses fairly by cracking the whip over each equally.

Fair dinkum

The urban myth surround this expression is that dinkum is of Chinese origin and means 'true gold'. It's supposed to have come from the goldfields during the rushes, the legend claiming that when the Aussie diggers heard the Chinese crying 'Dinkum!' every time they struck gold, the word caught on. Not true, I'm afraid. 'Dinkum' is an English dialect word brought to Australia by white settlers. It originally meant 'work'. In *Robbery Under Arms*, Rolf

Boldrewood writes, 'It took us an hour's hard dinkum to get near the peak'. From this came fair dinkum – originally meaning 'a fair day's work for a fair day's pay'. And then the meaning broadened to the one we know today: true or genuine, as in, 'Are you fair dinkum?' (I apologise if I'm exploding your favourite language myth!) Sometimes abbreviated to 'fair dink', in the great tradition of Aussie diminutives. (See Diminutives.)

Fair go

'Give us a fair go, mate!' a bloke might protest if he thinks he's not being treated fairly. It's a plea to be reasonable; a plea for sportsmanship. Australia was once called 'The land of the fair go' – the notion being that being fair to everyone, even-handed and reasonable, was a defining characteristic of this country.

Fang

This is a word with a long history, and a number of meanings in Australia.
1. Trying to borrow money from someone is 'fanging' them from the notion that 'putting the bite' on someone is 'putting the fangs in'.
2. To 'fang' the car is to drive very fast; while to drive around pointlessly, doing wheelies and screechies and trying to impress the girls, is 'fanging around'. (Possibly from the name of the legendary racing driver Juan Fangio.)
3. An old Aussie nickname for a dentist is 'fang farrier'. (In real life, farriers are blokes who fiddle with horseshoes in the way dentists fiddle with teeth.)

Federation

The formation of the Australian colonies into a single nation on 1 January 1901. The 1880s and 1890s were peppered with conferences and conventions as politicians, organisations, and citizens generally campaigned for Federation, to deal with such national matters as defence, tariffs and immigration. New South Wales politician Sir Henry Parkes (1815–96) is often called 'the Father of Federation' because of the key role he played, notably with his Tenterfield Oration on 24 October 1889, which galvanised support for Federation.

Federici's ghost

Frederick Federici was a handsome Italian bass baritone appearing in Melbourne in 1888, at the height of the **Marvellous Melbourne** era. During a performance of *Faust*, in which he played Mephistopheles, he left the stage in a cloud of smoke, vanishing into a stage trap door. Under the stage, Federici fell from the ladder under the trap door, and died a short time later. Before long the story began to circulate that Federici's ghost was haunting the Princess Theatre. His spectral appearances were reported by staff working alone, late at night, in the dimly lit theatre. He was usually described as 'a man in a top hat and a black evening cloak' who vanished into thin air the moment he was spotted (shy creatures, these ghosts). Sadly, when a dental hospital was built next door to the Princess, it blocked out the moonlight that filtered in through the high windows in the theatre – and without the misty moonlight, reports of ghostly appearances ceased. A rather prosaic end for such a theatrical ghost.

Fettler

The name given in Australia since at least 1887 to the workers who build and maintain railway lines. In most state railways they worked for what was called the 'Way and Works Branch' and their job was to maintain the 'Permanent Way' (what us non-railwaymen call 'the tracks'). Their work was celebrated by Banjo Paterson in his bush ballad 'The Flying Gang':

> I served my time, in the days gone by,

In the railway's clash and clang,
And I worked my way to the end, and I
Was the head of the 'Flying Gang'.

Fiddly-did

One pound (from the rhyming slang 'fiddly-did' = 'quid'). One of my father's favourite expressions. Disappeared with the arrival of decimal currency on 14 February 1966. That great event was heralded by a jingle sung to the tune of 'Click Go the Shears':

In come the dollars, in come the cents,
To replace the pounds and the shillings and the pence.
Be prepared for changes when the coins begin to mix,
On the 14th of February, 1966.

First Fleet

The group of ships which reached Botany Bay in January 1788. There were 11 ships and around 1500 people – convicts, sailors, soldiers, officers and civilians. All these people, and the supplies with which to launch the convict colony, were under the command of Captain (later Governor) Arthur Phillip. Descendants of those earliest European settlers now call themselves 'First Fleeters', and on Sydney Harbour there are still ferries named after some of the 11 ships in that fleet, such as the *Sirius* and the *Supply*.

Fisher's ghost

Perhaps the most famous ghost story to come out of colonial Australia. In 1826 a farmer and ex-convict named Frederick Fisher disappeared from his small holding at Campbelltown (now an outer suburb of Sydney). His friend George Worrall said Fisher had returned to England leaving all his property to him (Worrall). Four months later, John Farley ran into a local hotel late one night in an agitated state. He had, he said, just seen the ghost of Fred Fisher sitting on the railing of a nearby bridge. The story spread and police began an investigation. In a deep pool under the bridge where the ghost had appeared they found the remains of Fred Fisher. Worrall was arrested, put on trial for murder, and executed on 5 February 1827. No mention of the ghost was made at the trial. The story was frequently retold in books and newspaper and magazine articles, and in bush ballads. In 1924 Australian film director Raymond Longford made a movie called *Fisher's Ghost*, based on the legend. Campbelltown City Council now runs an annual Festival of Fisher's Ghost every November.

Five o'clock wave

See **Seven o'clock wave.**

Flash

The language spoken by the first convicts, and originating from the thieves' argot of London, was called the flash language. It's recorded in the first dictionary ever compiled in this land, *A Vocabulary of the Flash Language* (1819) by James Hardy Vaux, himself a convict. Many of those flash words found their way into the distinctively Australian dialect of English. Someone whose clothing and behaviour were showy and pretentious was originally called a flashjack (from 1898) and then just 'flash' (The 'jack' part in flashjack coming from the most common male Christian name.) Not a term of approval. There is also a positive use of 'flash' – something that looks good can be said to be 'looking pretty flash'.

Flash as a rat with a gold tooth

Dressed up in your best or newest clothes; looking very flash. If someone gets all dressed up to go out and then asks you how they look you could reply 'As flash as a rat with a gold tooth.'

Flash mob

1. A group of people, co-ordinated by mobile phone messages, who congregate in a public place for a piece of unscheduled performance art, and then melt away again. Like the crowd of several dozen who gathered at an intersection in a German city: each took off their left shoe, passed the shoe around the circle, put their own shoe back on again, applauded each other and left. This flash mob phenomenon appears to have begun in New York and to have rapidly spread around the world. Interestingly, in the phrase 'flash mob' the word 'mob' is being used in a distinctively Australia way. More broadly', 'mob' means a disorderly or lower-class gathering. But in Australia, 'mob' has the wider meaning of any mixed gathering or group – so it looks like it's the Aussie meaning being employed by the performance artists when they call their group a flash mob. Another small sign of the export power of Aussie English. (See also **Mob**.)
2. In earlier usage, 'the flash mob' could refer to the well-dressed crowd in the expensive seats.

Flat chat/flat strap

The source of both of these is probably the earlier phrase 'flat out', meaning 'at top speed', first recorded in 1932 and born out of the age of the motorcar: if your accelerator pedal is 'flat to the boards' (a related expression) then you're going as fast as you can. 'Flat strap' was originally 'as flat as a strap' – if you lay a leather strap down it will be about as flat as anything can get. 'Flat chat' is probably just a variation on that, one that caught on because slang expressions with a bit of rhyme seem to catch on – the key here being the rhyme of 'flat' and 'chat' rather than any particular meaning.

Flat dog

Queensland nickname for a crocodile; also called a long flat dog, or a gotcha lizard, or a mud gecko.

Flat out like a lizard drinking

Very busy: 'Are you busy, mate?' 'Busy? I'm flat out like a lizard drinking!'

Floater

See Adelaide food.

Flum

Both a verb and a noun. As a noun a flum is 'a fluke; a piece of luck', while the verb 'to flum' means 'to fluke (something)'. It appears mainly in sporting contexts, and mainly in New South Wales – in fact, it's possible 'flum' is a word known only in some parts of Australia. The experts at the Australian National Dictionary Centre suggest that 'flum' might come from the sugary dessert called 'flummery', which started as a Welsh word and dates back to 1623. Perhaps if things turn out sweetly for you, then you have flummed it. Or it might be from 'flummoxed', meaning 'confused or bewildered'. 'Flummoxed' began life as an English dialect word and is first recorded in Dickens's *Pickwick Papers* in 1837. In this case, if you have a stroke of luck that leaves people flummoxed, then you have pulled off a flum. The experts remain divided. 'Flum' is first recorded in a glossary published in a notorious newspaper, the *King's Cross Whisper*, in 1967; then in 1972 it turned up in a glossary from Parramatta Jail. But where it came from (apart from being another piece of Aussie verbal invention) remains unclear.

Fly cemetery

A fruit slice. This is one of those Aussie kids' terms designed to make food more attractive (as in **Snot block** for a vanilla slice and **Rat cemetery** for a meat pie).

Fly-in fly-out

A form of employment in remote parts of Australia. 'Fly-in fly-out' means that workers are flown in to work in mining or pastoral areas and then flown back to Perth (or Adelaide, or their nearest capital city). This can be for a few days, or (more commonly) a few weeks. The most common turnaround time appears to be two weeks on, one week off, with 12 hour shifts. Fly-in fly-out is frequently abbreviated to FIFO, especially in job advertisements. Most common in Western Australia, this expression is also used by miners in the Mount Isa area of Queensland and in the Moomba oil and gas field in the Cooper Basin of South Australia. Fly-in fly-out may have arisen because mining companies gave up on building remote settlements or towns.

Flying gang

A gang of railway fettlers who are rushed to repair emergency problems with the railway track as they arise. (See also **Fettlers.**)

Flying doctor

See **Flynn of the Inland**, below.

Flynn of the Inland

The Reverend John Flynn (1880–1951), founder of the Presbyterian Church's Australian Inland Mission. His stated aim was to 'cast a mantle of safety over the outback'. He provided spiritual, medical and educational help to remote families living in the vast interior of Australia. In 1928 he founded the organisation that became the

Royal Flying Doctor Service. Originally called the 'Aerial Medical Service' it used the then new technologies of radio and aircraft to send medical help to isolated outback stations and communities. (See also In like Flynn.)

Fogger boller

Used in Australia to mean 'what-d'ye-call-it' or 'thingummyjig', or to name any unknown person, as in, 'Isn't that old fogger boller over there?' The expression was brought to Australia by the Irish, who spelled it in the traditional Irish way as faugh-a-ballagh. Presumably the modern Australian spelling preserves the pronunciation – although there's evidence that the older spelling was well known in the 19th century. The original Irish term was a battle cry meaning 'Clear the way!' Its first recorded use was as a regimental motto by the Royal Irish Fusiliers in 1798. It remains the motto of the Royal Irish Regiment today. And that meaning of 'clear the way' may explain why it's used as the name of a road in the Tarana Valley, near Oberon, in the Blue Mountains west of Sydney. And why it's used by Banjo Paterson as a jokey name for a racehorse in his comic bush ballad 'Father Riley's Horse':

> He had called him Faugh-a-ballagh (which is French for
> 'Clear the course'),
> And his colours were a vivid shade of green

Calling faugh-a-ballagh French is, of course, Paterson's joke. (Later in the ballad he says that 'Banshee' is 'Spanish for an elf'.)

Fly screen

The fine wire mesh that Aussies have over windows and doors to keep the big, blue-black blowflies out. (See also **Blowie.**)

Flying cane toad

The bitter nickname given to the myna bird, in recognition that it is (a) a non-native introduced creature, and (b) very destructive. The Indian myna comes from south-east Asia (the name is a Hindi word). It snatches territory and nesting sites from native birds and small mammals. In a poll on the most hated pests in Australia, the myna would score a place of honour – alongside the fox and feral cats and, of course, the ugly amphibian for which it has been named, the **cane toad**. In some parts of Australia there have been campaigns to wipe out whole flocks of mynas, but in most places it is simply cursed with a muttered comment of 'It's those bloody flying cane toads again!'

Footy frank

Frankfurters – especially of the type sold at football games. According to the good folks at the Australian National Dictionary Centre footy franks began life as a proprietary term of the Hutton's company but the term has expanded over the years – perhaps as much as the waistlines of those footy players who've retired from the paddock and eaten too many footy franks. They have become, says the ANDC, one of those defining Australian icons – modest consumer items that summon up in memory all the drama, the laughter and the tears of AFL Grand Finals at the MCG. And the expression 'footy franks' has itself taken wings and become a metaphor. A dull person can be described as having 'all the personality of a footy frank'. And if you're feeling the sweltering heat then you're 'as hot as a footy frank in the microwave'.

Fossick

I was watching an episode of the UK television program *The Antiques Roadshow*, filmed in Australia. An Aussie guest said, 'Here's something I found fossicking in the junk room'. The visiting English expert looked puzzled. After some explanation the

Pommy antiques expert said, 'Ah, yes, you mean rummaging'. We can easily forget that 'fossicking' is an Australian word. The verb 'to fossick' is first recorded from 1852, in the *Australian Gold Diggers' Monthly Magazine*. And that's where it comes from. Nowadays we can fossick around for anything, but originally you fossicked by looking for surface gold in loose dirt around the diggings. 'Fossick' seems to be another of those English dialect words that died out back in the UK while surviving here. A fossicker may have originally been a troublesome person, according to the *Oxford English Dictionary*. And at the gold diggings someone who came along to potter around your dirt heaps to pick up what you missed would certainly be looked upon as troublesome.

Four-bob Robbo

Four-bob Robbo lived in the Sydney suburb of Waterloo in 1897. He came into a bit of money and bought himself a horse and trap. The money was quickly spent and Robinson tired of the horse – so he turned to letting out the horse and trap for four shillings a half day. Almost immediately there was a run on this cheap rate for the hire of a horse and trap. So Robbo bought two other horses and traps and let them out for the same low rate. Neighbouring livery stables resented his undercutting their rates, and used to cry out in derision when one of his rigs passed by 'Four-bob Robbo!' The cry was taken up by children and became a Waterloo classic. It cost one person two pounds, when a magistrate ruled that 'Four-bob Robbo!', called out in the street, constituted insulting language calculated to create a breach of the peace. However, the term spread, and for a while any horse and trap was called by the street boys 'a Robbo'.

Four wheels in the city

In flash suburbs around Australia you'll find very expensive, top-of-the-line four-wheel drive vehicles employed for suburban use only. These are four-wheel drives that never see the bush. Instead, such a vehicle sits in a neatly cemented driveway sadly pining for the feel of real dirt and mud beneath its tyres. What is interesting is the number of nicknames they've attracted. In Melbourne, a city-bound four-wheel drive is a Toorak tractor or a Toorak shopping trolley; in Adelaide, it's a Burnside bus; and in Brisbane it's a Kenmore tractor. But in Sydney it's attracted a host of nicknames including a Balmain bulldozer, a Bronte buggy, a Double Bay or Mosman or Rose Bay shopping trolley, and a north shore tank or north shore Kingswood. It's seems that only in the television ads do these vehicles cross deserts and mountains – in real life they pick up the groceries from the supermarket and the kids from school.

Fremantle doctor

A soothing meteorological medicine consisting of a cooling afternoon sea breeze. Also known as the 'Freo Doctor'. The application of the word 'doctor' to a cooling sea breeze is recorded in Aussie English from 1870. The Fremantle doctor now shares its medical qualifications with a number of other refreshing breezes: Albany, Esperance, Eucla, Geraldton, the Nullarbor and Perth are all said to have their own 'doctors' – but the Fremantle doctor remains the best known. (See also **Southerly buster.**)

Full as a goog

See **Goog**.

Funnel-web

A venomous Australian spider whose bite can cause death to humans. They are large, dark-brown to black ground spiders. They live in burrows under rocks, logs and ground litter and in the summer months the males can roam at night in search of a mate. As well as being black and hairy, they are excitable and aggressive, and will readily raise their front legs and rear up into their strike position. (If you find a funnel-web let your cat deal with it – their venom is deadly to humans but harmless to cats.)

Furphy

In Australia a false or unreliable rumour is a furphy. The earliest recorded use is 1915, and, indeed, it seems to come from the diggers of World War I. The firm of J. Furphy & Sons operated a foundry at Shepparton in the late 1800s. One of their products was a water cart. These water carts were used by the Australian Army in World War I and (inevitably) became the place where diggers gathered and gossiped. The name Furphy was prominently printed on the back of each water cart, and became the name for the unreliable gossip exchanged there. When soldiers start swapping stories – especially about what the brass have got planned for them, where they'll be shifted next, and when they'll get some leave, they are bound to get it wrong – and, hence, to spread furphies.

The word 'scuttlebutt' has an identical origin. It means much the same – 'idle gossip'. On a sailing ship the scuttlebutt was the cask (or butt) of drinking water stored on the deck near the scuttle (or hatchway) where sailors gathered to exchange gossip.

By the way, each Furphy water cart had the following words of wisdom on the side: 'Good, better, best: never let it rest, until your good is better – and your better best.' That's the kind of motto our grandparents lived by (and it didn't do them any harm, either).

Fuzzy wuzzy angels

Papua and New Guinea islanders who acted as stretcher-bearers for wounded Aussie diggers during World War II. (The name was used affectionately, but sounds somewhat patronising today.)

Gabba, the

The Brisbane cricket ground, in the suburb of Woolloongabba. Although it may have first won its fame as a host for Test and interstate cricket, the Gabba is now a major, 35 000-seat sports stadium.

Galah

Officially a galah is a grey-backed, pink-fronted cockatoo. As such, the word 'galah' comes from the Aboriginal name for this bird (from the Yuwaalaraay language). But 'galah' has been extended to become an Australianism for a fool, a nincompoop, a simpleton, a **drongo**, **dill**, **drip**, dope, mug or **boofhead**, perhaps from the thought that such a person is a bird brain. (Australian English seems to have more words to describe stupidity than any other language on earth. Why, I don't know.) Then, from the noise that galahs make when they flock together we also get the expression 'galah session', meaning a private conversation, especially between isolated women on inland stations via outback radio. And there used to be another expression, 'galah pie', which was an old country dish much favoured by station hands and drovers.

Gammon

To kid someone is to gammon them; when you're mucking around, a lie told as a joke is 'a bit of gammon'.

Gardiner's gold

The Great Gold Escort Robbery in June 1862 netted Frank Gardiner's bushranging gang £14 000 worth of gold. Most that was never recovered. The attack on the coach carrying gold from the Lachlan River diggings happened near Forbes in NSW, and for many years afterwards locals remained firmly convinced that Frank Gardiner's share in the loot was still buried somewhere in the area. If only they could find it ...

Garth ghost, the

'Garth' was the name given to a stone house (back in the days when houses had names) in South Esk, near Fingal, in Tasmania. The house was built by a young English migrant for his new bride. With the house underway, but not completed, he sailed back to London to marry his fiancée – only to discover that she had undergone a change of heart. The jilted young man returned to Tasmania and hanged himself in the still unfinished stone house. His ghost was said to haunt the courtyard of the building on dark and stormy nights.

G'day

The distinctively Australian use of 'g'day' is recorded in *The Australian National Dictionary* as long ago as 1857, where the citation reads: 'Not one of them spoke to me, except to give me the occasional "Good day, mate".' The shorter spelling of the expression ('G'day') is first recorded in the *Bulletin* in 1927. It is, of course, an abbreviation of the rather more pedestrian English expression 'May you have a good day.' This form is very old indeed, being recorded in the *Oxford English Dictionary* as long ago as 1205. It had become the slightly elliptical 'Good day' by the time of Jane Austen, but it was Australians who managed to turn it into a single word: 'G'day'. And Mick Dundee, Steve Irwin and others have now made this familiar around the world (especially in America). So, when you meet a tourist, don't let them down. You'll make their day if you remember to greet them with 'G'day'.

Germaine Greer

Beer (rhyming slang) from Australian feminist, author, public intellectual and world-beating whinger Germaine Greer (b. 1939).

Get rinsed, to

To have a few alcoholic beverages – in other words, 'to get drunk'. Perhaps an extension of references to a few beers as 'a few cleansing ales' (when you've been 'cleansed' enough, you've been 'rinsed').

Ghosty

A game in which a bike is pushed along the street or footpath without a rider, and then released to coast by itself. The object of the game is to make the bike go as far as possible before it falls over.

Gibber

When I was a small boy a stone was called a gibber. In fact, a gibber was particular sort of stone – it was the kind of small stone that was suitable for throwing at gangs of other small boys in displays of swaggering infant masculinity in desultory battles that ranged up and down the street. This use of gibber is recorded in Sydney from 1790. In fact, in the 1830s the Sydney district called 'The Rocks' was nicknamed 'the gibbers'. Gibber comes from the Dharuk Aboriginal language. Stony parts of Australia have been called gibber country, gibber plain, or gibber desert. The community newspaper at Woomera is *The Gibber Gabbler*. But this remains a regional word, and elsewhere small boys used different names for the same small stones. Depending where you grew up in Australia you would have called these throwing stones 'boondies', 'brinnies', 'gonnies', 'goolies', 'ronnies' or 'yonnies'. And a number of these names also came from local Aboriginal languages.

Gidgee

1. There are two native Australian plants called gidgee: (a) the *Acacia cambagei* or 'stinking wattle', which gives off an unpleasant odour at the approach of rain; and (b) certain other species of wattle, including the poisonous Georgina gidgee or *Acacia georginae*.
2. A spear-like weapon for catching octopus, made from gidgee wood. According to one description, a gidgee was a short spear attached to a rubber loop – you held the end of the loop, pulled the spear back and gripped it so that you had tension, then released your grip to fire the gidgee. The word comes from the south-western Western Australian Aboriginal language Nyoongar.

Gilbert's ghost

Johnny Gilbert was an Australian bushranger and a member of Ben Hall's gang. He was born in Ontario, Canada, in 1842. Gilbert was trapped and shot dead by police near Forbes, in New South Wales, in 1865 (having been betrayed by a friend). This event was recorded by Banjo Paterson in his bush ballad 'How Gilbert Died':

> There's never a stone at the sleeper's head,
> There's never a fence beside,
> And the wandering stock on the grave may tread
> Unnoticed and undenied;
> But the smallest child on the Watershed
> Can tell you how Gilbert died.

Shortly before his death Gilbert had borrowed a racehorse from a squatter, promising to return it. When Gilbert was shot, the horse ran off into the bush and was believed to have run wild. However, according to the tale, some months later noises were heard in the squatter's stable yard late at night. The residents of the homestead ran out in time to see the ghost of Johnny Gilbert putting up the slip rails and fading into the moonlight. They ran into the stables and found, in his own box, the horse that Gilbert had borrowed.

Ginger Meggs

Australian comic strip character. Created by Jim Bancks (1889–1952). The comic strip first appeared in 1921 in the *Sunday Sun* newspaper. Ginger has a gang of mates, a girlfriend called Minnie, a rival in Eddie Coogan, and an arch enemy named Tiger Kelly. Following Bancks's death the comic strip was continued by a series of successors and continues to appear in newspapers around Australia, and around the world. The comic strip has inspired the movie *Ginger Meggs* (1982) and a 1991 stage musical by Jim Graham and Gary Downe.

Glue-pot

A wet and muddy section of a bush road, with potholes full of soft mud that will bog even your nice new four-wheel drive.

Giggle

1. Giggle house: secure accommodation for the terminally confused.
2. Giggle juice: any alcoholic beverage.

Go bag ya head

An expression of dismissal; another way of saying 'Drop dead'.

Goanna

The name given to Australia's large native monitor lizards. The word is recorded in Australia from the 1830s. This is another of those words you might assume was Aboriginal, when, in fact, it's a corruption of the Spanish word *iguana*. A goanna has a long head and neck, and a forked tongue. The body is usually black or brown with yellow bands or spots. The legs are short and powerful, and the tail is narrow and whip-like. The largest goanna in Australia is the Perentie, found in South Australia and the Northern Territory. It averages about 1.5 metres in length, but is known to grow to over 2 metres (making it the second largest lizard in the world, after the Komodo Dragon of Indonesia).

Gone to Gowings

This was formerly an advertising slogan used by Gowing Brothers department store in Sydney, now employed with a variety of meanings:
1. Deteriorating financially.
2. Ill, especially with a hangover.
3. Failing dismally, as of a racehorse, a football team, etc.
4. Having left; departed hastily without a specific destination in mind (or without leaving a forwarding address).
5. Drunk.
6. Gone nuts, cuckoo, insane.

Sadly, now Gowings itself has gone … and the expression (with all its meanings) is an echo from a fast-fading past.

Good oil, the

As far as I can discover in my researches the word 'oil' is World War I slang. It certainly turns up in W. H. Downing's 1919 collection of war slang called *Digger Dialects*, where oil is defined as being 'news' or 'information'. And this slang usage of 'oil' is definitely an Australian invention. Bill Ramson's note (in his 1990 edition of

Digger Dialects) suggests that 'oil' was used to mean 'the substance essential to the running of a machine'. Both 'oil' and 'dinkum oil' date from 1915, he says, and had very wide currency as Services' slang. Sometimes information was just 'the oil' and sometimes it was qualified as 'the dinkum oil' or 'the straight oil' or 'the good oil'. There was even a publication in 1915 called *The Dinkum Oil War News*. It must have spread quickly, because by 1916 C. J. Dennis could write: 'Now that's the dinkum oil from Ginger Mick'. In any army with stretched supply lines, essentials are often in short supply, and I wonder (it's a bit of pure speculation) if the diggers in World War I compared reliable information to oil because both were needed and both were scare?

Good onya

Well done! A bit of encouragement shortened from 'Good on you' – and sometimes shortened even further to 'Onya'! (Yet another expression Aussies love to abbreviate.)

Good-oh

'Good-oh' is a general term of approval in Australia – or used to be. I suspect it's declining in currency. It's an example of that oddly Australian construction that sticks an 'O' on to the end of something. Thus we talk about the 'salvos', or call an 'ambo' to an accident that may involve a 'derro' or a 'wino'. From the same bizarre stable came such expressions of approval as 'right-oh', 'whack-oh' and 'good-oh'. Interestingly, the earliest Australian citations for 'good-oh' seem to come from World War I, but there is an earlier New Zealand citation (from 1905). So perhaps the exclamation 'good-oh' was first heard in the land of the long white cloud, and became a part of Aussie English when the Anzac fighting force was formed. It is certain that the Anzacs brought a lot of their slang back with them to civilian life – including, it would seem, 'good-oh'. (See also **Whack-oh-the-diddle-oh.**)

Goodoo

An indigenous name for the Murray cod (*Maccullochella peelii*) – from the Kamilaroi language of northern New South Wales and Southern Queensland. In fact, it's probably a much better name for the fish than 'Murray cod' since the finny creature is not really a cod at all (certainly in the sense of the original European sense of cod). The name 'goodo' appears in 1898 in K. Langloh Parker's *More Legendary Tales,* and exactly one hundred years later was used by Robert G. Barrett as the title of his novel *Goodoo Goodoo.* (See also **Whales.**)

Goog

Egg. Sometimes as 'googie egg'. Hence the expression 'as full as a goog', which usually means drunk, but sometimes means that one has eaten one's fill. This can be expanded to 'as full as a goog at a Christmas party'. The earliest citation is from Sid Baker's 1941 *Dictionary of Australian Slang* – but it's obviously older than that. How Australians came to call eggs 'googs' I don't know, and, apparently, neither does anyone else. But once you accept that, the rest is clear: an egg is completely full of its contents, so to be 'as full as a goog' is to be completely full – filled to the shell with no room for any more. Sid Baker suggests that 'goog' might originally have referred to the roundness of eggs, but it remains uncertain.

Goose

Why do Aussies call someone a goose if they do something stupid? Why not a duck or some other bird? Well, for a start, 'goose' is a popular word in slang expressions. *Cassell's Dictionary of Slang* has 55 different expressions using 'goose' in one construction or another. And amongst these, 'goose' has been used to mean 'a fool' since the 16th century. This goes back to the belief (strong in folklore) that the goose is an unusually stupid bird. If you thought a duck was dumb, well, proverbial wisdom insists the goose is worse, being unusually slack-jawed and slow on the uptake. You might get a budgie to understand binomial theorem, but never a goose. Whether this folklore is true, or a gross calumny on the name of a fine and noble bird, I do not know. However, this belief that geese have the IQ of sea anemones is the reason for the word's colloquial use.

Got their licence off a Weeties packet

An expression of complaint about a bad driver.

Gotcha lizard

A listener reported that in a crossword puzzle the clue offered was 'Oz croc' and the answer was 'gotcha lizard'. He added: 'No one I've spoken to (and that includes 70 and 80 year olds) has ever heard the expression before', and then asks: 'Have you ever heard of an Australian crocodile being so described? If so, when and where?' The answer is 'yes' and 'in Far North Queensland'. (It could be that the 70 and 80 year olds had not heard of it, because the expression is relatively new.) And 'gotcha lizard' is not the only odd expression they have up in the pointy bit at the top end of Queensland. In those same northern tropical parts a crocodile can also be referred to as a 'mud gecko' or a 'flat dog' or a 'long flat dog'. Crikey!

Government house

1. The official residence of the representative of the Crown, originally in each colony, now in each state.
2. Nickname given to the main building on a large sheep or cattle station.

Govie

The national capital Canberra is a government town, and 'govie' is a Canberra word for a government-built house (to provide low-cost or subsidised housing). A 'govie' that is no longer owned by the government, and has been done up by its owners, is called an ex-govie (subtle class distinctions are involved here).

Goyder's Line

In 1865 surveyor George Goyder plotted a rainfall line across South Australia, below which agriculture was possible, but above which the lack of rain meant that grazing might be possible but agriculture was out of the question. Goyder's line starts on the west coast near Ceduna and goes south-east across the Eyre Peninsular to reach Spencer's Gulf near Arno Bay. Goyder's Line became a National Trust of Australia Heritage Icon in 2003.

Grass castle

A sprawling outback property. There were once cattle stations in the Northern Territory, and in the north of Western Australia, bigger than some European countries. Their economies were fragile, being dependent on the tall cattle grass that grew after the rainy season – a few bad seasons, or the bank foreclosing on the mortgage, or a natural disaster or two (flood, bushfire, cyclone), and the whole enterprise could collapse. The phrase appears to have been coined by Mary Durack in the title of her 1959 book *Kings in Grass Castles*, in which she told the story of her pioneering pastoralist family, and in which she wrote 'We are kings in grass castles that may be blown away with a puff of wind.' Sometimes the expression refers to the head station, or homestead, rather than the whole property. Mary Durack's expression was borrowed by the news media from the 1970s onwards to describe the palatial mansions built by crime bosses who ran the drug trade (from 'grass' as slang for marijuana).

Granny Smith

A green-skinned apple suitable for either eating or cooking. Named after Maria Ann Smith (1799–1870), who first cultivated this type of apple at Ryde in Sydney.

Great Australian salute

The irritated wave of the hand that shoos away annoying blowflies.

Grid

Bicycle – possibly because the metal frame of the bike suggests a grid of bars with openings between them; recorded from 1927.

Group settlement

A 1920s settlement scheme whereby the underdeveloped south-west of Western Australia was to be settled by British migrants, many of them ex-soldiers. (The scheme was run in co-operation with the British and Australian national governments.) However, the properties were small and the infrastructure primitive, limiting the success of the scheme. Someone who settled on one of these places was called a 'grouper' – not to be confused with a 'groupie' (a different species entirely).

Grouse

Good, or very good. A general word of approval. According to June Factor's excellent dictionary *Kid Speak*, young Aussies are just as likely to call something they like 'grouse' as they are to say 'cool' or 'awesome'. This is an encouraging sign that an excellent Aussie word is not about to die out. But where does it come from? The experts don't know. All the authorities say 'origin unknown'. One suggestion is that it may come from an old lowland Scots word, 'crouse', which (apparently) had much the same meaning. This may well be true, but there is no evidence. Other possible sources are the British moorlands bird, the grouse (something as bright as a bird could be said to be 'grouse'). Then there's the verb 'to grouse', meaning 'to complain' – and since meaning reversal happens in language, that's a possible source. The first citation for 'grouse' is from 1924, but where it arose from, or what was bubbling in the lexicon before 1924, remains a mystery.

Grosvenor's ghost

Munro Plains (inland from Townsville, in Queensland) has laid claim to its own ghost. The spectre is said to be the spirit of 19th-century English migrant Dick Grosvenor, who died when he fell headfirst into a large flour container and suffocated. Late night travellers claimed to see his whiskered, flour-covered ghost in the distance on moonlit nights.

Gully

A small valley; an eroded watercourse; a dry, water-worn depression. The word is very common in Australia and is frequently used as a place name. Hence such mythical places as 'Snake Gully' and 'Gunn's Gully'.

Gully raker

1. A thunderstorm that brings heavy rain – the expression is most commonly used in this sense in the New England district of New South Wales.
2. One who musters unbranded cattle from country that's not easily accessible.
3. A cattle thief.
4. Banjo Paterson applies the expression to stockmen who round up wild horses (**brumbies**) in remote, rough and rocky places:

   So, off to scour the mountain side
   With eager eyes aglow,

To strongholds where the wild mobs hide,
The gully-rakers go.

Gully wind

An evening wind, often strong, that blows off the Mount Lofty ranges over Adelaide in summer when the wind turns south-easterly.

Gum tree

The popular Aussie name for any tree or shrub of the genus *Eucalyptus*, almost entirely Australian apart from a very few tropical species in New Guinea and other nearby islands. The name comes from the thick, viscous sap exuded by a number of these eucalypts. These are the sort of trees that grow all over Australia; there are so many gum trees here they even wrote a song about them:

Give me a home among the gum trees,
With lots of plum trees,
A sheep or two, a k-kangaroo,
A clothesline out the back,
Verandah out the front,
And an old rocking chair.

As long ago as 1898 Edward E. Morris in his *Austral Dictionary* listed some 44 different (popular) names for different types of gum trees.

Gumsucker

A person from Victoria – an old nickname, no longer used. The legend says that back in the colonial era the bushies of the Garden State would sit around yarning, and, instead of chewing on a blade of grass, would chew on a wad of gum prized off the bark of a nearby gum tree.

Gun

This has both good and bad meanings.

1. 'In the gun' means unpopular (not good news if you're in the gun with the boss).
2. 'Under the gun' means pressed for time (the notion being that you're not ready for the starter's gun to fire).
3. Someone who is 'a gun' is very good at what they do (usually found in the combination 'gun shearer').

Gunyah

An Aboriginal name for a rough bark hut or temporary shelter. From the Dharuk language, and recorded from around 1790.

Guyra poltergeist, the

In 1921 the house of a local council worker in Guyra (in northern NSW) was disturbed nightly for a month by showers of stones thrown through windows and the rocking of the dwelling 'as if by giant hands'. Police and enthusiastic volunteer investigators failed to find any human explanation for this activity – which ended as mysteriously as it began.

Had the bean

Broken; doesn't work any more; no use.

Ham and beef shop

A delicatessen is one of those (usually small) shops filled with all kinds of delightful food items. The *Macquarie Dictionary* defines it as: 'a shop selling cooked or prepared goods ready for serving, usually having a noticeable proportion of continental or exotic items'. The word 'delicatessen' appears to have been coined in America in the late 19th century from a group of related words found in several European languages (including Greek and French) that originally meant 'delicacies or relishes for the table'. That's a name that seems to make sense, bearing in mind the range of stock such shops carry. However, the odd thing is that when I was a boy they weren't called 'delicatessens' but 'ham and beef shops'. Why this was so I have no idea, since they always sold a great deal more than just cooked and sliced ham and beef. The greengrocer is known as the 'fruit and veg' shop, but this fairly accurately describes his stock. Not so in the case of this odd expression, which is now largely obsolete. And the local delicatessen is now called the deli (hey, why bother to say more syllables than you have to?).

Hanrahan

See **Said Hanrahan.**

Happy as Larry

I've been asked more than once for the origin of the expression 'as happy as Larry' (meaning 'very happy'). The source is not certain, but I'll tell you what we know. In the first place, this is definitely an Australian term. It has spread around much of the world, but it started here. Sidney J. Baker, in his classic book *The Australian Language* says that while we can't know for sure, it's possible that it comes from an Australian boxer named Larry Foley (1849–1917). Why he was regarded as a happy pugilist is lost in the mists of time, but apparently he was. 'Happy as Larry' is first recorded in 1905, but was probably part of the spoken language well before that. There was an older expression, 'a Larry Dooley' or 'a Larry Foley', meaning a fight. And, I guess, if you liked a fight that would make you as happy as Larry.

Happy little Vegemite

Vegemite® is a popular salty spread Aussies eat on toast for brekkie; no one else in the world seems to like the stuff, so young Aussies are sometimes called 'happy little Vegemites' (and there was once an advertising jingle with these words as the refrain). (See also **Vegemite®.**)

Hashmagandy

A type of stew. First recorded in this sense as soldiers' slang in World War I for 'an insipid and monotonous army dish'. However, it may be older than that. In the colonial era old or sick animals (sheep, cattle, horses) were taken to a 'boiling down factory' where the fat was separated from the carcases to make tallow for candles. In 1893 'hashmagandy' was used for the remainder of the animal's carcase that was raked out of the bottom of the boiling-down vat at the end of the process. This, it seems, was fairly foul stuff. And it is likely that soldiers who were familiar with this stinking substance were the ones who first applied the unflattering name to army stew.

Hatter

A prospector working alone in the bush. This was unusual, because in the remote bush it was common to work with a mate – for safety as much as friendship. But a man was a hatter if 'his hat covered all his friends and family' – that is, there was no one for him to look after but himself, and no one to look after him. Hatters tended to become ratty: extremely eccentric, if not totally mad.

Haunted hills of Gippsland, the

In pioneer days of the 19th century Moe (in Victoria) was just a tiny township. According to legend, one day Moe was disturbed by a stampede of wild bush cattle through the town. The animals were described as 'wild eyed and terrified'. Strangely, there was no drover behind the mob. So what started them running? A few of the braver citizens rode into the hills where they said they found the bodies of scores of cattle, and the cold ashes of a drover's camp fire – but no sign of the drover. Later the legend grew when another drover claimed his mob of cattle had been spooked into a stampede, in the hills above the town, by the sound of an invisible stockwhip cracking.

Haunted homestead at Drysdale, the

'Coriyule' was a pioneering homestead at Drysdale (Victoria), overlooking Port Phillip Bay. Late in the 19th century the wife of the manager of the property fled from the house on a stormy night, terrified by the sound of a piano tinkling in the deserted front room, a tinkling that was then joined by an eerie whistling. The house became known locally as the Haunted Homestead. However, a later owner claimed to have explained the mystery. Retired Presbyterian minister Rev. Archibald Hamilton Ross noticed similar phenomena during a wild storm. Upon investigation he found the piano-like notes were coming from heavy raindrops striking against the small diamond panes in the front windows – each pane producing a slightly different note. The sound of the wind blowing through the old conservatory explained the whistling part of the puzzle – and the ghostly reputation of the homestead disappeared in a puff of common sense. (Disappointing really – a bit like discovering that the mysterious clanking in the cellar in the brother-in-law getting into the port.)

Have a gander

Take a look. If the goose is the bird with the lowest IQ (as popular speech would have us believe) and if blokeyness also reduces intellectual power then the most aimless creature of all must be the male goose – the gander. And that was the original meaning of this expression: to take a gander meant to wander aimlessly. Then it meant wandering around looking for something, and then just looking.

Hills hoist

As a child we had a clothes line that ran the length of the backyard and got in the way of games of backyard cricket. Until, that is, the old wooden support poles were pulled out and replaced by a metal, rotary clothes line called a Hills Hoist. Adelaide motor mechanic Lance Hills invented this ubiquitous bit of Aussie backyard furniture as a space saver. On the market since 1945, it is now an Aussie icon.

Hip pocket nerve

Political expression: the most sensitive nerve in a voter's body – the nerve that will twitch first when governments take any step that might increase the cost of living.

Head like a busted sofa

Wild or unruly hair. If you're having a bad hair day (a *very* bad hair day) then you'll have a head like a busted sofa. (Paints a pretty picture, doesn't it?)

Head like a half-sucked mango and a body like a burst sausage

Aussie English has a nice collection of insults, and this is one of them. If someone says this to you, what they mean is that they find you unattractive (but you'd worked that out, hadn't you?).

Hell's bells and bootlaces

A way of saying: 'Hey! That's a surprise!'

Hogan's ghost!

Jonathan Green says that 'Hogan's ghost!' is (or was) used as a general expression of amazement and is Australian in origin. *The Australian National Dictionary* records 'Hogan's ghost!' from 1930 – and adds that its origin is 'unexplained.' I do remember a parallel American expression: in the old Superman comics Perry White (editor of the *Daily Planet*) used to exclaim 'Great Caesar's ghost!' in moments of exasperation. 'Caesar's ghost!' is recorded in the US from the mid 19th century as a 'mild oath' and Australian author John O'Grady (in his 1977 autobiography *There Was a Kid*) sees the two expressions as interchangeable. *The Australian National Dictionary* suggests that 'Hogan's ghost!' might possibly be a euphemism for 'Holy ghost!', making it a softened blasphemy. However, that doesn't explain the parallel with 'Great Caesar's ghost!' So I suggest that the 'Hogan's ghost!' version might have been inspired by a Banjo Paterson bush ballad called 'The Road to Hogan's Gap' – about a surprisingly dangerous place to travel to. The bush ballad tells the story of a bloke who wants to serve a writ on Hogan, and is being given directions by a local to find Hogan's place. According to the local, the track is rough and steep and littered with dead animals. Paterson writes:

> It's like that song 'The Livin' Dead'
> Up there at Hogan's gap.

And that might just have inspired the 'Hogan's ghost!' Australian variation on the earlier American expression.

Homestead

The most common name for the main building, or group of buildings, on larger sheep and cattle stations. This is an old English word but it took special meaning in Australia, as the cluster of buildings on a remote homestead could almost become a small town.

Home unit

A dwelling place. What would be called a flat in London or an apartment in New York can be called a home unit in Australia. Home units (like apartments) are built in blocks, and are either rented or purchased, usually under a form of title called 'strata title'.

Hoon

The *Oxford English Dictionary* records 'hoon' as Australian and New Zealand slang for a show-off with limited intelligence, adding 'origin unknown'. Hoon is most often applied to young male drivers who are more interested in attracting attention than in being cautious. Sid Baker, in *The Australian Language*, suggests 'hoon' might be a contraction from the houyhnhnms, the anthropomorphic horses in Swift's *Gulliver's Travels*. The problem with this idea is that the horses are civilized – it's their human slaves, the yahoos, who are the dills. 'Hoon' might be of

New Zealand origin, since New Zealand has many other related expressions: 'hoonish', 'hoon bin', 'hoon chaser', 'hoondom', 'hoonery', 'hoon it up' and so on.

It's often been suggested that 'hoon' is a contraction of 'hooligan' or, perhaps, a combination of 'hooligan' and 'goon'. Another proposal is that it's rhyming slang for 'baboon', while yet another suggestion is that it's based on 'buffoon'. All are possibilities. *Huhn* is German for 'chicken' and a more unusual suggestion is that a 'hoon' might originally have meant someone running around like a headless chicken. And there is, apparently, another (very similar) German word for an ancient mythical race of clumsy giants. Lots of possible sources for hoon – no certainties!

Hooley dooley

An expression of surprise. The story starts late in the 19th century with an Australian boxer named Larry Foley (1849–1917). Early in the 20th century his heavy hitting in the ring had been turned into a popular expression, 'to give someone Larry Foley', meaning to hit them, beat them, punish them. For some unknown reason this expression changed over time to 'to give someone Larry Dooley'. Then it changed again, being shortened to 'holy dooley' with the word 'holy' acting as an intensifier. In other words, if you'd been hit with surprise (as staggering as a hit from a boxer) you'd cry 'Holy dooley!' By roughly the middle of the 20th century the origin of the expression had been forgotten and the two words were turned into a rhyming pattern, 'hooley dooley' – typical of how expressions change and grow over time. (See also **Happy as Larry**.)

Hoop snake

A carnivorous reptile able to grab its tail in its mouth and roll after its intended victim at a terrifying pace; reputed to be deadly, but no attacks on humans have yet been recorded. Closely related to the **drop bear**.

Hoops

Jockeys are sometimes known as 'hoops' because of the coloured bands on their silks. The contrasting coloured bands can be seen on their blouse, sleeve or cap.

Hooroo

'Hooroo 'is a distinctively Australian way of saying 'goodbye'. It's so distinctive to us that you'll find it in the *Macquarie*, *The Australian National Dictionary* and the *Australian Oxford* but it's missing from the full *Oxford English Dictionary* and from *Webster's*. 'Hooroo' is first recorded in the *Bulletin* in 1906 in the expression 'Hooroo. See yer termorrer.' It's based on the earlier expression 'hooray' – also used in Australia (but only here) to mean 'goodbye'. This is first recorded in the *Bulletin* in 1898 with the following explanation: 'In many places the salutation "good-day" or "good-night" is simply "Hooray!"' 'Hooray' or 'Hurrah' or 'Hurray' is, of course, a general shout or cheer and goes back to at least the 17th century. But only in Australia did 'hooray' come to mean 'goodbye' – and only here was 'hooray' changed to become 'hooroo'. And the 'H' is often dropped so it becomes simply 'Ooroo'!

How's your mother's chooks?

Back in the old days this was a way of saying 'G'day, how ya goin'?' Back in those days lots of people kept chooks in their backyards, so it sort of made sense. (When people stopped keeping chooks, they stopped saying it.)

Hughie

In the outback during times of drought it was common for struggling cockies to say 'Send it down, Hughie!' as an appeal for rain. 'Hughie' (spellings vary, sometimes it's 'Hewie') was an informal outback way of referring to God, in the context of God's control of the weather, especially rain. There are many stories that try to account for the origin of the expression, but none that is clearly convincing. For instance, a 1912 citation from Narrandera suggests the name may have been inspired by an amateur meteorologist name Mr Huie who had an unusually good record in forecasting rain. Another suggestion is that it may have come from the name of an early government Minister for Agriculture, or perhaps even from our early Prime Minister Billy Hughes. There are a string of such stories, but none stands out above the others as the clear source of the expression.

Humphrey B. Bear

A man in a bear suit – also a fictional character who starred in his own TV show for preschool children from 1965 to 2006. The occupants of the suit changed over the years but the suit remained the same: shaggy brown, with a tartan waistcoat and an oversized yellow bow tie, the whole ensemble topped with a straw boater. Generations of small Aussie kids grew up knowing the Humphrey song:

> What a funny old fellow is Humphrey,
> He gets in all manner of strife,
> He leads a very exciting life,
> And honey's his favourite fare,
> Which is hardly so very surprising,
> He's a really amazing old bear,
> What a funny old fellow is Humphrey,
> Humphrey the fun loving bear!

Humping bluey

Carrying a swag; walking the outback bush tracks from property to property looking for work (or else looking for a free feed and a handout). What swaggies did was to 'hump' (or 'carry') their 'swag' (or 'bluey').

Humpy

A shack; a shed; a bush shelter; a roughly built house. Comes from an Aboriginal word.

Hunger

Aussies have a number of expressions that express hunger: 'I'm so hungry …

> … my stomach thinks my throat's been cut.'
> … my stomach's flapping against my backbone.'
> … I could eat a horse and chase the rider.'
> … I could eat the crutch out of a low-flying duck.'

Huntsman spiders

Huntsman spiders are large, hairy, flat-bodied brown spiders that (in the wild) hide under the bark of trees. In modern driveways they're inclined to hide behind the sun visor of your car – and frighten the life out of you when they fall into your lap, perhaps in the middle of heavy traffic. These huntsman spiders have had a number of different nicknames over the years. As child I remember that we called them 'tarantulas' – perhaps to increase the scare factor (although the name does seem to suit their large, long-legged, hairy appearance). Earlier they were nicknamed 'triantelope' – an odd word that appears to be a combination of 'tarantula' and 'antelope'. Huntsmen were also given the nickname 'Clarence', at one time – although no one knows why. I find it a surprisingly bland name. A scream of 'Honey, there's a Clarence in the bathroom' has much less impact than a terrified scream followed by the shout of 'Tarantula!'

Iceberg

A person who takes early morning swims during the coldest days of winter (and not in a heated pool either!).

Iced VoVos

The Iced VoVo is the brand name of a popular sweet biscuit made by the Arnott's company. It was registered as a brand name in 1906. Iced VoVos are a cakey biscuit topped by two strips of pink fondant and a strip of strawberry jam, which are topped in turn with coconut. According to an oral tradition long passed down among the biscuit makers, the name is based on a German colloquial expression meaning either 'cake' or else 'Grandma's cake'. Whichever it is, the Iced VoVo remains an indelible part of an Australian childhood. (The only unanswered question: is Iced VoVo a plural expression? Is it possible to have an IcedVo?)

Icy pole

An ice block; a confection of flavoured frozen water; originally a proprietary name, but now moving in the direction of becoming a generic label.

Illywhacker

A small-time confidence tricker. The earliest citation is from Kylie Tennant's 1941 novel *The Battlers*, but the word, we must assume, is a good deal older than that. In fact, it was probably part of the spoken language in the 19th century. Once in danger of being forgotten, 'illywhacker' was revived by Peter Carey as the title of his 1985 novel. What is the source of the word? No one knows. However, an illywhacker is someone who 'whacks the illy' – which seems to mean someone who 'hits the suckers' (perhaps by selling shares in the Sydney Harbour Bridge, or by playing the old three-card game with them). Now, if the sucker is called the 'illy', can this be related to the word 'silly'? (Perhaps by the sort of slang word formation that drops the opening consonant?) If so, then 'hitting the sillies' becomes 'whacking the illies' and one who does it is an illywhacker. Well, it's a possibility at least.

I'm not made of wood and water!

This is something Aussie mums used to say to their kids if they felt they were being nagged; it means 'I can't do everything at once, you know!' (It's probably based on such a mum feeling as if they were being treated like a **wood-and-water joey**.)

In like Flynn

This phrase means 'a dead certainty' and it's commonly thought to be a reference to the ease with which Aussie born Hollywood movie star Errol Flynn charmed (and seduced) women. More specifically, many believe it to date from Flynn's 1942 statutory rape trial, in which he was acquitted. The phrase has been associated with Errol Flynn since at least 1945, when an article in the journal *American Speech* stated that it referred to Flynn's swashbuckling cinematic feats. As an action hero, everything seemed to come easily to him on the silver screen.

It's clear from other evidence, however, that the phrase does not stem from the 1942 rape trial. American researcher Barry Popik has found several uses of the phrase prior to Flynn's trial, one as early as July 1940, in reference to a party of people being told they would have access to the New York World Fair with the words 'Your name is Flynn ... you're in.' Furthermore, the sexual connotations of the phrase did not clearly appear until the 1970s. Early uses are not references to seduction. But it's possible that the phrase still refers to Errol Flynn because he was certainly famous long before the rape trial.

Another theory links the phrase with Edward J. Flynn (1891–1953), a US Democratic machine politician from the Bronx. Flynn's candidates reputedly always won. The date of the phrase's appearance fits with this explanation, but there is no solid evidence of a connection.

On the other hand, 'in like Flynn' may simply be rhyming slang, originally not referring to anyone at all. David Niven (in his book *Bring on the Empty Horses*) certainly claims that Errol Flynn was stuck with the expression (and hated it).

Gerry Wilkes includes the phrase in his *Dictionary of Australian Colloquialisms*, and, if it really is of Australian origin, there is another possible source: the Reverend John Flynn, known as **Flynn of the Inland**. The mission he took on was to cast a 'mantle of safety' over the isolated folk in remote communities. As such he was the inspiration behind the Flying Doctor Service. Might not his legendary nickname be the source of the expression? The expression 'Flynn of the Inland' was certainly well known from 1932, when Ion Idriess's book of that title was published.

Indigenous

Now often the preferred term for the original Australians, in preference to either **Aboriginal** or Aborigine. This was originally coined to function as a word that encompassed both Aborigines and Torres Straight Islanders, but is now used (especially by the politically correct) as the preferred term, even when only Aborigines are being referred to.

In-ground pool

This is a distinctively Australian expression for a domestic swimming pool set into the ground in a suburban backyard. In some states such a backyard swimming facility would be called a 'below-ground pool'. The contrast in both cases is with the **above-ground pool** – a cheaper and more temporary installation.

Inland

Another name for the outback.

Inlanders

People who live in the outback (the inland).

In the tin

In trouble, in the sense of being in a tight spot. Possibly the original form of the expression was 'in a tin can' meaning 'in a jam'. It dates back to the days when jam more commonly came in tins than in a glass jars. And the expression was partly rhyming (or half-rhyming) slang, and partly an appeal to the visual absurdity of the person 'in a tight spot' being jammed down into a tin can – about as tight a spot as one can imagine. This bit of Aussie slang seems to date from the 1940s.

Irishman's compass

An escaping Irish convict is said to have cut the image of a compass off the bottom of a map and pasted it into the crown of his hat. This was the 'compass' he consulted when he became lost in the bush. Hence the now dated expression, 'about as useful as the Irishman's compass'. (This is, of course, a gross calumny on a fine and intelligent race, which is merely reported here – not endorsed.)

Iron gang

Back in the early days a group of convicts made to work chained together (so they couldn't escape) was a called an 'iron gang'.

Ironbark

A type of gum tree; a source of tough, long-lasting hard wood.

It must be rough on the bay!

A verbal response to seeing a flock of seagulls in the city (for example, at the Melbourne Cricket Ground), well away from the waters of Port Phillip Bay.

I've been to Manly

Among Sydneysiders this used to be a jocular response to the question 'Have you been overseas?', because for most Sydneysiders getting to Manly meant catching a ferry across Sydney harbour. As overseas travel has become more common, this old joke has slowly faded.

J

Jackaroo

A jackaroo is a station hand in the outback. However, originally a jackaroo was a white settler who chose to live beyond the boundaries of close settlement, and later it came to mean a young man (often an English immigrant) seeking to gain experience by working cheaply at a sheep or cattle station. Sometimes the jackaroo was the bloke starting at the bottom, learning the trade, with a view to becoming a station manager. The *Oxford English Dictionary* seems to think that 'jackaroo' comes from a combination of the common name 'Jack' and the word 'kangaroo'. However, *The Australian National Dictionary* tells a different story (and is more likely to be correct on this one). It says that 'jackaroo' comes from an Aboriginal word, 'jagara', meaning 'a wandering white man' (combined, obviously, with the tail of 'kangaroo'). The female equivalent is 'jillaroo', but this is a much later coinage: 'jackaroo' is recorded from 1875 and 'jillaroo' from 1943.

Jack

A negative expression: to be 'jacked off' is to be fed up, and that might lead you to 'jack it in' – to give up on that something (or someone); just quit and walk away.

Jack Dancer

Cancer (rhyming slang). Put into wide circulation in the 1970s by an ABC-TV movie of this name starring Gary McDonald as a radio star diagnosed with cancer. Now adopted by some community groups working with cancer sufferers, sometimes in the expression 'waltzing with Jack Dancer'.

Jackie Howe

Jackie Howe (1861–1920) was a champion Queensland shearer. He was a legend among shearers, a **gun** shearer or **ringer** – he once shore 321 sheep in a single day, back in the era of hand shears. He has given his name to two items of Aussie clothing: (a) the sleeveless pullover worn by Aussie Rules players, and (2) the blue singlet once worn by rural workers and now commonly worn by truckies and brickies' labourers.

Jarmies

Pyjamas; or a nightie; or any nightwear.

Jarrah jerker

Timber-getter, bush worker (especially in Western Australia, where the great jarrah forests grow).

Jeff's Shed

The Melbourne Exhibition Centre – from Jeff Kennett, Premier of Victoria 1992–99.

Jelly cake

A lamington-style cake. Its making is described thus: a plain sponge cake, cut into cubes, dipped in pink almost-set jelly and covered with desiccated coconut, sometimes with the addition of jam and cream in the middle. Also called a pink lamington.

Jiffy

In Aussie English a very short period of time is called a jiffy, as in 'How long is this going to take?' 'Ah, just a jiffy.' There is, however, a claim floating about that 'jiffy' has a literal meaning; that it means precisely 'one hundredth of a second' – exactly that, no more and no less. Well, all the authorities I consulted agreed that 'jiffy' is not a mathematical term and has no precise measurement. It is simply, they say, 'a very short period of time'. The word 'jiffy' first appears in English in the late 18th century, the oldest citation being from the English translation of Rudolf Erich Raspe's *The Surprising Adventures of Baron Münchhausen*. That source suggests that it may have been an arbitrarily invented word, creatively coined for comic purposes. It has given rise to the phrase 'jiffy quick' meaning 'very fast' (a more common expression in the US than here) and to the proprietary names 'jiffy bag' (meaning a padded post bag) and 'jiffy pot' (meaning a pot for growing seedlings, made of peat).

Jim Jones

A fictional character whose story is told in an early ballad of the convict era, 'Jim Jones of Botany Bay':

> I'll give the law a little shock: remember what I say,
> They'll yet regret they sent Jim Jones in chains to Botany Bay.

Jimmy Woodser

Someone who drinks alone, rather than with mates taking turns at 'shouting' rounds. From 'Jimmy Wood', a character in a bush ballad of that name by Barcroft Boake (1866–92):

> He wouldn't take a liquor with a man,
> Not if he was to be hanged, drawn, and quartered,
> And yet, he drank—construe it as you can—
> Unsweetened gin, most moderately watered.

The Australian National Dictionary suggests there may have been a real person of that name (and habit) who was immortalised by Boake:

His signature is on the scroll of fame,
You cannot well forget him, though you would, sir,
The man is dead, not so his homely name,
Who drinks alone—drinks a toast to Jimmy Wood, sir.

Jindyworobak

A nationalist movement among a group of Australian writers. It was founded by South Australian poet Rex Ingamells. His aim, he said, was 'to free Australian art from whatever alien influences trammel it'. He insisted on a recognition of 'environmental values' and an understanding of Australian history and traditions. He edited the *Jindyworobak Review* from 1938 to 1948.

Job and knock

An agreement between a boss and a worker whereby the worker can leave early if he or she finishes the job quickly (sometimes called 'job and finish'). It can be used, for example, on an extremely hot day when everyone is tired and the job is going slowly, to speed the job up. This is achieved by working thorough all lunch breaks and smoko breaks (and then heading for the pub nice and early).

Joe Blow

An average Aussie; an ordinary person; the man on the street.

Jubilee cake

A plain cake containing sultanas or other dried fruit, created for the 100th anniversary of the founding of South Australia in 1936.

Jumbuck

A sheep; a good feed of meat walking around on four legs – which explains what happens in 'Waltzing Matilda':

> Down came a jumbuck to drink at the billabong,
> Up jumped the swagman and grabbed him with glee,
> And he sang as he shoved that jumbuck in his tucker bag,
> You'll come a-waltzing Matilda with me.

The origin of 'jumbuck' is unknown, but *The Australian National Dictionary* suggests it may have begun life as a pidgin word, a corruption of an English expression such as 'jump up', perhaps referring to the characteristic occasional leaps of moving sheep.

Jump-up

'Jump-up' is one of those bush expressions that city folk just don't know. It turns up in the centre of Australia, in parts of Queensland and South Australia, and in the far west of New South Wales. A jump-up is the point where a road or track rises abruptly from one level to another, as in, 'Aw, mate, we'll never get the truck over this jump-up.' 'Jump-up' can be used where a road or track has been cut by a water course of some kind, causing a gully with steep sides. And it's a commonly used term for a slight but abrupt rise, often in the otherwise flat country.

K

Kakadu

The name Kakadu comes from the Aboriginal Gagadju language – the main language spoken in the area at the start of the 20th century. As far as I've been able to discover, Gagadju is the correct name for the people who inhabited the area, and the language they spoke. The present name, 'Kakadu', is just an Anglicised version of that word. Aboriginal people have inhabited the site for more than 20 000 years, and evidence of their culture can be seen (for example) in the many Kakadu rock paintings, which are probably the world's oldest surviving graphic artwork.

Kanga cricket

A modified form of cricket designed to be played on almost any surface without the need for protective gear. Also known as 'kangaroo cricket'. Promoted by the Australian Cricket Board since 1984 as a way of introducing primary school kids to a range of skills.

Kangaroo

One persistent verbal myth is that the word 'kangaroo' doesn't mean the familiar marsupial macropod, but rather 'I don't understand'. The myth claims that when Captain Cook, in

1770 (at Endeavour River, in north Queensland), gestured at a kangaroo and asked its name the local natives replied that they didn't understand him. But he took their utterance to be the name, and the mistake has continued ever since. That story, however, is of recent origin and lacks confirmation. It's true that in the Sydney region local aborigines called this animal 'patagorong' or 'patagorang'. However, in 1787 it was claimed that 'kangaroo' was the name used in Tasmania, and (later, in 1835) in the Darling Ranges of Western Australia. Those claims seem unlikely, given the large number of Aboriginal languages in Australia. What is more likely is that 'kangaroo' was the local name of the particular type of kangaroo Captain Cook was pointing at, at the time – and that it was English-speaking settlers who carried the word around Australia.

Kangaroo court

A kangaroo court is officially defined as 'an improperly constituted court having no legal standing, especially one held by strikers, mutineers or prisoners'. More broadly, the notion is that in a kangaroo court the accused will not receive justice, but that rough punishment will follow almost immediately upon accusation. So any unofficial court that punishes people unfairly is a kangaroo court. Oddly, this expression appears to be Australian influenced, but not of Australian origin. In fact, the phrase appears to have been born in the United States. The earliest citation is from Texas in the second half of the 19th century. The suggestion has been made that the term 'kangaroo court' was born on the goldfields of California in the gold rushes that began in 1848. The phrase may have been coined because there were Australians who'd joined the rush, and they were teaching the Yanks a word or two; or because the first such 'rough justice' tribunals were aimed at punishing 'claim jumpers' – and anyone who's a 'jumper' can be nicknamed a 'kangaroo'. So perhaps originally the expression may have referred to the accused, rather than the fact that the so-called 'court' leapt to judgment in a single bound, with the agility of an Australian macropod.

Kath-and-Kim-speak

This is a deftly observed slice of Aussie English reproduced with affectionate fidelity by the television series *Kath and Kim*. It incorporates some distinctive pronunciations (such as 'Hi' pronounced 'Hoi', 'bye' pronounced 'boy', and 'cool' pronounced 'coo-well' ... among others) together with some distinctive vocabulary items. Hence in Kath and Kim speak 'gropable' means 'very annoyed', 'ravishing' means 'very hungry', 'clutching at spanners' means 'foolishly maintaining illusory hopes' and 'effluent' means 'prosperous' or 'financially secure'. Beyond the urgent instruction to 'Look at moi, look at moi, look at moi!' is the fact that Kath-and-Kim-speak is an acute insight into a colourful bit of Aussie English. If you ever find yourself expressing agreement by saying 'Ditto, twofold' you'll know that you're celebrating the verbal rainbow that is Kath-and-Kim-speak.

Kelpie

An Aussie breed of dog, short-haired with pointy ears – very tough, and good at rounding up sheep.

Kidman

No, not Nicole but Sir Sidney Kidman (1857–1935), famous as 'the Cattle King'. Starting out as a stockman, he built up a string of cattle stations stretching from Queensland, through New South Wales, and into South Australia. At his peak, the area of land he owned was greater than the size of England.

King cobra, to

To go to bed in your grubby work clothes and with your filthy work boots on! (One step worse than **black snaking it**.)

Kitchener bun

A doughnut-like cake filled with cream or mock cream, and often jam as well. Reportedly, this was originally known as a 'Berliner' and was given the more patriotic name of 'Kitchener bun' during World War I. The name is used particularly in Adelaide.

Kiwi

We're familiar with the use of the word 'Kiwi' to mean a New Zealander, but in World War I the diggers would call a soldier who was very smartly dressed, in precise uniform, with all his leatherwork highly polished, a Kiwi. This is an Aussie soldier mind you: if he was full of spit and polish he was a Kiwi. A quote from 1916 expands on this, and calls such diggers 'Kiwi kids', these being considered bad bargains in a battle – all show and no fight. And a quote from a diggers' newspaper called *Southern Cross* from 1917 says the army consists of two types: soldiers and Kiwis. It was also used as a verb 'to Kiwi up'. This use of 'Kiwi' to mean a highly polished soldier came from the most famous boot polish in Australia at the time – Kiwi brand boot polish.

Knock 'em down

A violent thunderstorm in the Northern Territory with strong winds, lashing rain and plenty of lightning and thunder; they tend occur only at the end of the wet season, and take their name from the fact that they knock down the two-metre-tall cattle grass.

Koala

Sometimes called a 'koala bear' or 'native bear', but the koala is not related to any kind of bear. Koalas have soft, thick fur; a large, leathery, hairless nose; round ears; and no tail. The fur is grey or brown on the animal's back and white on the chest. The word is Aboriginal, from the Dharuk language. The word is recorded from 1798, but it was 1808 before the familiar spelling was settled on: both 'coola' and 'kool-la' turn up in early documents. Because of their cuddly 'teddy bear' like appearance, they are probably the most popular native Australian animals. Koalas make some memorable appearances in Australian literature, notably Blinky Bill (in the stories of Dorothy Wall), 'Bunyip Bluegum' (in Norman's Lindsay's *The Magic Pudding*) and Two-Thumbs in *Two-Thumbs: The Story of a Koala* by Leslie Rees.

Kookaburra

When I saw a large kookaburra sitting in a lordly fashion on our Hills hoist – watching (with fearless curiosity) as I hung out the towels – I wondered about his name. The word 'kookaburra' comes from the Wiradjuri Aboriginal language and is first recorded in English in 1834, although for the first 50 years or so the spelling varied wildly. For instance, Henry Kendall in one of his poems calls this bird the 'goburra'. This Australian member of the kingfisher family of birds was first known as the 'laughing jackass', with early settlers hearing his call as a laugh that mocked their efforts to carve some farmland out of the bush. 'Laughing jackass' is recorded as early as 1797. The kookaburra's habit of making its first loud outburst at dawn led to it also being called 'the settler's clock' or 'the bushman's clock'.

There is one other oddity about the kookaburra's cry that's worth noting. From the 1930s to the 1950s (and perhaps beyond that), whenever Hollywood had to create the impression of deep, tropical jungle the noise they invariably dubbed onto the sound track was the exotic laughing cry of our own kookaburras. You can hear it in the background of every Tarzan and Jungle Jim movie ever shot on the back lots of MGM or Columbia. So for many Americans the cry of the kookaburra is forever associated with the mythical Hollywood version of Africa.

Koori

The name by which Aborigines in New South Wales and Victoria prefer to be known. First recorded in 1834, it comes from the Aboriginal languages of central and northern New South Wales. Koori literally means 'man' or 'person'.

Kriol

Kriol is a language of northern Australia. It's sometimes been thought of as pidgin English, but in fact it's a language in its own right, with a vocabulary mainly based on English, but a structure and grammar typical of Aboriginal languages. Kriol is what scholars call a 'post-contact' language. Linguists have for many decades now been recording the various dialects of Kriol, developing spelling systems and word lists. And a group of Aboriginal Christians in the Northern Territory took on a challenge of biblical proportions: the translation of the whole Bible into Kriol (a task that has now been completed, and published by the Australian Bible Society). Many Aboriginal people in the region between Katherine, the Roper River and the Kimberley in Western Australia speak Kriol as a first language. Many more speak it as a second or third language.

Kylie

We think of this now as the name of the singing budgie – Australia's most successful pop export. But she is not the first to bear the name. Before Kylie Minogue there was the novelist Kylie Tennant, and (doubtless) other Kylies as well. This word 'kylie' is, in fact, the Western Australian word for 'boomerang', itself an east coast word from the Dharuk language. 'Kylie' comes from the Nyoongar Western Australian Aboriginal language and was first recorded in 1835. A hundred years later the word had a transferred usage in the game of **two-up** – the small piece of board on which the pennies were tossed being called a kip, stick, bat or kylie. How 'kylie' was transferred from boomerangs and two-up to a woman's name is not clear. Perhaps someone just liked the sound of it.

Lacca

This word for 'rubber band' is a piece of regional Australian colloquial English. The *Macquarie ABC Dictionary* lists several regional variations, including 'lacker band' and 'lackie band' (or 'lackey band' – all meaning 'rubber band'. So, where do all these (clearly related) expressions come from? The answer appears to be: from a Hindustani word *lăkh*, which went into both Portuguese and Spanish as *lacca*. It originally meant 'the dark, resinous encrustation produced on certain trees'. Because of the uses this resin was put to, this word became the source for more common words such as lacquer and shellac (products which, apparently, come from this resin). And because rubber similarly begins life as a resin (or gum, or, more accurately, latex) exuded from a tree, the word 'lacca' (and its variants) came to be used as a slang word for rubber.

Lag

A criminal, originally a convict transported to Australia; most often heard in the expression 'old lag', implying a consistent and diligent application to a life of crime.

Lair

Someone who is overdressed, in a style they think is rather flash, and vulgar in their behaviour – a show-off, a larrikin – can be called a lair. 'To lair it up' or 'to lairize' means to behave in a brash, flash and vulgar manner. The earlier form of the word was 'lairy', which developed from an old bit of the flash language, 'leary'. In his *Vocabulary of the Flash Language* James Hardy Vaux says that being 'leary' was the same as being 'fly': vigilant, suspicious, cunning, not easily robbed or duped; a shop keeper or person of this description was called a 'fly cove' or a 'leary cove'. By 1898 'leary' had become 'lairy' and had come to refer mainly to style: cheap and flashy, and socially unacceptable. Being described as a lair is never a compliment. (See also **Larrikin**.)

Lamington

One of Australia's national foods. A lamington is a square of sponge cake, soaked in chocolate sauce and dipped in desiccated coconut. (Mind you, the best lamingtons also have jam and cream in the middle!) Originally, lamingtons were created to find a use for stale cake. Today, lamingtons are rarely made from stale sponge cake, and are all the better for it. The best guess we have is that lamingtons were invented in Queensland some time around 1900, and were named in honour of the Governor of Queensland at the time, Baron Lamington. (His full name was Charles Wallace Alexander Napier Cochrane-Baillie, he lived from 1860 to 1940, and was Governor of Queensland from 1896 to 1901.) The earliest citation for the word 'lamington' (meaning these small cakes) is from 1909. Now, assuming you have your sponge cake already cut into cubes, here's how to turn those cubes into lamingtons:

Ingredients:
3 tablespoons cocoa
4 tablespoons boiling water
25 g butter

vanilla essence

500 g icing sugar

desiccated coconut

Method:

Mix the cocoa and water together. Add the butter, vanilla and icing sugar. Cover the cubes of cake in icing and roll in the coconut.

Lamington drive

A fund-raising activity for voluntary organisations, consisting of selling home-made lamingtons door-to-door.

Land lice

Nickname for sheep, especially used by cattlemen. Indicating a similar level of disrespect for the animal that once carried our nation on its collective back, a sheep can also be known as 'a maggot taxi'.

Lapper

An adolescent driver who does laps around suburban streets, usually late at night with a loud stereo and a noisy exhaust. The 'lappo' is the car in which the lapper drives his laps. In some parts of Australia the lapper is known as a 'lappy' – sometimes with the slight variation that his 'lapping' consists of driving up and down the same piece of road repeatedly after doing U-turns at the ends of each lap.

Lagerphone

An Australian folk musical instrument. To make a lagerphone, loosely nail about 300 beer bottle tops to a broom stick. This can then be rattled or thumped rhythmically. Like most Australian folk instruments it provides rhythm not melody. (See also **Wobble board**.)

Larrikin

An old word for a young bloke who stirs up a bit of trouble; a hundred years ago it meant a young hoodlum, a gang member. The *Oxford English Dictionary* says that 'larrikin' is 'chiefly Australian'. It's recorded from 1868, and in those days it meant the violent members of the 19th-century equivalent of bikie gangs. But over the years the term softened, so that by 1898 Edward E. Morris (in his *Austral Dictionary*) could say that it was often used to mean 'a playful youngster'.

There are a bunch of urban myths surrounding the origins of 'larrikin'. One claims it comes from 'larking' (as in 'larking about'), as pronounced by an Irish-born policeman giving evidence in a Melbourne magistrate's court. But as the *Oxford English Dictionary* notes: no trace of the incident has been found in the local papers of the time. So that one's a myth. Then there's suggestion that is comes from the common male name 'Larry' – the 'kin' part being either a diminutive (referring to a 'little Larry') or a claim of kinship ('Larry's kin'). Again, there's no evidence to support this notion.

However, there is at least some evidence to support the idea that 'larrikin' is another of those English dialect words that survived in Australia after it died out in its homeland. The *English Dialect Dictionary* records 'larrikin' as a Warwickshire and Worcestershire word meaning 'a mischievous or frolicsome youth'.

Larrikin lexicography

This book.

Lasseter's reef

Lewis Hubert Lasseter (who called himself 'Harold Bell Lasseter') (1880–1931) claimed to have discovered a gold reef of extraordinary size and richness somewhere in the sands of central Australia – and then lost it again. Hence it's often referred to as 'Lasseter's lost reef'. A well-equipped expedition guided by Lasseter left Alice

Springs on 21 July 1930 to try to relocate the reef. In September of that year the expedition abandoned the search, but Lasseter carried on. A search party later reported finding his body at Shaw Creek in the Peterman Range in March 1931. Lasseter's story has been told in many books, most notably in *Lasseter's Last Ride* by Ion Idriess (1931).

Lazy wind

A very cold wind; a bitterly cold wind; it's 'lazy' because 'it won't blow around you – it blows straight through you!'

Leak

Aussie for urinate. The most common term among men, although Barry Humphries coined some more colourful ones for his character Barry McKenzie: 'point Percy at the porcelain' and 'rinse the prince'.

Lebanese lawn

Concreted front or back yard, especially when painted green. Ideal for those who prefer a low-maintenance home. Sometimes this is called either 'Italian grass' (thus switching the ethnic slur from one group to another) or 'Leichhardt lawn' (from the Sydney suburb where this efficient practice is reputedly common).

Lemon time

A break in the footy, now a dated expression. In AFL lemon time, or 'lemons', was at three-quarter time; in rugby it was at half time. At some stage the lemons supplied to players were replaced by oranges, but the old name hung on. Today the players have sports drinks, but older fans can remember players eating quartered oranges on the field in the break. And before the oranges, it was lemons.

Light globe

What the rest of the world calls a light bulb is commonly called a light globe in Australia.

Lobster

A $20 note – it's exactly the same shade of red as a boiled lobster: 'Hey, mate! Ya still haven't paid me that lobster you owe me!'

Logodile

A floating log which cunningly disguises itself as a crocodile, and thus frightens the life out of the humans with which it shares the waterways.

London fog

Aussie name for a lazy labourer, because, you see, he 'won't lift'.

London to a brick on

An Australian phrase popularised by legendary radio race caller Ken Howard. 'London to a brick on' is a statement of betting odds in which the punter is prepared to bet the whole city of London to win a single brick – a statement, in other words, of supreme confidence. Often the phrase is shortened to just 'London to a brick'. There are earlier examples of the same kind of statement in British English, such as 'bet all Lombard Street to a China orange'; or 'bet a million to a bit of dirt'. But from the 1950s onwards, the distinctive nasal tones of Ken Howard on the radio every Saturday afternoon employed the expression 'London to a brick on', often when he was tipping the outcome of a photo-finish, and made it part of Aussie English.

Long paddock

The grass that grows beside the road on the stock routes; during a drought, when the grass is dying and the paddocks are brown, stockmen used to take their herd of cattle out on the open road, travelling long distances, to eat the grass growing by the sides of the road – these cattle were said to be 'on the long paddock'.

Loo

Apart from 'dunny', the most common Aussie name for the toilet is, I would think, the loo. But where does loo come from? Well, Rudolf Brasch suggests it comes from the days before modern plumbing, when folk would empty their chamber pots from upper windows into the gutters below. Before doing so they would shout to passers-by 'Watch out for the water!' – but they said it in French: '*Gardez l'eau!*' However, I see problems with this. In the first place, why would the English lower classes shout a warning in French? And secondly, loo meaning 'toilet' is not recorded until 1922 – long after any such practice had well and truly ended. The alternative suggested by Alan S. C. Ross is that it probably derives from 'Waterloo'. As such it's a play on words: where do you go to dispose of water? To the 'Waterloo' – or the loo for short. It seems the most likely explanation.

Lucky country

Description of Australia coined by Donald Horne (1921–2005) in his book of that name, published in 1964. The book was a critique of Australian society in the 1960s but its title, although widely used, was often misunderstood. Horne defined Australia at the time as 'a lucky country run mainly by second-rate people who share its luck'. His point was that Australia was living on its luck rather than on its creativity or energy. He even said that one of Australia's great national festivals (**Melbourne Cup Day**) is mainly a celebration of luck.

Lurk

An easy to way do something; a short cut to success. A scheme for doing your own work in the boss's time is called a lurk. Sometimes a **bludger** can be a real 'lurk merchant'.

LVS

The accusation has been made that many Aussies suffer from so-called LVS or Loose Vowel Syndrome. This is the verbal habit of causing vowels to disappear from words. It's LVS that turns the two syllable 'police' into the one syllable 'p'lice' – a pronunciation much favoured by former New South Wales premier Neville Wran. In a similar way 'careers' can lose a vowel and become 'c'reers'. Australians, of course, have a long history of turning 'Saturday' into 'Sat'dee' and the name of this country into 'Straya'. But I think this sort of thing has been going on for as long as English has existed. Long ago LVS turned the 'forecastle' of a ship in the 'focsle' and the 'boatswain' into the 'bosun'.

M

Macadamia

It may come as a surprise to some to learn that the delicious macadamia nut has been known by a number of different names over the years. It used be known, for instance, as a 'bopple' or the 'bopple nut'. This name was corruption of Mount Bauple in Queensland, where macadamia trees grow in profusion. And because of its Queensland source the macadamia was once known as 'the Queensland nut'. So where did the name 'macadamia' come from? Well, it was given to this particular nut in the middle of the 19th century by botanist Frederick von Müller, and he named it in honour of Scottish-born chemist John Macadam, who was secretary of the Philosophical Institute of Victoria at that time. Macadamia is sometimes abbreviated to 'macca'.

Macquarie Street/Island/Harbour etc.

Lachlan Macquarie (1762–1824) was governor of the colony of New South Wales from 1810 to 1822. And he seems to have spend a great deal of that time riding around the place saying, 'I name this bit after me. And this bit. And this other bit over here.' Hence all the Macquaries all over the place, the Lachlan River (from his Christian name), and Elizabeth Street (from his wife's name).

Mad as a cut snake

As mad as a cut snake can mean 'angry' or 'crazy' or 'eccentric'. This Australian coinage was first recorded in 1917. And the earliest version of the phrase was shorter, just 'as mad as a snake'. The longer version is first recorded in 1932. It most probably comes from nothing more complicated than observations of how Australian snakes behave in the bush. Since Australia is home to some of the most venomous snakes in the world, settlers very quickly learned to be wary of them. A disturbed snake would strike out aggressively – hence 'mad as a snake'. Snakes around the farmhouse had to be killed, of course, often by chopping them into a couple of pieces with a hoe or a spade. The resulting bits would thrash about madly before expiring, hence 'as mad as a cut snake'.

Mad as a meat axe

A variation on the above ('angry' or 'crazy' or 'eccentric'), first recorded in 1946. The source of the expression is not clear, since tools (even tools with a sharp cutting edge) are not inclined to go crazy. However, it may be a case of transferring the attitude of the homicidal manic to the weapon he's waving. And as an expression it probably caught on, and has persisted, because of the neat alliteration between the madness and the meat axe. Both this and the above expression are part of a whole group of Aussie expressions that start with the words 'As mad as ....' The group includes as mad as a beetle; as mad as a dingbat; as mad as a Chinaman; as mad as a goanna; and as mad as a gum tree full of galahs.

Mad Monday

The Monday after the weekend on which a sporting team has won the grand final. The 'madness' consists of the unbridled celebrations by the victors, sometimes marked by themed dressing up ('This year we're all sports commentators' or 'This year we're all schoolgirls') and fuelled by alcohol. Often remembered with dull, thumping embarrassment on Tuesday.

Maggot bag

The humble meat pie is often regarded as being one of the culinary icons of Australia. A 'meat pie and tomato sauce' is as Australian as Aussie Rules, or kangaroos, or Slim Dusty. But we display our affection in an odd way – by giving the meat pie some rather off-putting schoolboyish nicknames. Perhaps the most common is 'maggot bag'. To ask the nice lady at the canteen for 'A maggot bag and blood, thanks, love' is to ask for a meat pie and tomato sauce. 'Maggot bag' is used in much of Queensland, northern New South Wales and South Australia. An equally appealing alternative is 'rat's coffin'. This one turns up in Sydney and parts of Victoria. In those places, if you get hungry at the footy you might nick off to buy yourself a hot rat's coffin. How can we be so unkind to such nice food?

Magic Pudding

The Magic Pudding is a classic Australian children's book by Norman Lindsay, first published in 1918 and still in print. It has given the Aussie language the expression 'cut and come again', which is the Pudding's own description of its ability to regrow any piece sliced off it. It also had the ability to be a steak and kidney pudding for main course and then a plum pudding for dessert. When trying to allocate limited resources someone may well say, 'Our funds are not a magic pudding, you know. The bank account's not "cut and come again". Once it's spent, it's spent.'

Magoos

The second-string players in a sports club – both from rhyming slang ('magoos' = 'twos' = 'seconds') and from the short-sighted

American cartoon character 'Mr Magoo', created in 1949, with the voice supplied by Jim Backus.

Magpie

Magpie is not a distinctively Australian word – there are black and white birds in England also called magpies. Their name came about because as early as the year 1250 these birds were called 'pies', meaning that they were 'pied' – that is, 'decorated or mixed' (in the same way the 'pied piper' was so named). This use of 'pie' probably comes from the Latin *pica*, meaning 'painted or embroidered', as if a black bird was painted or embroidered with white. Then the birds called 'pies' were given a personal name, much as the birds called wagtails were given the name 'Willy'. And the name these pies was given was the common and popular name 'Margaret', playfully shortened to 'Mag'. The result was magpies. When European settlers landed on our shores they saw a remarkably similar black and white bird and so named it, too, 'magpie'. However, I am told that the European magpie belongs to the crow family and the Australian magpie to the butcherbird family. They may dress alike, but they are only the most distant of relatives.

Mahogany ship, the

The wreck of a Spanish (or possibly Portuguese) sailing ship, built of mahogany, which, according to local legend, lies buried in the sandhills to the west of Warrnambool, in Victoria. The story is that the wreck was first seen in 1836 and continued to be seen from time to time until it disappeared forever beneath the drifting sands in the 1880s.

Major Mitchell cockatoo

A pink and white cockatoo with a scarlet crest. Named for explorer Sir Thomas Mitchell (1792–1855).

Mallee bull

Big, tough and healthy; anyone who's 'as fit as a Mallee bull' is really fit.

Maluka

An Aboriginal title for the person in charge; the boss. It became widely known through Mrs Aeneas Gunn's books *We of the Never-Never* (1908) and *The Little Black Princess* (1905), describing life on a remote Northern Territory cattle station, where her husband was known to the locals as Maluka. Mrs Gunn left the property (and wrote the books) after her husband's sudden death: 'The tribe mourned for their beloved dead – their dead and ours – our Maluka, "the best Boss that ever a man struck".'

Malt sandwich

A bottle of beer.

Man from Snowy River, the

Legendary character created by Banjo Paterson. His bush ballad 'The Man from Snowy River' first appeared in the *Bulletin* on 26 April 1890. Six years later it became the title of Paterson's first collection of ballads, *The Man from Snow River and Other Verses*, and was an instant national best-seller. It is still frequently republished, sometimes in illustrated editions for younger readers. It has been the basis for three movies, a television series and an arena spectacular. The hero of the story remains unnamed in the ballad. Paterson stressed that the ballad was not based on a real person. He said he wrote it to describe the cleaning up of wild horses in the district where he grew up – around Yass, hilly country near the headwaters of the Murrumbidgee. He said: 'I had to create a character, to imagine a man who could ride better than anyone else, and where else would he come from except from the Snowy?

And what sort of a horse would he ride except a half-thoroughbred mountain pony?' To this day many Australian readers still find the climax of the story heart-stopping:

> But the man from Snowy River let the pony have his head,
> And he swung his stock whip round and gave a cheer,
> And he raced him down the mountain like a torrent down
>   its bed,
> While the others stood and watched in very fear.

(See also **Clancy of the Overflow** and **Saltbush Bill**.)

The title of the ballad has entered the language, and newspapers will sometime refer to rocky hillsides or mountain properties as being 'Man from Snowy River country'.

Man who rode the bull through Wagga, the

A catch phrase like **dog on the tuckerbox**, that turns up in Aussie folk tales and bush ballads:

> I've dropped me swag in many camps
> From Queensland west to Boulder,
> And struck all sorts of outback champs
> And many a title holder.
> But though I've heard the episode
> By drover told, and dogger,
> I'm still to meet the bloke who rode
> The big white bull through Wagga.

Dame Mary Gilmore once said that the expression was based a real incident that happened during her childhood in Wagga. A circus came to town, including a bull that the circus proprietor challenged all comers to attempt to ride. A local man said he would ride the bull – not just in the circus but right through the town. Dame Mary names him as a local auctioneer, a Mr Buffrey, and says he succeeded in riding the bull down the main street, with the animal behaving as quietly as a lamb.

Man with the donkey, the

Private John Simpson Kirkpatrick (1892–1915) became known as 'the man with the donkey' on the beaches of Gallipoli. On 25 April 1915, the day of the Gallipoli landing, he obtained a donkey, and from then on, day and night, he worked carrying wounded from the front lines to the beaches. After three weeks of tireless work both he and the donkey were killed by shrapnel from an artillery shell.

Maroon

This is a colour that might be described as a shade of magenta, or a particular kind of brownish-crimson, or as 'claret coloured'. But how should it be pronounced? Many Australians pronounce it ma-*roan* (to rhyme with 'groan'). Others complain this is wrong – it's ma-*roon* (to rhyme with 'moon'), they say. It's an interesting point, and I suggest that ma-*roan* is a regional pronunciation. I grew up in New South Wales pronouncing it ma-*roan* , as do some other folk from other parts of Australia. Most other English users – and all dictionaries – say it's ma-*roon*. Perhaps some leniency should be allowed. Australian English does have (slight) regional accents, so perhaps we can allow both ma-*roon* and ma-*roan*. And here's a thought based on the origin of the word. It appears to come from the French *marron* – a particular type of southern European chestnut, which is, supposedly, a brownish-crimson or claret colour, hence the English word. At a guess I'd say that the ma-*roan* pronunciation is a little closer to the French original, while in Britain (and elsewhere) the pronunciation has been anglicised, along with the spelling.

Marvellous Melbourne

The famous slogan used to describe Melbourne during its boom years in the 1880s. Following the flood of citizens and money drawn to the colony by the gold rush, Melbourne developed rapidly, becoming the commercial and social centre of the Australian colonies.

Mate

This is a word found throughout the English-speaking world to mean 'a friend' or 'a partner'. It appears to have come into English around the 14th century from a Germanic source word meaning (more or less) 'companion' – making the key sense of the word unchanged over many centuries. But in Australia the word 'mate' took on a special complexion. This was because of the difficulties and dangers of life in the bush during the early years of the various colonies that were to become the nation of Australia. Although 'mate' is first recorded here in 1834, it was more towards the latter part of the 19th century that it took on its distinctive Australian colouring, when a mate came to be 'one with whom the bonds of close friendship are acknowledged; a sworn friend'. Used in this way it suggested a high level of trust: the bush was a dangerous place and it was safer to work in pairs, but you had to trust the bloke you were working with; he had to be a real mate. This is the sense in which Henry Lawson used the word in all those classic short stories. Then, in 1914, the mates went to war and the word was infused with wartime suffering and heroism. Today it is probably somewhat weaker. But in Australia mate is still a form of address implying equality and goodwill. Some people will, today, use the word 'mate' ironically, even sneeringly. But despite this, it is a stubborn little word, and refuses to die.

Mateship

The whole concept of having mates and of being a mate is called 'mateship'. The word is recorded as early as the 1860s, and became one of the defining characteristics of life in the bush in the pioneering days: 'In the days,' as Henry Lawson called them, 'when the world was wide'. Lawson was the great chronicler of mateship in his short stories and bush ballads.

Meatworks

What Australians call an abattoir – an establishment where meat is processed and packed, or a slaughterhouse.

Melba

Operatic soprano Helen Mitchell (1861–1931) adapted the name of her home city, Melbourne, to create her stage name of Nellie (later Dame Nellie) Melba. She was notorious for the many 'farewell tours' she gave. Hence anyone who says 'goodbye' and then hangs around is said to be making 'as many farewells as Nellie Melba'. She inspired chefs to create dishes that still bear her name, such as Peach Melba (a confection of ice-cream and peaches flavoured with raspberry sauce) and Melba toast (thinly-sliced bread toasted to crispness).

Melbourne Cup Day

On the first Tuesday in November the nation stops to follow a horse race. The Melbourne Cup is run on that day each year – and has been since 1861. Mark Twain visited the Melbourne Cup in 1895 and wrote: 'Nowhere in the world have I encountered a festival of people that has such a magnificent appeal to the whole nation. The Cup astonishes me.' It's a handicap race run over 3200 metres and carries over a million dollars in prize money.

Messages

Shopping. When I was a child, if I was sent out with a small shopping list and instructions to buy the items on the list I would be told 'do the messages' or 'run the messages' – in other words 'do the shopping'. This always was a very odd expression, and I wonder if it's still used by the current generation of mothers when sending their kids on shopping errands?

Message-stick

A piece of wood carved with significant markings that can be read and understood by the recipient. A method of communication once used between Aboriginal communities. The title of the long-running ABC program produced by the ABC's Indigenous Programs Unit *Message Stick* commemorates this form of communication.

Methodist gate

A rickety old farm gate which is so hard to budge that only a Methodist can open or close it without swearing.

Milk bar

1. A small shop selling milkshakes, soft drinks, ice-cream sodas (called in Aussie English 'spiders'), confectionery, snack foods and hamburgers (but no smallgoods, bread or grocery items). Such shops have now entirely disappeared from the landscape.
2. A small shop selling a range of soft drinks, snack foods, smallgoods, bread and other grocery items; a corner store – what is now sometimes called a 'convenience store' or 'deli' or 'mixed business'.

Migaloo

A white person – from the Mayi-Kutuna Aboriginal language of the Leichhardt River area of north Queensland. In *The Other Side of the Frontier* Henry Reynolds writes: 'She looked at me not as an individual, or as a male, or as a well-meaning academic, but as a white man, a migaloo ...' In the 1990s a rare albino humpback whale seen off the coast of Queensland was given the name Migaloo – suggesting the word has developed a wider meaning outside of Aboriginal English.

Milo

Someone who is a little bit slow on the uptake. (Both Milo® and Quick® were brands of milk flavouring, and anyone who wasn't quick must be a …) Aussie kids' slang.

Min min

Mysterious lights that are sometimes seen floating over the ground in the outback at night. The south-western Queensland town of Boulia has made the min min light the centre of its tourist industry. Hundreds of people over the years have told of seeing the min min light in the Boulia district. The light got its name from the old Min Min pub and mail exchange which used to stand on the boundary of two big sheep and cattle stations. According to locals, soon after the Min Min grog shanty burnt to the ground the ghostly min min lights began to appear. The earliest of these reports are from 1941 (more than 20 years after the shanty had burnt to the ground). Others have claimed that the min min light is an ancient Aboriginal spirit guarding the land. However, Professor Jack Pettigrew, of the University of Queensland, claims the lights are simply an inverted mirage of light sources which are, in some cases, hundreds of kilometres away over the horizon. Which makes him, I think, a bit of a spoilsport.

Minties

Chewy peppermint flavoured lollies, manufactured since 1926. Famous for many years for their slogan 'It's moments like these you need Minties.' (Those words would be printed under a cartoon in which things were going disastrously, and hilariously, wrong.) The result was that the slogan entered the Aussie lingo. So the next time you have an embarrassing accident, if you hear a friend say 'It's moments like these you need Minties' you'll understand why.

Mitchell grass

A hardy, tussocky grass that thrives in semi-arid parts of Australia. Important as feed for sheep and cattle. Named for explorer Sir Thomas Mitchell (1792–1855).

Mob

A lot; a bunch; you can have a mob of sheep or a mob of cattle or I could talk about my mob (meaning my friends) or your mob (meaning your friends).

Moke

Horse. Originally this meant 'a donkey' and it seems to have come to Australia from a regional dialect word found in Hampshire and Devon.

Moleskin

Heavy cotton cloth. Moleskin trousers are much favoured in the bush.

Molly-dooker

A left handed person. Dooks (or 'dukes') is a long-standing nickname for the hands (rhyming slang: 'Duke of Yorks' = 'forks', an old name for the fingers or hands). Molly suggests femininity or doing women's work. Left-handers are not, in fact, either weak or effeminate, but this name enshrines a common long-standing suspicion of left-handers. (After all, 'left-handed' in Latin is sinister!)

Moo juice and cow cordial

In the language of Aussie kids, moo juice is full cream milk while cow cordial is low fat milk.

Mooch

This is a word much beloved of C. J. Dennis's 'Sentimental Bloke', who says that he is:

> Jist moochin' round like some pore, balmy coot,
> Of 'ope, an' joy, an' forchin destichoot.

The glossary at the back of my edition of *The Songs of a Sentimental Bloke* says that mooch (when used by the Bloke) means 'To saunter about aimlessly'. The word 'mooch' must have been both common and popular in late 19th and early 20th century Australia, because it also appears in Rolf Boldrewood's bushranging classic *Robbery Under Arms*, where one of the characters says: 'I don't see but what bushranging … ain't as safe a game … as mooching about cattle duffing' ('duffing' being the Australian equivalent of cattle rustling – stealing cattle). Originally 'mooch' had about it a definitely criminal tinge, and was used to mean pilfering or stealing, before becoming the more law-abiding 'loafing or loitering'. Since it derives from an Old French word meaning 'to hide or skulk' the criminal meaning was the earlier one. More recently 'mooch' has come to mean cadging or sponging. Indeed, in certain circles it remains part of the current argot. For instance, according to the citations, drug users talk about mooching drugs off their fellow users. Still, I like to think of it as employed by that lovable larrikin, the Bloke. If someone asks: 'How did you spend you weekend?' you could always reply: 'Just mooching about.'

Morphine

An idiot; a real, brainless dropkick – because morphine is a 'slow working dope'; sometime 'morph' for short.

Mozzie

Aussie for mosquito. You need to remember the insect repellent if you want to keep the mozzies at bay and 'aveagoodweegend.

Motza

A large sum of money, apparently from the Yiddish word for bread, *matse*.

Muckadilla

A disorganised messy person (a bit of Queensland slang).

Mug

The great Australian comedian Roy 'Mo' Rene was especially fond of the word 'mug'. In the expression 'Whadda ya take me for, a mug?' he used 'mug' to mean someone who was gullible and easily taken in. Roy Rene also used mug to mean 'face', as in 'What an ugly mug!' And these variable meanings point us to the fact that the word has a long and varied history.

The *Oxford English Dictionary* has no fewer than 15 entries for 'mug' – eight nouns and seven verbs. The earliest form of the word I could find is the verb 'to mug', meaning to drizzle with light rain. This is recorded from the 14th century and is thought to come from a Norwegian source word. This suggests to me that it's connected to the Viking invasions (and settlements) of parts of Britain – particularly in the north of England.

The earliest noun is 'mug', meaning an earthenware vessel, bowl, pot or jug – and this is recorded as a northern dialect word, putting it smack in the middle of the area most influenced by the Vikings. The original Norwegian word, apparently, referred to a vessel used especially for warm drinks. Maybe it referred to the sorts of drinks you'd need to keep warm when the weather was 'muggy' (meaning, in those days, drizzling with rain).

Later, in the 18th century, we find mug meaning 'face'. Lexi-cographers think this arose because drinking mugs made to represent grotesque human faces were common in the 18th century. (I take it that the Toby jug, or character jug, is a survival of that habit.) This led to verbs such as 'mugging', meaning 'pulling faces', and the theatrical verb 'to mug up', meaning to apply makeup. From the same source we get 'mug shot', meaning the police photograph of a criminal.

Then in the 19th century 'mug' began to be used to mean 'a stupid or incompetent person; a fool; a simpleton'. This may also go back to those faces on drinking vessels, which may have often depicted grotesque faces of leering stupidity. This, then, leads to other combinations such as 'a mug's game' – a thankless task, a foolish or unprofitable activity.

Also in the 19th century, 'to mug' was to read or study hard. You'll sometimes still hear someone talking about 'mugging up' on a particular topic or subject. Perhaps there's a connection here, in that this sort of swotting ('mugging up') is what a 'mug' (a stupid or incompetent or gullible person) has to do to pass an exam. In time, the exam itself came to be called a mug, although this usage seems to have been born in, and died out in, the 19th century. There are other uses and developments of 'mug', some related, some unrelated – but that's probably quite enough to be going on with. And from that history you can readily see where 'Mo' got his spluttering use of the word, still common among Aussies. (See also **'Ave a go, ya mug.**)

Mulga

Originally the word 'mulga' referred to a species of the Acacia family, to which the wattle also belongs. Mulga especially applies to the widespread shrub (or tree) the *Acacia aneura*, which has grey-green foliage, is regarded as useful fodder for grazing animals, and yields a distinctive brown and yellowish timber. This is found throughout the dry inland of Australia. The word is first recorded used in this sense from 1848. The earliest citations are from the journals of explorers such as Mitchell and Stuart. Then the meaning of the word was extended more widely, until it virtually became a synonym for 'the bush'. And so you got such combinations as 'mulga country', 'mulga flats', and 'mulga paddocks'. Some could say they were 'going up the mulga' meaning they were going up the bush. 'Mulga madness' is said to be something that overtakes you when you live in the middle of nowhere. And the National Party has, occasionally, been referred to as the 'mulga mafia'. The word was originally an Aboriginal word, from the Yuwaalaraay language – where it was probably something more like *malga*.

Munted

A Perth mother reported this as a playground slang word her children had picked up. Anything which has gone wrong is described as 'munted'. Where does it come from? Well, there is an old South African slang word, 'munt', which meant a Black African, a servant, and was usually employed as a term of contempt. So, if a 'munt' is someone who was despised as likely to get things wrong, then anything that has gone wrong has been munted. Another point worth making is that a lot of former South Africans have settled in Perth, presumably bringing their language with them. Hence, the transfer of 'munt' and then 'munted' to the playgrounds of Perth is plausible.

Murdering sand hills, the

In the 1890s two brothers named Pollman, travelling by wagon through the Narrandera district, were murdered at their camp in the sandhills beside Deep Creek (a tributary of the Murrumbidgee). Several years later a drover and his young son were pushing a mob of sheep through the same district and camped at the same spot. The boy was on watch at night when he heard the sound of a wagon rattling down the bush track towards their camp site. He ran to move the sheep off the track, but no wagon could be seen – and the sound quickly faded. In the morning he told his father, an Irishman, who turned pale at the story of the ghostly sound and said (you need to imagine the Irish accent): ''Tis the Pollman ghosts driving their wagon down to the creek. Pack up quick, 'tis not safe to stay here.' At least, that's how the story goes.

Murray talk

At the Sydney Writer's Festival I sat on a panel discussing regionalisms with poet Les Murray. And he had a wonderful collection of regionalisms from his part of the world (the mid-north coast of New South Wales) to share with us. Around his way, Les told us, no one says 'please' – instead they say: 'I suppose ya couldn't ...' And instead of 'thank you' they say, 'Good onya!' Les also insists that in his patch of Australia (an old dairying and logging area) no one ever gets fat: instead they 'put on condition'. And if, on the other hand, you've lost weight the locals will tell you that you're looking 'tucked up' or that you've 'fell away a bit'.

Murrumbidgee sandwich

A goanna between two sheets of bark. Supposedly the standard diet of bushmen during a prolonged or severe drought. (Also **Borroloola sandwich**.)

Muster

The *Macquarie ABC Dictionary* says that 'muster' means to assemble people, such as troops or a ship's crew, for a particular purpose; or to round up livestock, say for shearing or branding; or that any group of people who come together can be called a muster. The word has a particular Aussie application. Where an American ranch would have a round-up an Australia sheep or cattle station would have a muster, and this was because of the military beginnings of white settlement here. The colony was first run by soldiers, and muster is a military term. The first census conducted in Australia was called a muster for just this reason. The word was being applied to livestock by the 1840s. And in the 19th century it gave rise to many combinations, such as 'muster bell', 'muster book', 'muster day', 'muster clerk', 'muster roll', 'muster yard', and so on. The word 'muster' came into Middle English in the 14th century from an Old French word that meant 'to exhibit, or display'. By the early 15th century it was being used to mean an assemblage of troops, which is the meaning that arrived with the convict colony, and that grew into the word we know today.

Mythical towns

Part of what Russel Ward called 'the Australian legend' has always been those mythical outback towns – places you won't find on any map, but which symbolise the remoteness of life in the bush. When I was a boy the one I heard mentioned most often was Bullamakanka. It scores an entry in the *Macquarie Dictionary*, where it's defined as 'an imaginary remote and insignificant town'. Bullamakanka belongs on the same imaginary map as 'Oodnagalahbi', and 'Woop Woop' (which turns up in such expressions as 'from the back of Woop Woop', meaning 'from far, far away'). Then there was the mythical town of 'Bundiwallop', sometimes known as 'Bandywallop', under which variation it used to appear on the children's television program *Mr Squiggle*. And when I was compiling the *Word Map* dictionary I came across another of these mythical town names: Wheelyabarraback. Each exists only in the Aussie imagination – where they paint a mental picture of dry, dusty, remote existence (the verbal equivalent of a Russell Drysdale painting).

Nark

Someone who's always complaining; someone who finds a problem with anything and everything you suggest; a bit of a **whinger**; or someone whose complaining (or incompetence) spoils everyone else's work. According a specialist glossary, in the shearing industry a nark was a troublemaker who interrupted the rhythm of the shed. It appears that a nark shearer could only hurt himself, but a nark shedhand would slow down the work of all the men handling the fleece

Native

In the early days of the colony the word used for Australia's indigenous inhabitants. But also, from the 1820s, non-Aboriginal people who were born in Australia were called natives. So the Australian Natives' Association was founded in Melbourne in 1871 and all its members were white settlers – but settlers who'd been born in the colony. The Australian Natives' Association was a welfare organisation that also took part in public debate supporting such issues as Federation and votes for women. 'Native' was also used as a label for local flora and fauna. Hence the earliest name for the koala was the 'native bear'.

Nature strip

For some Aussies the nature strip is the strip of grass outside your front fence bordering the footpath, but in other places 'nature strip' refers to the median strip in the middle of road that the council has planted with flowering shrubs.

Ned Kelly

1. A Victorian bushranger who lived from 1855 to 1880, famous for fighting a battle with police wearing home-made armour. He lost the battle and was hanged at Melbourne jail. As a result, anyone who is a thief or a cheat can be called 'a bit of a Ned Kelly'. At the same time, someone who is foolhardy, or fearless in the face of overwhelming odds (much the same thing, really), is said to be 'as game as Ned Kelly'. (See also **Such is life**.)
2. Rhyming slang for 'belly.'
3. In World War I soldiers' slang, red wine was called 'Ned Kelly's blood'.
4. In the bush a crow could be called a 'Ned Kelly' or a 'Kelly crow' – apparently from the attacking, thieving behaviour common to crows.

New chums

A 19th-century Australian expression for newly arrived migrants. It especially designated those who were yet to learn the ways of the bush.

Neenish tart

A neenish tart is a small pastry case filled with mock cream and iced in two colours – white and brown or pink and brown. But is this a distinctively Australian culinary item? And, if so, where does the name come from?

When this question was being debated in the columns of the *Sydney Morning Herald* in 1988 a certain Mrs Evans claimed that neenish tarts were first made in her home town of Grong Grong. She nominated Mrs Ruby Neenish, a friend of her mother, as the originator. Mrs Evans said that in 1913, running short of cocoa and baking for an unexpected shower tea for her daughter, Ruby made do by icing her tarts with half-chocolate, half-white icing. From then on they were known as neenish tarts. This would certainly account for the popularity of neenish tarts in country Australia.

The earliest reference to the word 'neenish' is for 'neenish cakes', not tarts, and appears in a 1929 cookery book published at Glenferrie in Victoria. However, the citizens of Orange, in New South Wales, claim that the first true neenish tart recipe appeared in the *Orange Recipe Gift Book* – from where it was reproduced in many other cookery books, especially Country Women's Association cookbooks.

However, there is an alternative spelling of neenish as 'nienish' or 'nienich'. Those who think that this was the original spelling claim that the treat was originally of Viennese or German origin. The word certainly has a Germanic ring to it, but, personally, I love the story about Ruby Neenish and I'm sticking with that!

Nervous Nelly

Aussie name for a timid, cautious person.

Never-never

1. The outer outback; the vast inland of Australia, especially the most remote parts of the Northern Territory and Western Australia. It's recorded in this sense from 1833, and was put into wider circulation by Jeannie Gunn, under her married name of Mrs Aeneas Gunn, in a book about the exploits of her and her husband on a Northern Territory cattle station, published in 1908 as *We of the Never-Never*. (It seems that J. M. Barrie borrowed the expression from Australia to use as the name of Peter Pan's island home, Neverland.)

2. At one time 'never-never' was the name given to lay-by and other time-payment schemes, as in 'We're buying a new fridge on the never-never' – the implication being that you'd never get the wretched thing paid off!

Neville

Another bit of Aussie kids' slang. A Neville is someone who is good at school, dresses like a geek, and is universally disliked. Neville is short for 'Neville no friends'. This is sometimes expressed in the longer version, 'Scott Neville', meaning ''s got no mates, never will'. Another variation on this same theme is 'Nigel No Friends', or 'nof' for short (kids can be cruel).

Nimbin

The northern New South Wales town of Nimbin has been known, since at least the late 1960s, as a hippy haven. In fact, the word 'Nimbin' has become synonymous with ageing hippies and 21st-century followers in their organic, green, alternative, meditating, tarot-reading footsteps. Jim Wafer (writing in the newsletter of the Australian National Placename Survey) says there are two theories as to the source of the word. First, that Nimbin comes from a local Aboriginal word for 'camp, hut or house'; or alternatively (and Nimbin folk always like to be alternative) that it comes from another Aboriginal word meaning 'a little man who dwells in mountains or rocks'. If that latter suggestion is correct it appears that a nimbin was originally a small man with supernatural powers, the Aboriginal equivalent of Ireland's leprechauns, or England's 'little folk' and 'fairy folk'. A colourful idea, and one that would well suit the hippies still living there. Sadly, it seems likely that the more mundane meaning of 'camp, hut or house' is the real source – but the linguists are uncertain, and are still studying the matter.

Noah

Shark (rhyming slang: 'Noah's ark' = 'shark').

No flies on ...

If someone is smart and cluey you might say 'There's no flies on them'. The implication is that they are so busy, or move so quickly, that flies don't get a chance to settle on them.

Noodle, to

To go through the dumps of opal mines at Coober Pedy or Lightning Ridge to find missed 'potch', opal that has no play of colour and is of no value; fossicking through opal waste dumps for opals (often a tourist activity).

No worries

This is a way of saying 'relax, everything's okay'; when someone gets wound up about something an Aussie will often say, 'No worries, mate – she'll be apples' to help them relax. By the way, the Aussie expression 'She'll be apples' began life as rhyming slang: 'apples and spice' = 'nice'.

Nong

A nong is someone who's not too bright. It's one of a large number of Aussie English expressions for stupidity, **drongo**, **ratbag**, **galah**, **boofhead** and **mug** being some of the others. The question has been raised as to whether or not 'nong' is a racist expression. One of the major groups of Aboriginal people in Western Australia is the Nyoongar people. So the question that's been asked is: does 'nong' derive from 'Nyoongar', being an early racist reference to non-English speaking Aborigines? I'm pleased to say this appears not to be the case.

'Nong' is an abbreviation of 'ning-nong', and 'ning-nong' (in turn) quite possibly derives from an old Yorkshire expression for an idiot: 'ning-nang'. This is recorded from 1865 as Yorkshire slang for a crook horse, a worthless old nag. However, an English dictionary of slang published in 1700 records the word 'nigmenog' meaning 'a very foolish fellow' and that may also have contributed to the emergence of this expression 'ning-nong'. (A variation on that – 'nig nog' meaning 'an idiot' – was used in *The Goon Show* scripts in the 1950s.)

'Nong' as part of Aussie English appears to date not from the colonial period, but from World War II. 'Nong' is recorded from 1944, and the earliest citation is from an RAAF newspaper for the troops. The longer form 'ning-nong' does not appear in print until 1957 (in *They're a Weird Mob* by 'Nino Culotta' – the pen-name of John O'Grady). This suggests that originally both the longer and shorter forms were in circulation together, although I suggest that today the longer form has largely died out and only the shorter form survives.

Nullarbor nymph

Between 1971 and 1972 there were reports of supposed sightings of a half-naked young woman living wild, among the kangaroos, on the Nullarbor Plain, which stretches over a thousand kilometres between South Australia and Western Australia. The initial reports described a blonde white woman among some kangaroos. The story was supported by badly shot amateur film of a young woman apparently wearing kangaroo skins and holding a kangaroo's tail. The reports were later exposed as a hoax, with the young woman in the film being identified as 17-year-old model Janice Beeby.

OBV

Old Bush Vernacular – a reservoir of classic Aussie English expressions. Most Aussies don't speak OBV all the time. Those who do wear blue singlets, drive utes, and listen to Slim Dusty. But there is a reservoir of Old Bush Vernacular that lurks beneath the surface of urban Australians. Somewhere inside that pale-faced, anxious stockbroker in his grey suit is the spirit of a weather-beaten stockman in a battered old Akubra.

Ocker

An ocker is a rather boorish, loud, over-assertive Australian male. The source of the word is found in the name of a character in the television series *The Mavis Bramston Show*, from the 1960s. There was a series of sketches devised by Ron Fraser in which he played a character called 'Jack' and Barry Creyton played 'Ocker'. Jack kept referring to Ocker by name and so dinned the name into the mind of the viewer as being associated with boorish behaviour. The word 'ocker' has spawned such derivatives as 'ockerish', 'ockerism' and 'ockerdom'. But where did the character get the name Ocker? Well, he would have been christened by his loving parents 'Oscar' – and in the long tradition of abbreviating proper names 'Oscar' becomes 'Ocker', just as Barry becomes 'Bazza', Garry becomes 'Gazza', and all the rest of them. The nickname 'Ocker' for 'Oscar' is recorded from 1916, and the wider term 'ocker', meaning an exaggerated Australianism, is first recorded in 1968.

Offsider

Offsider, in the sense of 'assistant, friend or mate', is an Australianism, an expression coined here. The *Oxford English Dictionary* knows nothing of this meaning, and thinks an offsider is either 'the animal on the offside of a team' or a player who is offside in certain sports. The Australian meaning arose from a bullock driver's assistant being called an offsider. He was so called because he walked on the offside of the bullock team, while the bullocky himself walked beside the leader and cracked the whip. From this, 'offsider' was extended to anyone who was an assistant in any occupation or enterprise. The earliest citation for this distinctively Australian use of 'offsider' is from 1879. It's nice to know that when you refer to your mate as your offsider you're recalling the role the bullockies played in building Australia.

Old bloke

A nickname for your father (but not one to use when the old bloke can hear you!).

Old Dart

The 'Old Dart' means 'the old country', most commonly Great Britain, especially England. This is a piece of Australian slang that can quite confuse visitors who come from the Old Dart, and have never heard it before. The earliest citation is from 1908, from a book called *Quinton's Rouseabout and Other Stories* by Edward S. Sorenson. As to where it comes from, the *Oxford English Dictionary* says only 'origin uncertain' – so a bit of detective work is called for here.

There is an earlier Australian slang word, 'dart', which could mean 'a plan, an aim, a scheme' but which could also mean 'a favourite or fancy'. It appears to have died out before World War II. It's first recorded in a book called *The Sydney Slang Dictionary*, published in 1882, which says that a 'dart' is 'an object of attraction, or an enticing thing or event, or a set purpose'. Rolf Boldrewood used the word in that sense in his classic novel *Robbery Under Arms*. But we can, I think, go back one step further, because during the gold rushes 'dart' was used to mean 'a scheme or dodge' or 'a favoured location or object' or 'a course of action'.

A book about the gold diggings published in Victoria in 1859 says that 'dart' was used by diggers as 'the designation of stuff worth washing, as contradistinguished from that considered worthless'. In other words 'dart' was 'pay dirt' – a mixture of soil and rock from the diggings that was worth washing for its gold content. And from this the lexicographers suggest that 'dart' is a corruption (or regional pronunciation) of 'dirt'.

And that looks like the story: the Old Dart meant 'the Old Dirt' meaning 'the Old Pay Dirt' – the good stuff, something desirable as a goal.

One hand salute

Brushing away flies (especially while trying to eat food at a barbecue); sometimes called 'the great Australian salute'. (See also **Blowie**.)

Onkaparinga

Since 1926 'onkaparinga' has been an Australian word for a woollen blanket. In that year Onkaparinga (with an upper-case 'O') was registered as a trade mark by the South Australian Woollen Company Limited. The word comes from the place where their factory was located, Onkaparinga in South Australia, on the southern edge of Adelaide. The city, in turn, was named after the Onkaparinga River, on the banks of which it stands. And the name of the river, in turn, comes from a local Aboriginal word meaning 'women's river'. The district was explored and settled, and the name first applied by the settlers, in the mid 19th century. But there's more to the story of the word than that. 'Onkaparinga' also became Australian rhyming slang for 'finger' – although this is a more recent development, first recorded from 1967. So your onkaparingas are your fingers (or they could just be called your 'onkas' for short).

Optics

How things look. Used by Australian politicians, their minders, and political journalists in such expressions as 'the optics of the last few days have not been good for the Health Minister.' This use of the word 'optics' seems to have been born in America (in a 1998 book by James Scott called *Seeing Like a State*, which is described as providing 'a comprehensive understand of the optics of state power') but for some reason seems to have become a more common part of the political lingo here than there.

Orstralia

The way pommies with plummy accents mispronounce 'Australia'. (Ya gotta feel sorry for them, haven't ya?) The Queen used to say it this way, but she doesn't any more – someone must have set her straight.

Our accent

Writing in an online journal called *The Vocabula Review* American linguist Keith Hall says: 'Having an Australian accent is a mixed blessing. It sounds reassuringly normal in Australia, but can be a liability in the rest of the world. Some people love it, most people hate it, but few are unmoved by it. It always seems that no one knows what to do with Australian English. Australians often appear to be embarrassed by it; the English think it sounds like South African; South Africans think it sounds like New Zealandish; New Zealanders hate it; Americans are baffled by it; and Asians refuse to believe that it is English at all.'

I get a sneaking suspicious that he doesn't like the way we speak!

But that sort of comment fails to take into account that fact that Americans seem to love the voices of Paul Hogan and the late Steve Irwin ('the Crocodile Hunter'). And Britain seems to love the way Rolf Harris, Barry Humphries, Germaine Greer, Clive James and Kylie Minogue speak. On that evidence an Australian accent is certainly not 'a liability in the rest of the world'.

Australian linguists have long classified the Australian accent as existing along a spectrum from 'broad Australian' to 'educated Australian'. By 'broad Australian' they mean the sort of 'Dad and Dave' accents adopted by an earlier generation of Aussie actors, such as Chips Rafferty and Bill Kerr (and the sort of thing recorded under the entry on **Strine**). By 'educated Australian' they mean the sort of voices that were once heard reading the news on the ABC (if you remember John Chance and James Dibble you'll be on the money).

In more recent years the suggestion is that the extremes have been dwindling, and the Aussie accent is moving towards the middle – a mid-point which is neither trying to sound posh, nor is very flat and broad. And I suspect the comments by Keith Hall reflect the views of someone who is unaware of what's been happening to the Aussie accent over the last few decades.

The bottom line is that Aussies don't need to 'bung it on': just speak naturally and the world will listen.

Outback

The inland; the bush; the mulga. The earliest recorded use of 'outback' is from the Wagga Wagga *Daily Advertiser* from 1869. It started life as two separate words, then became hyphenated, and it wasn't until 1922 that became a single word.

Overflow

An imaginary outback cattle station invented by Banjo Patterson in bush ballads such as 'Clancy of the Overflow'. Back in the old days, cattle stations had names like 'One Tree Station' and 'Nevertire Station' and the Overflow was meant to be that sort of name – 'Overflow Station':

> And Clancy of the Overflow came down to lend a hand,
> No better horseman ever held the reins;
> For never horse could throw him while the saddle girths
>   would stand—
> He learnt to ride while droving on the plains.

(See **Clancy of the Overflow**.)

Overlander

In the days before railways, and today's 'road trains' (semi-trailers with multiple trailers), were used to move cattle, huge mobs of animals were walked great distances, from Melbourne to Adelaide, from the Queensland coast to the Northern Territory, etc. The drovers who moved these huge mobs were called 'overlanders'. In 1946 Aussie movie legend Chips Rafferty starred in a film called *The Overlanders*. It told the story of a small group of drovers crossing three states of Australia and 2000 miles, with over a thousand head of cattle. The film was set in 1943 and was based on the true story of a cattle drive organised by the government to empty the land of people and supplies in the face of a possible Japanese invasion. Meanwhile, the original overlanders have been celebrated in folk songs:

> There's a trade you all know well
> And it's bringing the cattle over,
> On every track to the gulf and back
> They know the Queensland drover.

So pass the billy round boys,
Don't let the pint pot stand there
For tonight we'll drink the health
Of every overlander.

Oxygen thief

An idiot; a useless person; a waste of space – another piece of slang
that appears to have been coined by Aussie kids.

Oz

Nickname for Australia. First recorded in the *Bulletin* in 1908, but
with a different spelling: 'Oss'. However, it was recognised that this
spelling failed to capture the way 'Aussie' is actually pronounced,
and in 1944 the spelling Oz first turned up – perhaps influenced
by L. Frank Baum's children's book *The Wizard of Oz*, and the 1939
MGM movie thereof, starring Judy Garland.

P

Paddock

1. A field for keeping sheep or cattle in.
2. A sports field.

The word goes back to 16th-century England, where it meant a small field or enclosure. However, in Australia the meaning changed, and paddock was used for any block of land enclosed by a fence, with no reference to its size (although paddock always implies a size on the large rather than small side).

Paddock chicken

A wild rabbit.

Paddymelon

Despite the name, not a fruit or vegetable but a small member of the wallaby family. Which explains the (otherwise confusing) line in the folk song 'The Old Bullock Dray':

> Everything has got a mate that shows itself to view
> From the little paddymelon to the big kangaroo.

Pakapoo ticket

Any writing that is difficult to decipher was once labelled a pakapoo ticket. I remember being told, as a child in school, 'This exercise book looks like a pakapoo ticket, Richards.' From that use it was extended to describe anything that was untidy or disorderly, as in 'Tidy up your room, it looks like a pakapoo ticket'. The earliest citation for this sort of use is from Eric Lambert's novel *Twenty Thousand Thieves* (1951), based on his wartime experiences, in which an officer complains that the platoon's pay book 'looks like a pak-a-poo ticket'.

The origin of the expression is the presence of large numbers of Chinese on the Aussie gold fields, because with them came a Chinese gambling game played with slips of paper marked with columns of characters. Because of the inability of Aussies to read these Chinese characters, such slips looked like untidy scribblings. To Australian ears, the name of this game sounded like 'pakapoo'. The earliest citation for this (original) use of the expression is from 1886. 'Pakapoo ticket' is another distinctively Australian contribution to the English language.

Paling fences

The paling fence is a ubiquitous bit of Australiana. It seems that no Australian suburban landscape is complete without paling fences all over the place. But why are they called paling fences? Where does the word come from? In fact, 'paling' is a very old English word, dating back to the 14th century. Originally it was called a 'pale' – a wooden stake driven into the ground to form a fence. As such it came from the Latin *palus*, meaning 'stake'. By the 15th century this had become a verb: the act of 'paling' was the action of constructing a fence. And then the verb was turned back into a noun (and an adjective) to describe the fence that had been made as a paling fence and the boards it was made out of as palings. And that's the story behind your backyard fence.

Paperbark

A type of gum tree having papery, often peeling, bark.

Parents' retreat

A part of the house where the parents can get away from the kids, and have a bit of quiet and privacy; an increasingly popular architectural feature of Aussie houses produced by a combination of (a) ageing baby boomers, and (b) the 'full nest' syndrome, where adult kids refuse to leave home.

Parrot on the biscuit tin, the

A biscuit-chewing parrot sitting on a perch has long been the trademark of Arnott's biscuits, makers of such iconic Aussie food as **Saos** and **Iced VoVos**. Arnott's Biscuits began in 1865 when Scottish immigrant William Arnott opened a bakery in Hunter Street, Newcastle. The company's trademark parrot is believed to have been first drawn by William Arnott's daughter-in-law, Leslie Arnott. It was registered as a trademark in 1907. In 1997 Arnott's was taken over by an American firm, the Campbell Soup Company, who promised not to Americanise the products or dispense with its Aussie icons. The trademark has given rise to expressions such as 'as cocky as the parrot on the biscuit tin', and the old army joke where one soldier asks another what he does in civilian life and is told 'I shoot parrots for Arnott's biscuit tins!'

Paterson's curse

A biennial herb, *Echium plantagineum*, native to the Mediterranean area, but widely naturalised in settled parts of Australia, having blue-purple flowers. There are eradication programs set up in most states to get rid of this noxious weed. It's also known as 'Lachlan lilac', 'Murrumbidgee sweet pea', 'Riverina bluebell', and 'Salvation Jane'.

Pause the game

A father reported: 'After dropping my daughter at school this morning, I was walking back across the playground when I heard the following "Pause the game! Pause the game!"' It struck me that this is likely to be a recent coinage from computer games. I remember some thirty years ago when children wanted a break in the middle of a schoolyard game they would call out 'Barley!' Why 'barley'? Well, barley (or its abbreviation 'bar') has been used in this sense in children's games since the 14th century! It is staggering to think of an oral tradition surviving for so long – but it has. Perhaps barley (used in this way) was a corruption of 'parley' (from the French verb 'to speak') – in other words, a truce called for negotiations. It still must be used, because it's recorded by June Factor in *Kidspeak,* her book of current Aussie kids' slang. However, computer games may be slowly putting paid to a 700-year-old tradition with 'barley' and 'bar' giving way to 'pause the game' (which someone else may have to explain, 700 years from now).

Pavlova

Both Australia and New Zealand claim to have invented pavlova – the dessert made of a large, soft-centred meringue, topped with whipped cream and fruit. According to one story: in 1935, the chef of the Hotel Esplanade in Perth, Herbert Sachse, created the pavlova to celebrate the visit of the great Russian ballerina, Anna Pavlova. On the other hand, the first appearance in print of the word 'pavlova' (referring to a dessert) is from New Zealand seven years earlier, in a booklet put out by Davis Gelatine called *Davis Dainty Dishes.* However, since the pavlova we now cook includes no gelatine, that may be a reference to some other dessert and not to the meringue-based one we know today – which may, indeed, be an Australian invention. At any rate, the origin of the name is not in dispute: it was named in honour of the great Russian dancer Anna Pavlova, who toured Australia and New Zealand in 1926.

Perentie

See **Goanna**.

Pergola

In other 'Englishes' you'll encounter this word, borrowed from Italian and first recorded in 1675, meaning a wooden framework with trailing plants growing over it. However, Aussie English gives this a slight twist. It seems that here, and only here, pergola shifted to also mean 'a shelter or sunshade with open sides, supported on poles' – with the grape vine (or passionfruit vine or whatever) no longer a part of the picture. Well, given our climate there's a clear need to be sheltered from the sun but open to the breeze. But what do you call such a thing? Well, we borrowed a word for such a structure from Italian via British English.

Perk

Some benefit on the side; an extra bit that you get for doing the job; or an advantage that comes with the job: 'Working at the cinema is a great perk – I get to see all the latest movies for nothing!'

Phar Lap

Phar Lap (1926–32) was Australia's most famous racehorse. He won many races, including the 1930 Melbourne Cup. Much suspicion was expressed in Australia when Phar Lap died in California, probably due to colic. The remains were returned to Australia and mounted in the Melbourne Museum, where they can still be seen. The horse's legendary courage gave rise to the expression 'a heart as big as Phar Lap's'.

Phlegm cake

Aussie kids' slang for a vanilla slice, also known as a 'phlegm sandwich' or a 'phlegm slice'. It's also known as a 'pus pie', 'snot-block', 'snot-box', and 'snot-brick'.

Phil Garlick

A Phil Garlick is 'a bit of a dill' – especially a dill who takes foolhardy risks. From the name of a famous Sydney speedway driver of the 1920s, Reginald Gordon 'Phil' Garlick. He had a reputation as a daredevil who took great risks on the steeply banked Maroubra speedway track. He died in an accident at the Maroubra track on 8 January 1927. His headstone at the South Head Cemetery, near Sydney, overlooking the ocean, is a bust of the famous racer wearing his helmet and with a steering wheel in his hands. His name lives on as a warning not to take foolish risks.

Pigrooter

A political commentator described a minister of the crown as a 'right-wing pigrooter'. The expression 'pigroot', perhaps surprisingly for urban Australians, actually describes the behaviour of a horse. First recorded in 1900, 'pigrooting' describes a bucking horse that 'kicks upwards with the hind legs, its head down, and its forelegs firmly planted'. Apparently a pigrooting horse looks as though it's trying to stand on its front legs. From the *Bulletin* in 1900 comes the statement: 'I saw a colt after much buck jumping and pig rooting get rid of rider, saddle and girth'. 'Pigroot' is a piece of distinctively Australian slang. When it was more widely known there were metaphorical extensions of this expression – so a car started in gear, and jerking along, could be said to 'kangaroo' or to 'pigroot'.

Pilliga Yowie

A wild, hairy creature surviving in small numbers in the most remote parts of Australia. According to some scientists it shares DNA with the drop bear and the hoop snake. Others, however, claim it is more closely related to the bunyip. The debate continues. (See also **Yowie.**)

Pink lamington

A lamington-style cake which is pink, rather than chocolate, in colour. (For the recipe, see **jelly cakes.**) Originally lamingtons – both the pink and chocolate varieties – were a way of finding a use for old cake. However, this tends to make very dry lamingtons and is not recommended. It's perfectly all right to make your lamingtons with fresh cake. (I'm glad we cleared that up.)

Platypus

A monotreme – that is, an egg-laying mammal; one of only two such in the world, the other being the echidna, also found in Australia. It has webbed feet, a muzzle like the bill of a duck (hence references to the 'duck-billed platypus'), and a broad, flattened tail. The male platypus also has a hollow claw-like spur behind each ankle, connected to a poison gland. They are amphibious animals that live in burrows beside creeks. The word 'platypus' comes from two Greek source words and means 'flat-footed'. The platypus was named as early as 1799. Leslie Rees wrote a children's classic book about these animals called *The Story of Shy the Platypus* (1944).

Now, the question that troubles some people: what is the plural of platypus? Well, 'platypi' is a mistake because it's putting a Latin ending onto a word constructed from Greek roots. If you go back to the Greek, you would have to use 'platypodes' – but if you did, you would puzzle everyone, so there's no point. Since 'platypus' is now an English word it's perfectly all right to turn it into a plural using the normal pattern of English grammar:

platypuses. However, Professor Pam Peters (in her *Australian English Style Guide*) notes that there is a rising trend to treat the word like 'sheep' so that 'platypus' is used as both the singular and the plural, as in 'Seven platypus were found in the creek'. And that strikes me as a sensible solution.

Plonk

Wine – although this can be extended to refer to any alcoholic beverage. Coined by Aussie diggers in World War I as a corruption of the French *vin blanc*.

Poddy calf

A young calf, probably being hand fed and not yet branded.

Poisoner

The nickname drovers, stockmen and shearers often gave to the unfortunate soul employed to cook for them.

Policeman bird

North Queensland name for the jabiru – the Australian stork. One suggestion is that this nickname comes from the fact that the bird is quite solitary, but it's more likely to come from its almost silent, stalking approach. Like many other wading birds the jabiru depends upon a stealthy approach to its prey. 'Jabiru' is recorded by E. E. Morris in his 1898 dictionary, *Austral English*. He says it was named after a Brazilian stork with a similar appearance. 'Policeman bird' is recorded from 1928.

Pommy

The legend is that Pommy comes from the letters P.O.M.E., standing for 'Prisoner of Mother England' – in other words, a convict. Unfortunately for believers in the legend, the word entered

Aussie English too long after convict transportation ended for this to be true. The most likely explanation is that it started as a form of rhyming slang to describe new immigrants from England. An elderly letter-writer to the *Sydney Morning Herald* in 1983 recalled schoolchildren, before World War I, chanting 'immigranate, pomegranate' at new arrivals. From this sort of 'immigrant/pomegrant' rhyming slang was the word 'Pommy' first formed. There may also have been a suggestion that the pink cheeks of the new arrivals resembled the pomegranate fruit. But that is where it comes from. Probably. With such oral folklore we can never be 100 per cent certain of anything!

Poofle valve

Sometimes as 'foofle valve' or 'foofer valve'. 'Don't bust ya poofle valve' means the same as 'Don't bust ya boiler' – in other words, don't strain too hard or you'll do yourself an injury. It seems to refer an undesignated part of the body (or of an engine or mechanical device) prone to breaking down. To computer users, 'poofle valve' can function as what they call a 'highly technical name for an undesignated electronic component'. Searches on the web show that 'poofle valve' is employed on lots of websites – but explained on none of them. Thus we resort to those familiar words (the dictionary maker's friend): origin unknown.

Possum

Originally this was the Native American Indian word (from the state of Virginia) 'opossum.' By 1613 it had been shortened, and in this form it was transferred to Australia and applied to a group of tree-dwelling, long-tailed marsupials. There are many different types: brush-tailed, ringtail, pygmy, honey, dormouse and flying possums. They seem to have adapted to encroaching civilisation by taking up residence in the roof cavities of suburban homes. They sleep there by day and then go out at night, with much loud thumping on porch and carport roofs, to hunt and socialise.

Possum knockers

Small rounded cakes or scones. Quite possibly this expression originally described cakes or scones that came out of the oven as hard as rocks, and were suitable only for throwing at possums.

Power poles

Power poles across Australia all carry much the same overhead cables (telephone cables, power cables, and so on) but they carry many different names. For instance, in Tasmania they're 'hydro poles'; in Victoria, 'SEC' poles (from the initials of the old State Electricity Commission); and in Queensland 'utility poles'. In New South Wales they're still, rather oddly, called 'telegraph poles'. That name refuses to die, despite the death, long ago, of the telegraph as a form of communication. (Possibly the use of 'Telegraph' on various newspaper mastheads keeps the word alive.) And in South Australia they're 'Stobie poles', and are made from concrete, with sides of steel. They take their name from engineer James Cyril Stobie, who lived from 1895 to 1953, and who designed them for the Adelaide Electric Supply Company in 1924 to compensate for the lack of hardwood (and the wide-spread presence of termites) in South Australia.

Power Without Glory

A novel by Frank Hardy, published in 1950 and turned into a mini-series by the ABC in 1976. It's a fictionalised account of the life of Melbourne businessman and ALP powerbroker John Wren (under the name of 'John West'). Wren responded by pursuing Hardy, who was tried for criminal libel in 1951. The case coincided with an anti-communist referendum (Hardy was a member of the Communist Party) and attracted enormous publicity. Frank Hardy was acquitted, and later wrote about the case in his book *The Hard Way*.

Prad

Horse. An English dialect word that died out in Britain but survived in Australia. Originally it sprang from the Dutch *paard*, meaning 'horse.' Behind the Dutch word appears to be the Late Latin source word *paraverudus* ('horse').

Prang

An accident; a crash; a smash; when you run your car **flat chat** into a tree that's a real, proper prang.

Property

In the bush any tract of land suitable for either growing crops or grazing domesticated animals is called a property. Some properties are farms (growing crops) and others are stations (grazing sheep or cattle) but all are properties. What might be called a 'farm' or a 'ranch' in other parts of the world is always a property (or else a rural property) in Australia.

Pub with No Beer

A hugely popular hit song in the late 1950s for Slim Dusty, written by Gordon Parsons. Said to be partly based on an earlier bush ballad by Queenslander Dan Sheahan written in 1944 when he found his local pub out of beer due to war shortages and a big booze-up the night before by troops. Many pubs claim to be the original 'pub with no beer' but if the Dan Sheahan story is correct the title belongs to the Day Dawn Hotel in Ingham in north Queensland. Gordon Parsons is said to have invented the colourful characters who make up the verses of the song, but the famous words that 'there's nothing so lonesome, morbid or drear' than being stuck in the legendary dry pub may come from Sheahan's original version.

Qantas

Australia's national airline. It began in 1920 as the 'Queensland and Northern Territory Aerial Services'. The company then consisted of four men: the chairman, two pilots and a mechanic. In 1921 the Qantas fleet comprised two war surplus biplanes – an Avro 504K and a Royal Aircraft Factory BE2E. In its first year it carried 1100 passengers. You could say it got off to a flying start (or, on the other hand, you could avoid the bad pun).

Quart pot

Another name for a billy; sometimes shortened to 'quart'.

Queenslander

An old high-set weatherboard house surrounded by verandas. Authentic examples can date back to the 1800s but nowadays the term is sometimes applied loosely to any older house that is up on stumps.

Quick smart

Very quickly.

Quokka soccer

A joking threat to treat the cute quokkas of Rottnest Island as soccer balls. Quokkas are short-tailed wallabies. The word 'quokka' is from the Western Australian Nyoongar language, and is recorded from 1885.

Quoll

A carnivorous marsupial, sometimes called a 'native cat'. Recorded by Joseph Banks in his *Endeavour Journal* of 1770 – putting it among the first group of Aboriginal words to be recorded in English. Quolls are apparently under threat because of their inclination to eat those poisonous imports, the **cane toads**.

Racing chook

A Tasmanian native hen – from its distinctive and fast style of running.

Rain boots

Rubber boots for wet weather (equivalent of the British 'gumboots').

Rainbow serpent

A common motif in the art and mythology of Aboriginal Australians. It frequently appears in **rock art**, and is said to inhabit certain permanent waterholes, where it is often described as a protector of its people and a punisher of law-breakers.

Ranga

Red haired people can be called 'bluey' or 'ginger' or 'bloodnut', but these days the red-heads seem to be most commonly called 'ranga'. This is a contraction of 'orangutan' – an ape with reddish-brown hair native to the forests of Indonesia and Malaysia. This label 'ranga' is the most recent word for red-heads, appearing only in the early 21st century. But be warned – being called *aranga* in America doesn't mean you're red-headed – it means you're a monkey!

Rat coffin

A meat pie – a 'rat coffin with blood' is a meat pie with tomato sauce. (See also **Maggot bag**.)

Ratbag

When Keith Dunstan wrote his book *Ratbags*, he wrote about Australians most would think of as eccentric – nonconformists in their ideas or behaviour. A ratbag is an eccentric person or a troublemaker, and the suggestion is that this may have arisen in World War I as a result of the troops calling their ration bags 'rat bags' for short. There is an urban myth claiming that some of the volunteer packers of these ration bags slipped in propaganda leaflets, giving rise to the expression 'rat bag ideas'. It's a nice story, but unfortunately the word 'ratbag' is recorded a quarter of a century earlier. The oldest citation for 'ratbag' comes from 1890 – so World War I diggers can't be the source. 'Ratbag' actually derives from the now obsolete expression 'to get a rat', meaning 'to get a wild idea into your head'. If you are a 'container' for a ratty idea, then you are a ratbag.

Rats of Tobruk

Name given to the soldiers who held the port of Tobruk against the might of Rommel's Afrika Korps. The siege of Tobruk lasted from April to November of 1941. More than half the troops in the Tobruk garrison were Aussie diggers – the Australian 9th Division and the 18th brigade of the Australian 7th Division. The story is told in *Tobruk* by Peter FitzSimons and in the novel *We Were the Rats* by Lawson Glossop. The movie *The Fighting Rats of Tobruk* (1944) starred Peter Finch and Chips Rafferty.

Ratter

Someone who enters your opal claim or mine to steal opal.

Raw prawn

A cheat; a swiftie; a raw deal. If someone tries to trick you or deceive you – and you see right through their little dodge – then what you say is, 'Don't come the raw prawn with me, mate!'

Razor gang

Any committee in any parliament (state or federal) given the task of cutting government spending.

Redback

A venomous little Aussie spider. It belongs (broadly speaking) to the family of spiders known overseas as the 'black widow'. The redback name comes from the red (or sometimes orange-red) stripe on the upper abdomen of the female of the species. Redbacks are said to be Australia's best-known spiders. They're found everywhere and thrive in populated areas. Their bite is painful and toxic, but rarely fatal. Hundreds of bites are reported each year but less than 30 per cent require antivenom treatment. Before the antivenom, redback bites caused about a dozen known deaths. So iconic has the redback become that it's given its name to a cricket team and a beer, and been celebrated in a best-selling song by Slim Newton:

> There was a red-back on the toilet seat
> When I was there last night,
> I didn't see him in the dark,
> But boy! I felt his bite!
> I jumped high up into the air,
> And when I hit the ground,
> That crafty red-back spider
> Wasn't nowhere to be found.

Red rattler

Older suburban railway carriages, burgundy red in colour, on the Sydney suburb electric train circuit – not noted for their passenger comfort. They were draughty, noisy and, lacking automatic closing doors, they flew along with doors wide open (and schoolkids hanging out in the breeze).

Reg Grundies

Undies (rhyming slang). Often shortened to 'Reg' or elaborated to refer to your 'Reginalds'. Reg Grundy (b. 1923) was a television producer best known for the plethora of game shows his company churned out.

Remittance man

Common 19th-century expression for a migrant to Australia supported by regular payments from his relatives back in the old country – usually because they wanted him kept a safe distance away, and well out of sight.

Removalist

A common enough looking word meaning 'a person or firm engaged in household or business removals' – but it happens to be an Australian coinage, first recorded by the great Sid Baker in 1959. What embedded this word so deeply in Australian English was probably David Williamson's 1971 play *The Removalists*. The play was made into a movie in 1975, and has often been revived and set as a study text for students.

Rhino

One popular old bush song is called 'On the Road to Gundagai', with the chorus of: 'We camped at Lazy Harry's on the road to

Gundagai ...' It appeared in the first edition of Banjo Paterson's *Old Bush Songs* in 1905 and tells the story of a group of shearers on their way to the city to spend their pay cheques. Unfortunately, they stop at Lazy Harry's grog shop on their journey and waste all their money on booze (beer and rum-and-raspberry – see **Barmaid's blush**), while ogling the barmaids. Broke again, they have to forget about their city trip and head back to the bush. The song begins with these words:

> Oh, we started out from Roto when the sheds had all cut out.
> We'd whips and whips of Rhino as we meant to push about

Clearly 'rhino' here means money. But what is the source of this slang word? The full *Oxford* helpfully says 'origin unknown'. But the earliest citation (1688) is Irish, so there is at least the possibility that this was slang brought to Australia by Irish convicts and settlers. And since the last citation in the *Oxford* is from 1851 it may be one of those terms that survived in Australia after it died out in its homeland. But that still doesn't explain the origin. One suggestion is that back in the 17th century when this was coined the rhinoceros was thought of as a rare and exotic beast, 'worth its weight in gold'. Slang expert Jonathon Green dismisses this suggestion as smacking of 'lexicographical desperation'. He adds that 'rhino' began as underworld jargon and moved into general slang only in the mid 19th century.

Ridgy-didge

The old Aussie expression 'ridgy-didge' means 'all right', 'genuine', 'fair dinkum'. 'Ridgy-didge' is first recorded by Sid Baker in 1953, but there seems to be an earlier expression from which 'ridgy-didge' developed. In 1938 Eric Partridge recorded 'ridge' as an Aussie slang word meaning 'good', 'all right', 'genuine'. And although this wasn't recorded until the 1930s there's a suggestion that it might go as far back as the gold rushes – the word 'ridge' referring to gold (to a gold-bearing ridge, perhaps) – and that from this it came to apply to a gold coin, and then to anything that was the genuine article, that was 'as a good as gold'. And this slang word 'ridge' was then expanded (in the way that often happens with informal English) into the rhythmical rhyming expression 'ridgy-didge'.

Right as rain

Why do Aussies say 'as right as rain'? There've been expressions starting 'as right as ...' since medieval times, always in the sense of something being satisfactory, all right, okay or correct. As long ago as 1546, they used to say 'right as a line'. Later variations included 'as right as a gun', 'as right as my leg', 'as right as ninepence', 'as right as nails' and 'as right as the bank'. This one ('as right as rain') is a latecomer, first recorded in 1894. Quite possibly there's a lurking idea here that rain often comes straight down, and 'right' can mean 'straight' ('a right line' means 'a straight line'). But the alliteration of the two 'Rs' ('as right as rain' rolls off the tongue!) also played a role in why it was created and why it's survived.

Ringer

Someone who can 'run rings around' others. It has two meanings.
1. In a shearing shed the ringer is the fastest shearer in the shed (because he can 'run rings around' the other shearers).
2. On a cattle station all the stockmen are called ringers (because they can 'run rings around' the cattle).

Ripper

Really good! Terrific! Fabulous! This is sometimes heard in expressions such 'You little ripper!' or 'Ripper bewdy bottler mate!' 'Ripper' appears to have started in the 17th century in the expected, literal way: a ripper was a tool for ripping, or a person who ripped, or a murderer who ripped the bodies of his victims. But from the early 19th century it also became a slang term meaning 'a person or thing that was especially good, particularly an attractive young woman'. What is not explained, and is not obvious, is how this usage developed. None of the lexicographers I consulted were prepared to offer a guess, and I shall follow their sound example. At any rate, the slang use of 'ripper' seems to have died out in England in the early 20th century but to have continued here as part of Aussie English up to the present day. The first recorded use in Australia is from 1858, in one of Charles Thatcher's popular goldfield songs. (See also **Bewdy.**)

Road maps

Bloodshot eyes – the visible veins resembling tracks wandering over the map.

Rock art

Ancient rock art is found widely across Australia, with the style varying according to the region – ranging from stencil art (using, for instance, a hand as a motif) to the X-ray paintings of the Northern Territory and the dot paintings of the Central and Western deserts.

Rock choppers

Roman Catholics – from the initials R.C.; Australian slang recorded from 1908. Edmund Campion called his 1982 book about growing up Catholic in Australia *Rockchoppers*. (See also **Cattle ticks.**)

Roo

An idiot, fool or clumsy person. Mostly used on cattle stations. Possibly from the old saying, 'He's got kangaroos in his top paddock'.

Roo bar

Heavy metal protection on the front of a car, designed to protect the vehicle in the event of striking a kangaroo on a remote, outback road – always a possibility, especially at night.

Rooned

A literary attempt to capture vernacular Australian speech in John O'Brien's bush ballad, 'Said Hanrahan'. (See **Said Hanrahan**.)

Rort

Rort is a bit of Aussie slang meaning 'shrewd practices' or 'confidence trickery' or 'fraud'. In tracing the origins of 'rort', Sidney J. Baker says there was an earlier use of the word to mean 'the patter used by a showman to draw the public'. And, of course, in so doing showmen rarely told the truth. They would encourage the crowd to 'Step inside the tent, ladies and gentlemen, and see the horse with its tail where its head ought to be.' And if you were **mug** enough to fork over your two bob, what you saw inside the tent was an ordinary horse with its tail in its feed-box. The step from that sort of rort to any sort of fraud is not a big one – so that, perhaps, is the journey the word has taken.

Rosella

A rosella is a brightly-colour, seed-eating Australian parrot of the genus *Platycercus*. This attractive bird was first seen in the Sydney suburb of Parramatta, and takes its name from that suburb – or, rather, from the earlier name of that suburb. When Parramatta was first settled, in November 1788, it was named Rose Hill, after a British treasury official, a certain Mr Rose. But the name was changed a few years later to Parramatta, an Aboriginal word meaning 'head of the waters'. During the time when Parramatta was called Rose Hill, these brightly coloured birds were first identified and named. They were called 'Rose Hill parrots' (that name is recorded from 1789). This was shortened to 'rose-hillers' – and this, in turn, was corrupted to 'rosellas' (recorded as such from 1836).

The name 'rosella' was also applied, in the 19th century, to a shrub or small tree, used as a food plant and an ornamental plant.

The food made from the blossoms of the shrub was called 'rosella jam'. Later 'Rosella' was used as a proprietary name for a range of jams and other food products. And the name 'Rose Hill' was re-used to name another Sydney suburb.

Rosiner

Originally a rosiner was a stiff drink – a generous serve of spirits. It's a metaphor that comes from the world of violin playing, where 'rosin' (a solid substance distilled from turpentine) is applied to the bow of the violin in order to improve the sound. (By the way, this word 'rosin' is linguistically related to 'resin', which refers to various, often sticky, substances exuded by trees.) So, a stiff drink was a 'rosiner' on the theory that it would make you play better: 'put a bit of rosin on your bow'. This is listed as both Australian and Irish slang, although the earliest citation (from 1932) is from Australia. Behind this bit of Aussie slang is the older British slang term, 'to rosin', meaning 'to make drunk' – as long ago as 1734 alcohol was being called 'rosin'.

Rough as guts

A thug was called a 'rough' as early as 1911 in Australian slang, and 'rough as guts' seems to be a development of this, suggesting a thug so violent that he'll 'spill your guts' when he lays into you.

Rough end of the pineapple

Hostile or unfair treatment; a raw deal or inequitable treatment. Given in full this is often a statement about the rough end of a pineapple being employed to do unpleasant things to a sensitive part of the anatomy. It seems to date from at least the early 1960s.

Rough on rats

Unlucky. An expression of obscure origin, first recorded in 1885. When something very unfortunate or unlucky has happened it can be described as being rough on rats – although why this should be so is not entirely clear.

Rouseabout

A rouseabout is a general worker, an odd-job man, or (sometimes) a casual worker, especially on a sheep or cattle station. This meaning developed in Australia and New Zealand in the 19th century – it's recorded in this sense from 1861. Earlier 'rouseabout' had existed as an English dialect word (a Somerset word, to be precise) with the meaning of a restless, roaming creature. It seems to come from the verb 'to rouse', meaning 'to stir up to movement'. It was used of rousing game birds from their nests (so that they could be shot – not that you would have told them that at the time); and rousing a sleeping person from their bed. And 'rouseabout' was abbreviated, in the common Australian manner, into both 'rousie' and 'rouser'. (Not to be confused with 'roustabout' – an American expression meaning a wharf or circus labourer or ship's deckhand.)

Rum and raspberry

This revolting sounding concoction, also known as 'barmaid's blush', was (apparently) a favourite tipple of shearers and other outback workers in the 19th century. Rum was certainly the common (and popular) form of alcohol from the early days of the colony. In the hot, dry Australian inland beer only took its place after the spread of refrigeration. The raspberry cordial might have been added to the rum in notorious sly grog shops – such as the legendary Lazy Harry's on the road to Gundagai – to make the rum go further. As the shearers became drunker the proportions could be changed by the barmaid – including more and more water and raspberry cordial and less and less rum. (See **Barmaid's blush.**)

Rum rebellion

In 1808 the Governor of New South Wales was William Bligh, and he was no more popular with certain leaders of the colony than he had been with the crew of the *Bounty*. A group of leading colonists and officers of the New South Wales Corps under John Macarthur and George Johnston arrested Bligh on 26 January 1808. Later court hearings in London exonerated Bligh of any wrongdoing, court-martialled Johnson and cashiered him out of the army. The New South Wales Corps was disbanded. The event became popularly known as the Rum Rebellion since one of the key issues for the revolutionaries was keeping their monopoly of the profitable rum trade. (See also **Bligh under the bed**.)

Run

A sheep or cattle station can also be called a run. This is because the earliest squatters did not own their land, they simply had grazing (or 'running') rights – that is, the right to run sheep or cattle on the land. And the place where you would run your sheep or cattle was called a run.

Runaway hole

In the south-east of South Australia, which is limestone country with many underground caverns, there exist runaway holes – depressions in the ground that appear to be solid, yet in heavy downpours run-off water floods in and drains rapidly away through the porous bottom of the hole. Very often a tree grows next to these holes.

Said Hanrahan

A quotation from a bush ballad, usually uttered to identify someone who's being a prophet of doom, gloom and utter despair. The ballad is called 'Said Hanrahan' and was written by a bush priest, Patrick Hartigan (1878–1952), under the pen-name of 'John O'Brien'. It tells the story of a bunch of cockies who gather after church to squat on their heels, chew on a bit of bark, and talk about farming conditions. Hanrahan is the gloom merchant of the bunch.

> 'We'll all be rooned,' said Hanrahan,
> 'Before the year is out.'

… either from too little rain, or too much, or rain at the wrong time, or the river being too high, or too low, or the summer being too hot, or not hot enough. Whatever happens, Hanrahan is certain it will bring about drought, flood, bushfire, bankruptcy or the collapse of commodity prices (or, quite possibly, all of the above).

Salad dodger

A fat person.

Saltbush

The common name given to the wild alkaline shrubs growing on the dry interior plains of Australia. The areas dominated by such plants can also be called the saltbush (or, sometimes, the saltbush plains).

Saltbush Bill

Legendary character created by Banjo Paterson. He features as the hero in five of Paterson's bush ballads. The first of these ('Saltbush Bill') appeared in the *Bulletin* on 15 December 1894 and told the story of Saltbush Bill's adventures as a drover (the 'King of the Overland') outwitting an English **new chum**. The character was later adopted by Eric Jolliffe (1907–2001) in a long-running series of cartoons for *Pix* magazine and for his own publication, *Jolliffe's Outback*. (See also **Clancy of the Overflow** and **Man from Snowy River**.)

Saltpan

A large flat area of hard mud sometimes inundated by very high tides or flooding rivers.

Salvo

Australian abbreviation of 'Salvation Army'. Highly regarded in Australia for their practical approach: 'Christianity with its sleeves rolled up'.

Sandy blight

A painful eye infection, common in sandy arid areas (and used by Eric Jollife as the name of one of his outback cartoon characters, Sandy Blight). Henry Lawson wrote about the eye problem in his short story, 'A Vision of Sandy Blight.'

Sanger

This Aussie abbreviation of 'sandwich' is first recorded from 1943 – and it appears to have been born as World War II digger's slang.

SAO

The SAO (a large, square, flaky biscuit) was launched in 1906, and there are conflicting accounts of how it came to be so named. One is that is was the name of a sailing boat seen on Lake Macquarie where William Arnott (founder of the biscuit baking clan) had a home. Another is that the initials stand for 'Salvation Army Officer' and as William's son, Arthur Arnott, joined the Salvos this is a possibility. It has also been suggested that S.A.O. preserves the initials of another of William's sons: Samuel Arnott – but that doesn't explain the 'O' at the end. Finally, there's the notion that it was named after a trading vessel with a Portuguese name: the 'Sao …' something or other (in other words the 'Saint Something', 'Sao' being Portuguese for 'saint'). Which is the true story? We don't know. The true origins of SAO are lost in the mists of history.

Schmick

Stylish, excellent. Anything from clothes to restaurants can be schmick. The puzzling thing is where the word came from. At first glance it appears to be Yiddish, and to be related, in structure, to such familiar Yiddish words 'schmuck' (a foolish person) and 'schlock' (cheap goods). In fact, this is the claim made for it when it first appeared in the *Bulletin* on 10 April 1990. A footnote to the article said that schmick was 'New York Jewish slang: slick with a cheeky twist'. But there is no evidence for 'schmick' in New York or anywhere else before it turns up in Australia. There is a German word, *schmuck*, meaning 'nice, pretty, handsome, spruce', but the lexicographers can't see how a German word could have found its way into Australian English at such a late date. So 'schmick' remains a puzzle, but for the moment it seems to belong to Aussie English.

Schoolies

1. End of secondary schooling celebrations (short for 'schoolies' week').
2. The graduating students attending these celebrations.

Scozzie

A Scottish-born Aussie.

Scribbly gum

A gum tree with a trunk that looks as if someone has drawn (or scribbled) all over it. The scribbly gum is a eucalyptus tree with a very smooth, pale trunk. The distinctive brownish 'scribbles' are made by the larvae of the tiny scribbly moth. These larvae are harmless to the tree and, though found on many eucalypts, it's only in a few varieties that their 'artwork' becomes visible on the outside of the pale bark. Judith Wright celebrates the scribbly gum in her poem of that name:

> The cold spring falls from the stone.
> I passed and heard
> the mountain, palm and fern
> spoken in one strange word.
> The gum-tree stands by the spring.
> I peeled its splitting bark
> and found the written track
> of a life I could not read.

Scrub

The bush, the mulga.

Season, the

The sugar crushing season on the north coast of Queensland.

Selection/selector

By the 1850s squatters had acquired most of the agricultural land in the colonies, and had it locked up in large holdings. In response to popular clamour to 'unlock the land' systems were introduced allowing settlers to take up (to 'select') small farms of limited size with the land sold on credit. Most of these properties were too small to be viable, and life on them was a struggle. The story of typical battling selectors **Dad and Dave** is told by Steele Rudd in his book *On Our Selection*.

Sentimental Bloke, The

The Songs of a Sentimental Bloke (1915) is a yarn told in a series of highly colloquial verses by C. J. Dennis (1876–1938). The story of Bill, the larrikin from the inner suburbs of Melbourne, who marries his Doreen and settles down to raise a family won Dennis the title of 'the Laureate of the Larrikin', while his use of the Aussie dialect of the streets caused him to be labelled 'the Australian Burns' (as Robbie Burns was the poetic employer of Scottish dialect). The book was a bestseller and became a popular silent movie. Later it was turned into a stage musical, and John Derum toured Australia with a one-man show about Dennis and his creation called *More Than a Sentimental Bloke*. (See also **Mooch** and **Squiz**.)

Septic

An American (rhyming slang: 'septic tank' = 'Yank'). Not intended as a flattering expression. Not recorded until 1976, following the flood of American servicemen on R and R ('rest and recreation') leave in Australia from the Vietnam War, but it's possible it was part of the oral culture during World War II, when there were some famous tensions between Aussie soldiers and their American counterparts.

Seven-course meal

A six pack of beer and a meat pie.

Seven o'clock wave

A mythical wave released each day from the dam up the Murrumbidgee River from Wagga Wagga. Newcomers to the place would be told to get a surfboard and be at Wagga beach to catch the seven o'clock wave, which had been released earlier from the dam. (Ah, those visitors, they'll fall for anything, won't they?) However, some residents insist that it was the 'five o'clock wave'. (This is what I like: when people argue about the arrival time of something that doesn't exist!)

Shark biscuit

A bad surfer; especially one on a cheap surfboard made of foam, instead of a proper one made of fibreglass.

Sheila

An Aussie female. (The equivalent of **bloke**.)

Shearers

For much of Australia's history the economy was said to 'ride on the sheep's back', making shearers an important part of the Australian legend. Patsy Adam Smith wrote a comprehensive historical and anecdotal account of shearers and shearing in *The Shearers* (1982). Shearers feature in countless folks songs and bush ballads, in the paintings of Tom Roberts and in movies such as *Sunday Too Far Away* (1975).

She'll be apples

A general assurance that things will be okay. (Rhyming slang: 'she'll be apples and spice' = 'she'll be nice'.)

She'll be right

Not a statement that the words just spoken by a woman are correct (although they almost certainly are – regardless of the woman or the circumstances). Rather a general assurance that things will be okay.

Shiralee

D'Arcy Niland's novel *The Shiralee* has twice been filmed (once with Peter Finch and again with Bryan Brown). The word 'shiralee' is first recorded from 1892 as a synonym for 'swag', 'drum', 'bundle' or 'matilda'. Of course in D'Arcy Niland's book, 'shiralee' is used metaphorically to refer to the child, Buster, who is a burden to her father, an itinerant worker. Dr Dymphna Lonergan has traced 'shiralee' back to an Irish source word, and as there were certainly many Irish-born itinerant workers humping their shiralees in Australia in the 19th century, Dr Lonergan may very well have solved another linguistic puzzle.

Shirk

Today in Aussie English the verb 'to shirk' is a synonym for 'bludge', meaning 'to deliberately avoid doing something that you should do (probably because you're lazy)'. But it's not the meaning it always had. The oldest recorded meaning of the verb 'to shirk' (from the early 17th century) was 'to practise fraud or trickery instead of working as a means of living; to prey or sponge upon others'. And this verb grew out of the noun 'shirk': 'a needy disreputable parasite; one who makes a living by sponging on others, cheating at play, swindling or the like'. And this noun was a corruption of the word 'shark'. So 'to shirk' was originally 'to shark': 'to prey upon others'. That's the source from which the modern meaning developed over time. And I guess modern shirking is still a form of sharking – because it's preying on others in the sense of leaving others to do the work.

Shonky

According to Jonathon Green's *Dictionary of Slang*, the word 'shonky' is Australian and New Zealand slang, first recorded in the 1970s, with the meaning of 'unreliable, dishonest, crooked, … engaged in irregular or illegal business activities'. However, it turns out that this expression, which we think of as being quite harmless today, had its origins in anti-Semitism. Early in the 20th century the word 'shoniker' was an offensive term for a Jew in American slang. It may have derived from a Yiddish word, 'shoniker', meaning 'a petty trader or peddler'. By the 1930s this had been abbreviated to 'shonk' and was also an offensive term for a Jew. 'Shonk' was being used in that sense (at least in fiction) as late as the 1980s. However, around the 1970s, in Australia, at least, it became separated from its anti-Semitic past, and 'shonky' was being used generally to mean 'unreliable, dishonest, or crooked'. Most Aussies who use 'shonky' today would be quite unaware of its disreputable and offensive past.

Short of

Someone who is not quite up to the mark intellectually is usually described by Aussies as being 'something short of something'. The earliest version I can recall hearing was 'two bob short of quid' (and this even seemed to survive, for a while at least, the conversion to decimal currency on 14 February 1966). Much older is 'a shingle short of a roof', which seems to go back to at least the 1840s. Another classic is 'a few bricks short of a load' – but the list is a long one. It includes: 'a button short of a shirt', 'a bite short of a biscuit', 'a sandwich short of a picnic', 'a few Tim Tams short of a packet', 'a banger short of a barbie', and 'a sheep short of a paddock'. You can see how it's done – so you should now feel free to go and invent your own versions.

Shout

'Shouting' for drinks is a bit of slang that was coined in Australia and first recorded here in 1850. The expression originated in the time of the old pubs and taverns and grog shops where the noise level meant that in order to be served you had to raise your voice. The person who put together the collective order, then (literally) shouted that order to the bar, was the person the barman collected the money from, this being the simplest way (in all that noise) to work out who was paying for what. Well, those years have passed, and we no longer raise our voices, but we still shout a mate a drink. John O'Grady, in one of his very Aussie novels, has one character invite a workmate to join his 'choir'. When the bloke expresses surprise it's explained to him that this choir doesn't so much sing – rather it shouts. Then he understands!

Six and out

In the rules of backyard cricket if you hit a six (over the fence) you've also lost your wicket: you are six and out (and you have to climb over the fence and get the ball!).

Skerrick

A small amount; a small fragment; the slightest bit. Almost always used in the negative: we might say that we have 'not a skerrick' of something, but it would be unusual to say that we do have a skerrick – unusual, but not entirely unknown, as in 'How much is left?' 'Just a skerrick.' Skerrick is one of those words that began life as a British dialect word, came to Australia with the early settlers, and survived here in Aussie English while fading out of existence in the land of its birth. It's recorded in Australia as early as 1854 (in a book called *Gallops and Gossips in the Bush of Australia*) in the statement: 'I have plenty of tobacco, but not a skerrick of tea or sugar.' The 1823 edition of Grose's *Dictionary of the Vulgar Tongue* records the word 'scurrick', which is said to be thieves' cant for a halfpenny (it's recorded in the same sense, in the same year, in a *Slang, a Dictionary of the Turf, the Ring, the Chase* by 'Jon Bee'). And 'scurrick' is sometimes recorded as 'scuttick', and sometimes as 'skiddick', so it is probably the origin of 'skerrick' – especially as the meaning seems to match: a halfpenny being 'a small amount'.

Skip

The name non-Anglo Australians (of Italian, Greek, etc. background) give to Anglo Australians. From the popular television series *Skippy, the Bush Kangaroo*.

Skite

To boast or brag. This began in Australia as a British dialect word for an odiously conceited person. Then the noun gave rise to the verb 'to skite.' Dates from around the 1850s. (See also **Blow**.)

Sledging

Sledging is a kind of gamesmanship employed in cricket in which close-in fieldsmen attempt to upset a batsman's concentration with a steady flow of subtle suggestions or comments, or (at its worst) abuse and invective. The practice is said to be a distinctively Australian contribution to the noble and ancient game of cricket. However, since it's covered by Law 42 (paragraph 6) of the Laws of Cricket – and Michael Rundell's *Dictionary of Cricket* has a complaint about it from 1897 – sledging (whether under that name or not) has clearly been around for more than a hundred years. As for the name, according to Ian Chappell that was born around 1964 from the expression 'sledgehammer'. Over time the expression 'to sledgehammer' the batsman's concentration was contracted to 'sledging'. The term was, at first, not widely used outside the Australian Eleven. But word of the word crept out, and in 1984 Ian Chappell told the story of its origins.

Slip-rail

A rail in a stockyard fence that can be slipped back to create an opening.

Slouch hat

The Aussie slouch hat is one of the icons of Australian head wear (along with the legendary **Baggy Green** and the battered old **Akubra**). It's first recorded in the sense of the hat of the Australian soldier in 1927, but I suspect it comes from World War I. It's not recorded in W. H. Downing's *Digger Dialects* (a great book recording the soldiers' slang from World War I) but that may be because it was so familiar it didn't need explaining. The expression 'slouch hat' was used earlier, back in the early 19th century, to mean 'a soft hat with a broad brim which hangs down over the face'. However, in the case of the military version one edge of the broad brim was turned up, not down (originally in order to facilitate carrying a rifle with a bayonet fitted). And that's the slouch hat that became a symbol of patriotism and courage. Hence the old song that says:

> It's just an old slouch hat with the side turned up,
> But it means the world to me.

Slushy, the

The assistant to the poisoner in a shearing shed (see **Poisoner**).

Smithy

Sir Charles Kingsford-Smith (1897–1935). Pioneering Australian aviator. He set many early flying records and broke others. His most famous achievement was leading the four member aircrew that was the first to fly across the Pacific Ocean. He disappeared in 1935 while on a flight from England to Australia. It's believed his plane crashed in the ocean off Burma. His story was told in the movie *Smithy* (1946), with Ron Randell in the title role. Sydney's main international airport is named after him and the plane in which he conquered the Pacific, the *Southern Cross*, is on display at Brisbane Airport.

Snags

Aussies calls sausages snags – and this appears to be yet another bit of English regional dialect that survived (slightly changed) in Australia, while dying out in mother Britain. Snag is probably of Scandinavian origin (there's a Norwegian dialect word, 'snag', which means 'a sharp point, projection, stump or spike'). 'Snag' is recorded in English from 1577, and it was first used to mean 'a short stump standing out from the trunk of a tree, or a stout branch of a tree or shrub, left after pruning'. From this it came to mean anything that you might catch upon. For instance, a trunk or branch of a tree embedded in a river, and an impediment to navigation, was called a snag from at least the early 19th century. Thus any hitch, defect or obstacle came to be called a snag. And then, out of the blue, in 1941, the great Sid Baker recorded 'snag' as Aussie slang for sausage.

Where does this slang usage come from? The *Oxford English Dictionary* throws up its hands in defeat and says 'origin unknown'. However, both the *Macquarie* and *The Australian National Dictionary* suggest that snag (meaning 'sausage') comes from an earlier British dialect word. In the late 19th century the *English Dialect Dictionary* recorded 'snag' as meaning 'a morsel' or 'a light meal'. This is the word that became slang for 'sausage' in Australia. As the poet once put it:

Serve 'em curried or barbecued,
Serve 'em fried or serve 'em stewed,
They're always something out of the bag,
The humble, but wonderful, sizzling snag.
Served with potatoes or onions or peas,
Eaten indoors or outside in the breeze.
Swaggies would carry a few in their swag,

The handy, transportable, sizzling snag.
Turned into sangers with slices of bread,
'Give us more bangers!' is what they all said.
The symbol our country should have on its flag
Is the beautifully barbecued sizzling snag.
'I don't like sausages!' Uncle Alf said.
Now Alf is healthy, wealthy … and dead!
He would have survived if he'd eaten up bags
Of humble, high-vitamin, sizzling snags.
A horse at Randwick a week or so back,
Was running so fast that it burnt up the track.
The stewards asked who had been feeding the nag
On the humble, high-octane, sizzling snag.
What is it that melts with delight in the mouth?
That tickles the tonsils as it travels down south?
I know the answer (though I don't want to brag):
Your taste buds, my friend, have just struck a snag!

Snatch it

To resign from a job (mining industry jargon).

Snottygobble

Can you imagine snottygobble as 'a well-recognised delicacy'? Well, that's how they're described by the distinguished Australian writer Flora Eldershaw (1897–1956). The word 'snottygobble' does sound pretty revolting, but it turns out to be the name for several native shrubs or trees of the genus *Persoonia*. As variations the snottygobble fruit was also known (sometimes) as 'snotty gollion' or 'snotty goblin'. Not a great improvement, really. The name is first recorded from 1854. And, in case you're wondering, snottygobble is described in one quotation I came across as 'red berries'. And, it seems, the tree that grew the berries had another application: its red-coloured inner bark could be used to produce a dye that colonial ladies used to dye straw hats a 'vivid and lasting red'. Professor Roly Sussex describes the name 'snottygobble' as 'poetry, Ogden Nash, Monty Python and Dr Seuss rolled into one'. Well, perhaps, Roly … perhaps.

Snowy

Aussie nickname for a bloke with black (or very dark) hair.

Snuffle buster

What kind of a person would be described as a snuffle buster? It's such an odd name that it sounds meaningless, but back in the later 19th and early 20th centuries 'snuffle buster' was an Aussie nickname for a puritanical person. The verb 'snuffle busting' also turns up in the same period with a quote from 1895 describing someone as 'a snuffle busting son of a gun'. The more common Australian slang term for such persons is 'wowser' (see **Wowser**). This alternative nickname seems to have had a very short run in Aussie slang, but then slang tends to be the fastest changing part of any language. Perhaps it's time to revive 'snuffle buster' as a way of describing the PPC – the Pathetically Politically Correct?

Soggit

Picture this situation: you're having morning tea with friends, and dunking your biscuit in your tea or coffee when, without warning, the end of the biscuit falls off and plops into the hot brew. In Aussie English the lost bit of biscuit is now called a soggit. When you get to the bottom of the cup, and find the gooey mess, what you are looking at is a soggit. And there are possible metaphorical extensions: when someone is socially soggy and uninviting you might refer to them as 'a bit of a soggit'.

Sool

If you encourage your dog to bark and snap at someone then you have 'sooled your dog onto them'. Sometimes it's the word you use when giving the order to your dog: 'Sool 'im Blackie – go for 'im!'

Southern hemisphere

That part of the planet on the southern side of the equator. Its relevance here is that places or objects in Australia are (not infrequently) referred to as the biggest, heaviest, longest, tallest, smallest, etc. 'in the southern hemisphere'. The proper response to all such claims, of course, is to point out that most of the southern hemisphere is water.

Southerly buster

A cool southerly wind in the afternoon or evening at the end of a hot Sydney's summer day.

Southern Cross

The constellation of stars known as the Southern Cross is visible outside Australia, but, despite this, it has come to be regarded as the astronomical emblem of Australia. The stars of the Southern Cross appear on the Australian flag, and the team song of the Australian national cricket team is 'Under the Southern Cross I Stand':

> Under the Southern Cross I stand
> A sprig of wattle in my hand,
> A native of my native land,
> Australia, you little beauty.

Spare me!

An exclamation of exasperation: 'Don't keep coming at me with this rubbish!'

Spare me days!

An exclamation of surprise. The implication is that the speaker is so surprised that they might die – 'the days of their life' might be cut short. Sometimes abbreviated to just 'Spare me!'.

Speed Jordan

Flash Gordon was a popular American science fiction comic strip hero from the 1930s onwards. In Australian newspapers this was printed with the hero's name changed to Speed Gordon because of the underworld connotations of the word 'flash' (going back to the convict days – see **Convict words**). He was parodied on a weekly radio comedy series called The Bunkhouse Show, where he was played by Keith Walsh as Speed Jordan, a dim-witted yokel. This led countless schoolteachers, during the 1940s and 50s, to chide slow learners with 'Come along, son! Even Speed Jordan could understand this!' In fact, for many years Speed Jordan was a proverbial label for the slow-witted. The Bunkhouse Show was written by George Foster (who played 'Uncle Sassafras') and starred Leonard Teale (as 'the Kansas Kid').

Speedos®

Speedo® is the registered brand name of a type of swimwear, first established in Australia in 1929 when the McRae Knitting Mills manufactured the world's first swimsuit (the 'racer-back') made from silk and joined in the middle of the back. Speedo® introduced the world's first nylon swim briefs in 1957. What is special about Speedos® is the astonishing number of nicknames these swimmers have bred in Aussie English, simply because they are very snug-fitting. The following is (to the best of my knowledge) a comprehensive alphabetical list of all the nicknames given to Speedos® tight-fitting men's swimmers:

ballhuggers
boasters
budgie-huggers
budgie-smugglers
dick bathers (or DBs)
dick-pointers
dick-pokers (or DPs)
dick stickers
dick togs (or DTs)
dikdaks
dipsticks
cluster busters
cock chokers
cock jocks
cod jocks
fish frighteners
jammers
jimmy clingers
knobbies
lolly-baggers
lolly bags
meat-hangers
nut huggers
nylon disgusters
racers
racing bathers
scungies
sluggers
sluggos
slug huggers
tights
toolies
wog togs

A very small item of clothing to inspire so many names!

Speewah

A mythical outback station of vast proportions. The setting for many tall tales and bush yarns. The sheep on the Speewah are so big that it takes several days to shear each animal – and that's with half a dozen shearers walking over the sheep's back as they work. The kangaroos on the Speewah are as tall as mountains and the emus lay eggs so big a bloke can empty one out and live in it. The Speewah is often used a comparison to make the present situation look insignificant: 'Rain? Ya call this rain? This is nothin' compared to the rain we used have on the Speewah!' And by substituting others words for 'rain' (drought, bushfire, barbecue, etc.) the statement can be applied to almost any situation.

Spider

A tall glass of soft drink with a scoop of ice-cream floating on top (what Americans call a 'floater'). The earliest citation is from 1850 when a spider was an alcoholic drink, and there was no ice-cream involved. The original spider was a mixture of brandy and lemonade. A few decades later a spider might be a mixture of lemonade and sherry, or of beer and brandy. And all such drinks were called a spider because they would 'creep up' on the drinker, with an innocuous taste followed by a stronger alcoholic bite. Then in the 20th century the name was transferred to the soft drink and ice-cream concoction and the alcoholic reason for the label was forgotten.

Squatter

One who occupied a tract of crown land in order to graze livestock, having title to do so either by lease or licence. They didn't own their land – they simply squatted on it. These early graziers often ended up running sheep and cattle over areas as large as some European countries, and made vast fortunes doing so. Squatters became the wealthy elite of the colonies, and so their title bred a string of other words: 'squatterdom' (all the squatters collectively, or the government practice of leasing land to them); 'squatteress' (a weird word for a squatter's wife); and 'squattocracy' (the notion of the squatters as forming a kind of ruling class).

Squiz

Squiz means 'a look or a glance'. This strikes us as such a normal word that we may not realise that it belongs to us – it's a piece of Aussie slang. The earliest recorded usage of squiz is from 1913, from C. J. Dennis's *Backblock Ballads*. He used it again the next year in his legendary *Songs of a Sentimental Bloke*. In fact, all the citations in the complete *Oxford English Dictionary* are from either Australian or New Zealand authors. It's people like Katherine Mansfield, Vance Palmer and Frank Clune who map the growing usage of 'squiz'. As for the word itself, the most probable source is a blend of the words 'quiz' and 'squint' – making a squiz 'a questioning look'. Sidney J. Baker (in his classic *The Australian Language*) suggests it may have begun life as schoolboy slang.

Starlight Hotel

When you're 'staying at the Starlight Hotel' you're sleeping in the open air – and the implication is that you're doing so from necessity, not choice.

State nicknames

Queenslanders are 'banana benders' (or 'banana-landers'). Western Australians are 'sandgropers'. New South Welshpersons were (in colonial times) known as 'cornstalks'. Victorians (in the same period) were 'gumsuckers'. Folk from the Northern Territory are simply called 'Territorians' – although they used to be called 'Top Enders'. Tasmanians were, back in the colonial era, known as 'Vandemonians' – more recently they've either been straightforwardly 'Tasmanians' or else 'Taswegians' (modelled on such words as 'Glaswegian' or 'Norwegian'), this word apparently having begun life in the 1930s as sailors' slang. As for South Australians, there are two options – they were either called 'crow-eaters' or else 'magpies'. Of those two I suspect that 'crow-eaters' was more common in colonial times – especially north of the Goyder Line, where farmers tried to grow wheat in an excessively arid climate, failed, and suffered from a scanty diet as a result. Hence, 'crow-eaters'.

That is pretty much the complete and matching set. There appears to be no nickname for residents of the Australian Capital Territory (perhaps there's nothing amusing about having to live in Canberra!).

Station

In Australia, tracts of land suitable for growing crops are called farms while tracts of land suitable for grazing animals are called stations. Why stations? It goes back to the military nature of the foundation of modern Australia. Originally a station was an outpost of the colonial government where convicts and troops were stationed for a particular purpose. If the troops and convicts were not on the move, but were stationary (housed in barracks), their location was called a station. Such places were often called 'convict stations', while a remote spot was called an 'outstation'. This military language was adopted by churches who established 'mission stations' and by squatters who established 'sheep stations' and 'cattle stations'. If, in those colonial days, you were granted the right to occupy a tract of grazing land, then you were said to have 'right of station'. The earliest recorded use of station in this agricultural (or grazing) sense is from 1820.

Steak and kidney

Very old rhyming slang for 'Sydney', now obsolete.

Stickybeak

A spying, prying, nosey person who sticks their nose into other people's business.

Stockman

The Australian equivalent of the American cowboy.

Stockwhip

A whip used for controlling the movement of stock, especially cattle. The Australian stockwhip had its origins in the English hunting whip, but from the beginning of European settlement it developed into a unique form. A major difference is the solid handle; another is the use of stranded, vegetable-tanned kangaroo hide – the toughest leather for its light weight in the world. Stockmen don't whip the animals they are controlling; instead, they crack the stockwhip, moving the startled animals on by their response to the sharp, sudden noise. The stockwhip also became a source of entertainment with performers, Smoky Dawson (and many others) giving demonstrations of using the stockwhip with great precision.

Stone the crows

'Stone the crows' is an old-fashioned Aussie bush exclamation of surprise (or possibly exasperation or even disgust). My memory of the old *Dad and Dave* radio serial is that Dad Rudd was forever saying, 'Stone the crows, Dave ...' There are variations on this expression: sometimes it's 'starve' or 'stiffen' or 'spare' the crows. And the earliest citation for the phrase is, in fact, in the form of one of these variations. In a 1918 book called *Saints and Soldiers* we read: '"Starve the crows," howled Bluey in that agonised screech of his.' (It just had to be someone called 'Bluey' who first used the expression in Aussie literature, didn't it?) Given the date of its first appearance in print (1918), it may have become a popular expression as soldiers' slang during World War I. However, I can't find it listed in W. H. Downing's *Digger Dialects* (the best book on World War I Aussie slang), so I'm not sure. Today, it's only ever used for comic effect, as a deliberate bit of OBV (**Old Bush Vernacular**). As for the origin of the expression – none of the experts can suggest anything. A journalist once suggested that given the difficulty of hitting a flying crow with a stone – or even a crow sitting on a fence (they'd take flight before the stone hit) – successfully 'stoning a crow' would be so surprising an act that 'stone the crows' was a suitable expression of surprise. And that will have to do until a better suggestion comes along.

Stonkered

The way I've heard this word used, the verb 'to stonker' means 'to put out of action, to render useless'. As such it derives from an earlier word 'stonk', which meant 'a concentrated artillery bombardment'. It started as military slang and was probably echoic (or onomatopoeic) in origin – 'stonk' echoing the dull thud of the artillery. Now, anything that has been pounded by the artillery has been 'put out of action, or rendered useless', hence the broader (metaphorical) used of 'stonkered'. And a further extension of that same metaphor is the Australian and New Zealand use of 'stonkered' to mean drunk. Anyone who has pounded their brain with enough booze to put it out of action is as stonkered as if they were a military target pounded by heavy artillery.

Stoush

'Stoush' means a fight, but not necessarily a physical fight (for example, the headline 'Political Stoush' referred to a heated debate in the national parliament). 'Stoush' is both a noun and a verb: to 'stoush' someone is to bash them or fight them (either physically or metaphorically), while the fight itself is called a stoush. In typical Aussie fashion the Great War of 1914–18 was called 'the Big Stoush'.

The earliest citation for 'stoush' is from a report in the *Bulletin* in 1893. The source of the word remains a mystery, but the *English Dialect Dictionary* records a somewhat similar word, 'stashie', meaning 'uproar' or 'quarrel'. So 'stoush' may have started life as an English dialect word that immigrated, changed, and then lived on here while it died out back in the British Isles.

Stranglers

Trousers worn too high on the waist.

Strewth

An expression of surprise: 'Strewth, cobber, you gave me a fright, creeping up behind me like that'. An abbreviation of an older expression, 'God's truth.'

Strike me pink

An expression of surprise. Perhaps from the notion of blushing or going red in the face with astonishment.

Strine

In 1964 the *Sydney Morning Herald* reported that while English author Monica Dickens was autographing copies of her latest novel in a Sydney bookshop a woman handed her a copy and said, 'Emma Chisit'. Monica Dickens then autographed the book to Emma Chisit. The woman, unhappy with this response, said more forcefully, 'Nah! Emma Chisit?' The question she was formulating (in Broad Australian) was 'How much is it?' This is the kind of speech that has been labelled 'Strine' – a one-syllable contraction of the word 'Australian'.

The newspaper report of this incident inspired Dr Affabeck Lauder, the Distinguished Professor of Strine at the University of Sinny (pen name of Alistair Morrison) to write a series of articles on the subject, later collected in two books (*Let Stalk Strine*, 1965, and *Nose Tone Unturned*, 1966).

Here are a few of his examples of Strine (or Broad Australian) pronunciations:

Air fridge – average

Baked necks – bacon and eggs

Garbler mince – a couple of minutes

Naw shaw – north shore

Split nair dyke – splitting headache

Snow White and the Severed Wharves (and you can work that one out for yourself).

Do most Australians still talk like that? On the whole, most linguists seem to think not. (See also **Our accent**.)

Stringybark

A type of gumtree, genus *Eucalyptus*. The stringybark is a very tall, straight tree reaching up to 30 metres tall. The bark is rough, fibrous and stringy. Traditionally the bark was used by Aboriginal people for many things, including painting, shelters, canoes and dishes. Early white settlers found that both bark and wood of the tree had a wide ranch of applications. Many a settler's hut was made from stringybark lashed together with strips of greenhide leather. Hence the old folksong 'Stringybark and Greenhide':

Stringybark and greenhide,
That will never fail yer,
Stringybark and greenhide,
The mainstay of Australia.

Stump-jump plough

A plough fitted with a mechanism that will cause the blade cutting the ground to jump over the stumps of felled trees. Extremely useful in the development of the Mallee areas of New South Wales, Victoria and South Australia. The story is that a farmer named

Mullins came up with the idea, and that R. B. and C. H. Smith then put it into practice. The mechanism for the stump-jump plough was registered in 1877, patented in 1881, and is still used today. If you ask the average Aussie what inventions have come out of Australia, most will think of the stump-jump plough.

Stunned mullet

Someone who has a really dumb, open-mouthed look, like a fish in a fish shop window, can be described 'looking like a stunned mullet' – and if they keep on standing there with their mouth wide open you can ask them if they're trying to catch flies.

Such is life

Supposedly the last words spoken by Ned Kelly at Melbourne Jail on 11 November 1880, as he faced the hangman. The expression was taken up by Joseph Furphy and used as the title of his novel, published by the *Bulletin* in 1903. And the novel *Such is Life* also contains a memorable phrase in the form of its legendary open line: 'Unemployed at last!' Mind you, there are some narky historians who want to spoil it all by claiming Ned never spoke these words at his hanging. Instead, they insist, he said: 'Ah well, I suppose it has come to this.'

Sugarloaf

A place name given to almost any roughly conical hill – from the conical shape in which loaf sugar was imported into the colony in the early 19th century.

Sunbeam

An item of cutlery that comes back from the table clean and unused, so it can be put straight back into the cutlery drawer without washing up. As I child in Sydney I never heard this expression, but it was common in my wife's farming family – which suggests that this is a regionalism. The origin is plain enough: unused cutlery is as bright and shiny as a sunbeam.

Sundowner

A swaggie who arrives at a station supposedly looking for work in return for a feed, but who's very careful to arrive at the end of the day (at sundown) so that it's too late to do any work and he gets his feed for free.

Swag

A backpack consisting of all a bloke needs when tramping through the bush wrapped up in a blanket, and tied up with a bit of rope or an old leather strap. Back in the old days the blankets were a blue-grey colour and so a swag could also be called a bluey. Also called a drum or a matilda.

Swaggie

Short for 'swagman' – back in the old days, swaggies would tramp 'down the wallaby track' from station to station looking for work (or, more likely, for a hand-out and a free feed!). (See also **Wallaby track**.)

Swy

Another name for **two up** – from the German for 'two', *zwei*.

T

Tall poppy

When Nicole Kidman won a Golden Globe award an Australian newspaper ran a captioned photo accusing the actress of having 'dish-pan hands'. A subsequent letter to the paper accused it of falling for the 'tall poppy syndrome'. Used this way, 'tall poppy' is a distinctively Australian expression. According to *The Australian National Dictionary* a 'tall poppy' is a person who is 'conspicuously successful; frequently one whose distinction, rank or wealth attracts envious notice'. The earliest citation is (perhaps surprisingly) from way back in 1902. The origin of the expression is not difficult to guess: it comes from the nature of the flower – a single tall stem, with a single large flower on top. In a bed of poppies it's the tall one that spoils the symmetry. When someone stands out above the crowd they thus resemble a tall poppy. And cutting down such 'conspicuously successful' people is much like lopping the heads off the tall poppies in the garden.

Tasmanian devil

A small, fierce marsupial with savage teeth and jaws and a bad temper! Most have black fur with white markings; some are entirely black. They can grow up to about a metre in length, and are powerful for their size. They sleep by day in a cave or hollow log, and hunt by night, killing small animals or feeding on the carcases of dead animals. Warner Brothers made the Tasmanian devil internationally famous by turning it into a cartoon character who was repeatedly mistaken by Sylvester the Puddy Tat for 'a giant mouse!' – which then proceeded to savage him in cartoon after cartoon.

Tasmanian tiger

Also called the thylacine. Most scientists believe it to be extinct. European settlers hunted the animal to extinction because they thought it preyed on sheep and poultry. The last known Tasmanian tiger died in captivity, in Hobart Zoo, in 1936. It was a powerful, dog-shaped marsupial, with grey or brown fur and stripes across its lower back. But is it really gone forever? There are two possibilities:

1. There are occasional reports of supposed sightings of the Tasmanian tiger in remote and rugged parts of Tasmania.
2. Scientists have speculated on the possibility of recovering enough DNA to re-create the species. We await developments.

Tea

See Dinner.

Tea-tree (or Ti-tree)

A name given to a number of shrubs and trees, mainly of the genus *Melaleuca*. Early settlers deprived of real tea leaves are said to have made a kind of tea by boiling the leaves of these shrubs – with varied success, according to contemporary reports. One writer (in 1848) says: 'the flavour is too highly aromatic to please the European taste.' The first Europeans to have attempted this brew appear to have been Captain Cook and his crew. The small curly leaf was thought to (slightly) resemble the leaves of the real tea plant, and this (combined with desperation) may have inspired the original experiments in making 'Clayton's tea' (see Clayton's).

Temporary Australian

A bike rider not wearing protective headgear, or a car driver or passenger not wearing a seat belt.

Territory rig

See Darwin rig.

Thank your mother for the rabbits

A strange, old-fashioned way of saying cheerio and goodbye when someone was leaving – it was meant to be a sort of joke. It probably comes from the Great Depression of the 1930s, when rabbit was a source of cheap meat.

Thanks, Yanks

One of the most common complaints heard today is that Australians are adopting American slang. There is, of course, some truth in that – particularly among the young, who desperately imitate the lingo of black ghetto kids. But the traffic is not all one way. Americans, it appears, have picked up 'no worries' and 'aggro' and 'U-ey' and other Aussie idioms, and are using them often. There are various theories as to how this happened. Some experts think it came from the deliberate use of 'Aussie-isms' by American media commentators during the 2000 Sydney Olympics. But Aussie movies, songs and advertisements have also had an impact. Earlier, Aussie slang was carried back to the states by servicemen who'd spent their R and R here, and by American surfers who'd come here for the beaches and the waves. One expert claims that Australians are providing more new material for the American lexicon than any other country in the world.

That

In his 1965 book *Aussie English* John O'Grady pointed out that Aussies have a most unusual way of using the word 'that' – or, perhaps, a bunch of ways. Here are some of the examples he gives:

'Now that's a jockey for you; the old Georgie.'
'Aw, don't give me that, he's not that good.'
'That's a big building they're puttin' up there.'
'You reckon? I don't think it's that big.'
'You should've seen 'er face when I told 'er – she was that excited.'
'What's for lunch?' 'Aw, just bread and meat and that.'

In other words, what you find in Aussie English is one small pronoun used as an adverb and an adjective and as a vague verbal gesture that saves you having to think of what it is you're really trying to say. And it if annoys you, well, get used to it – it's not that bad.

That room

There's one room in your house that is labelled by nothing but euphemisms. I refer, of course, to 'the smallest room in the house'; or the WC ('water closet' being one of the many euphemisms). To one bloke I know it's 'the little house on the prairie'. To many Aussies, of course, it's the 'dunny'. An English friend of mine once announced that he was 'going to sit on the doughnut in granny's greenhouse', while someone else might announce that they are 'going to inspect the plumbing'. To Americans it's 'the bathroom' (even when they are not going there to have a bath) or else it's 'the john' or 'the rest room' (but they're not going there for a rest). Mind you, even 'lavatory' is a euphemism, since it comes from the Latin word for 'washing'. And even 'toilet' is a euphemism, coming, as it does, from a French word meaning a small washcloth. So, there's no real name for this place – just heaps of euphemisms. If fact, the Aussie word 'dunny' is probably the most honest name the room has! (See **Dunny**.)

They're a Weird Mob

The biggest selling book in Australia in the 1950s. *They're a Weird Mob* (1957) was written by John O'Grady (1907–81) under the pen-name of Nino Cullota – supposedly an Italian migrant journalist who, in the course of the book, turned into a Sydney builder's labourer. The plot is a romantic comedy, with Nino ending up marrying the boss's daughter. It was an instant and continuing success, mainly, it appears, for what it showed Australians about themselves. In 1966 it became a highly successful movie with Walter Chiari as Nino Cullota and archetypal Australian actor Chips Rafferty as the knockabout Aussie builder who becomes Nino's father-in-law.

Three Sisters, the

A rock formation at Echo Point, near Katoomba, in the Blue Mountains west of Sydney. The name comes from an Aboriginal legend which says that the three towering rocks are all that remain of three beautiful sisters of a Jamison Valley tribe who fell in love with three brothers from a Nepean tribe. The sisters were forbidden to marry the brothers by tribal law. The brothers responded by planning to launch a major battle between the tribes and seize the sisters by force. The wise old man of the Jamison Valley tribe turned the sisters into rock formations to protect their lives, then lost his own life in the ensuing battle – leaving them as rocks forever.

Thumbs in

An expression of agreement to join in a game or participate in a group activity (schoolyard slang).

Ticket of leave

A permit or a document that allowed a convict to live and work as a private individual (virtually as a free citizen) within a stipulated area. It was rather like being released on a good behaviour bond. Perhaps oddly, some ticket-of-leave men were even employed as police constables. After having held a ticket of leave for a certain period of time, a ticket-of-leave man could apply for a pardon. Mind you, the ticket of leave could also be revoked for bad behaviour. And a ticket-of-leave man could not move from one district to another without official permission, and even needed to carry a passport recording this permission.

Tie Me Kangaroo Down, Sport

Song written by Rolf Harris as an expat art student in London and first performed for other expats at a local café. When he returned to Australia he recorded the song and it became a number one hit in 1960. It tells the story of an Aussie stockmen 'lying, dying' who props himself up on one elbow and gives the mates gathered around instructions for caring for his livestock: kangaroo, cockatoo, koala and 'platypus duck' (well, it needed that extra syllable so the line would scan!). The song is a parody of the many Australian folk songs and bush ballads about 'the sick stockrider' or 'the dying stockman'. It's worth noting, in passing, that 'sport' is a word (like 'digger') that can be substituted for 'mate' in Aussie lingo.'

Tiggy touchwood

A professional sporting clash lacking real aggression or (especially) physical contact. Named after a children's game in which players can only be caught if they are not touching a tree or a piece of wood. The implication is that big, boofy footballers have been playing like kids.

Tin kettling

The custom of making a din, by rattling and banging kettles and tins, outside a bride's house on the night before the wedding. The custom was brought to South Australia by German settlers.

Tin lid

Rhyming slang: the 'kids' are the 'tin lids'.

Tinny (or Tinnie)

1. A can of beer.
2. A small aluminium boat with an outboard motor.
3. Someone who's remarkable for their good luck.

Toad buster

Those intrepid persons hunting down the dreaded cane toad as it spreads across Australia like ink soaking across blotting paper. The giant neotropical toad or cane toad, with its poison glands and toxic tadpoles, was introduced into Australia in 1935 to control cane beetles. As these ugly amphibians bred and spread out steadily from the Queensland cane fields, toad eradication became an occupation, and the job title 'toad buster' was born.

Toey

According to the *Macquarie ABC Dictionary*, someone who is toey is 'anxious, apprehensive'. They might be a bit restive, touchy, ill at ease and raring to go – those ideas also accompany the word 'toey'. A slang word of Australian origin, first appearing in the *Bulletin* in 1930, it was probably part of the spoken language before that. 'Toey' is a term that comes from the sport of racing, and was first used to describe a horse that wouldn't settle in the box at the start of a race. I take it that it was, at first, almost a physical description, the horse being 'up on its toes', rather than settled, and ready to race.

Tom Uglys Point

Landmark on the Georges River in Sydney. There are two stories as to the source of this unusual place name. One is that an early settler was a man with only one arm and one leg. In the local Aboriginal language the word for 'one' was *wogul* and so the man became known as 'Tom Wogul', later extended to 'Tom Wogully', and then corrupted to 'Tom Ugly'. The alternative, and more likely, story is that the name comes from an early settler on the north side of Georges River, Tom Huxley. The local Aborigines found his surname difficult to pronounce so they called him 'Tom Ugly' – a name which amused his neighbours and caught on.

Too right

An expression of agreement: 'Too right, Bluey, you're spot-on there.'

Top end, the

The Northern Territory

Top of the wazza

Aussie digger slang going back to World War I, when the original Anzacs were serving in the Middle East. Their home station, when they weren't fighting at Gallipoli or in Palestine, was in Egypt. 'Wazza' was the name given by Aussie diggers to the native quarters of Cairo – it comes, apparently, from one of the street names in that quarter. From this original meaning, 'wazza' was broadened out to mean 'the slum area of any city' and then broadened further to mean 'a dirty or untidy house or room'. Therefore 'top of the wazza' means 'the best of a bad lot' – or else anyone who's got to the top of the pile.

Torrens title

A simplified method of land registration devised by Robert Torrens (1814–84), the first premier of South Australia. It was introduced in that state in 1858 and is now widely used across Australia. For this achievement, Torrens was knighted in 1872.

Track, the

The Stuart Highway that runs between Darwin and Alice Springs.

Train smash

1. A hastily prepared meal with a variety of ingredients, cooked together and often served on toast, the most common being scrambled eggs and tomatoes. (The expression may have been rhyming slang for 'hash', and may have begun as Navy slang.)
2. Tomato sauce.

Transport

A semi-trailer; sometimes with an adjective, as in a 'cattle transport' or a 'sheep transport'.

Trap

Early colonial slang for a police officer or trooper: one whose job it was to trap offenders.

Treacle trousers

'Treacle trousers' used to be a jibe, a taunt, levelled at a person wearing trousers which are too short. So, in a book published in 1928, we read: 'There was a space of three inches between the bottom of each leg and top of each boot … other boys barracked him about it … calling him treacle trousers.' And from 1944 comes this quote: 'I was growing fast and as a gap between the top of my boots and the bottom of the legs of my trousers appeared slightly greater day by day I was greeted by the cry of "treacle".' I guess the trousers were thought to look like treacle – trickling down the legs and not getting all the way. This is a bit of distinctively Australian slang that has now largely disappeared.

Triantiwontygong

A triantiwontygong is a type of Bunyip peculiar to the Central Highlands of Victoria. During World War II – in the early 1940s, in fact – city children were being evacuated from Melbourne to the bush to escape any possible bombing. And the bush kids used this 'triantiwontygong' to scare, or embarrass, or confuse the city kids. 'Did you see that?' a child might say in a hushed whisper, pointing. 'No, don't look now! It's a triantiwontygong!'

However, one correspondent reports her father using the word 'triantiwontygong' as a generic term for large, hairy spiders. Interestingly, there was an older slang word, 'triantelope', used for hairy spiders such as **huntsmen**. The earliest citation for 'triantelope' is from 1845.

Then in 1921 C. J. Dennis published *A Book for Kids* in which he combined both words ('triantiwontygong' and 'triantelope') to create his own mystical creature, which he called 'the Triantiwontigongolope':

> It is something like a beetle, and a little like a bee,
> But nothing like a woolly grub that climbs upon a tree.
> Its name is quite a hard one, but you'll learn it soon, I hope.
> So try:
>   Tri-
>   Tri-anti-wonti-
>   Triantiwontigongolope.

So wrote C. J. Dennis – giving us three creatures with impossibly similar names.

Trooper

The uniformed law enforcers of the colonial era were called troopers, hence the role they play in 'Waltzing Matilda':

> Up rode the squatter, mounted on his thoroughbred,
> Down came the troopers: one, two, three,
> 'Whose is that jumbuck you've got in your tucker bag?
> You'll come a waltzing matilda with me!'

Troppo

Short for 'tropical'. Someone who's 'gone troppo' has gone mad in the heat and humidity; consequently, anyone who's acting strangely (a bit weird) can be said to have 'gone troppo'.

Trotting cob

The residents of Wonganilla (near Deniliquin in NSW) insist they have their own local ghost. At a spot called Trotting Cob a horseman appears, on the stroke of midnight, carrying his bloody head under his arm, riding on a snow-white cob (a short-legged, stout variety of horse). In the late 19th century, coach drivers reported seeing the figure trotting around and around the site of a wayside pub.

True blue

The expression 'true blue' means something like 'having steadfast loyalty' and we seem to have adopted it as an Aussie expression, perhaps because John Williamson's memorable song has so deeply penetrated the Aussie consciousness. John himself defines 'true blue' as 'being proud of things Australian such as our wildlife and bush and the honest, down-to-earth Australian character'. Fair enough. But, in fact, the expression 'true blue' is of Scottish origin. It was the Scottish Covenanters of the 17th century who adopted blue as their trade mark colour. The Covenanters were Scottish Presbyterians who, in 1643, signed the 'Solemn League and Covenant' in which the Scots (and their English allies) pledged to preserve Presbyterianism in Scotland. The name 'Covenanter' is particularly applied to those who adhered to the Covenants after they had been declared unlawful in 1662. Their fierce loyalty marked such Covenanters out as being 'true blue' – steadfastly loyal to the blue, as opposed to the royal red. The expression 'true blue' has since travelled around the world, and presumably it came to Australia with the early Scottish settlers here. John Williamson's adaption runs thus:

True Blue, is it me and you?
Is it Mum and Dad, is it a cockatoo?
Is it standing by your mate
When he's in a fight?
Or will she be right?
True Blue, I'm asking you …

Trugo

A sport that will never be an Olympic event. It's played by striking a disc with a mallet, and the object of the game is to score points by hitting the disc through a pair of goal posts. It was invented (or, perhaps, accidentally stumbled upon) at the Newport Railway Workshops in the western suburbs of Melbourne in the 1920s, and has been fading slowly ever since. At the time of writing there are still five Trugo clubs in Melbourne. Can it be revived? Should it be televised? Should it be made a body contact sport? We await developments.

Tucker

'Tucker' is a classic bit of Australian slang – 'tucker' means food, and the container in which you carried your food was your 'tucker box'. Hence, the word turns up in bush ballads about dogs sitting on tucker boxes, either nine miles or five miles from Gundagai (the distance depends on which song you're listening to at the time).

This use of 'tucker' is first recorded in Australia in 1858. At about the same time in England the shorter word 'tuck' is recorded, also meaning food. It's first recorded in *Tom Brown's School Days* (by Thomas Hughes) and from then on turns up in many school stories – especially Frank Richards's stories about Billy Bunter of Greyfriars, who was always after tuck. And this use of the word 'tuck' is the reason that canteens in schools are called 'tuckshops'. It appears that this usage developed as follows: originally (and we're talking 13th century, here) a tuck was a fold made in clothing, and the verb 'to tuck' meant to fold the end of a piece of cloth and 'tuck it away' out of sight. Well, food that you swallow also disappears, goes out of sight, and so (by extension) it was said to be 'tucked away'. And then that which was eaten (or 'tucked away') came also to be called 'tuck'. However, it seems that only in Australia was the extra syllable added, so that food grew from being 'tuck' to 'tucker'.

Tumble off the twig

Die. Death probably has more euphemisms than any other word in contemporary language: 'passed away', 'passed on', 'deceased', 'has left us', 'has gone to their final reward', and so on – all the expressions you recall from Monty Python's dead parrot sketch. This is Australia's contribution: 'tumbled off the twig'.

Two-pot screamer

This is someone who can't hold their alcohol, and gets drunk easily (on two pots, or glasses, of beer). In some parts of Australia such a person is also known as a cadbury: from an old advertising campaign which claimed each block of Cadbury's chocolate contained 'a glass and a half' of milk. Getting tiddly on a glass and half makes you a 'cadbury'. (By extension, it can mean someone who gets very silly after smoking a small amount of dope.) In other places the two-pot screamer is known as an 'omo' – from Omo laundry liquid, which advertised: 'Only a third of a cup needed'.

Two bob watch, as mad (or silly) as a

Any wristwatch that cost only two bob (two shillings = twenty cents) was bound to be pretty useless. And anyone playing up in a crazy or foolish fashion is about as reliable (and useful) as a two-bob watch.

Two up

A national institution based on placing bets on the tossing of two coins. Sometimes the game is called 'swy' (a corruption of the German word for 'two', *zwei*). The game is an old one, and in the early days of the colony it was called 'chuck-farthing'. But the name 'two up' is definitely an Aussie invention. And there's a whole language that goes with it: the man in charge of the ring is the 'boxer', and when he decides that all bets have been taken he calls for the onlookers' attention and for the spinner to toss the coins with the words 'Fair go, spinner' – meaning 'Give the spinner a fair go'. The group playing the game are called a two up 'school'. There's a vivid (if frightening) description of an outback two up game in Kenneth Cook's novel *Wake in Fright*. (See also **Swy**.)

U-ey

A U-turn, which is always 'chucked' not driven, as in 'He spun the wheel and chucked a u-ey.' Also spelled 'uey'.

Ugg boots

Basically this is a sheepskin boot with the skin on the outside and the fleece on the inside. As far as I have been able to discover the boot was named (and probably invented) by a man named Frank Mortel back in 1958. Frank's wife looked at the first boots he made and said they were ugly, so Frank called them 'ugg' (for 'ugly') boots. The name is now the subject of international legal wrangle. An Australian manufacturer of ugg boots (called Ugg Holdings) was bought out by a giant American Corporation – Deckers Outdoor Corporation. Deckers now claims to own the expression 'ugg boots' as a trade mark belonging to them. They are now threatening to sue every little Australian manufacturer or retailer who uses the expression 'ugg boots'. It's a nasty thing to do, but they won't get away with it, because 'ugg boots' is a generic expression, and generic expressions cannot be copyrighted. The ugg boot is as fair dinkum Aussie as the Hills hoist, the Harbour Bridge and the Holden ute – so for an American company to try to claim the name is behaviour best covered by the expression 'the ugly American'.

Ugly tree, the

The mythical source of all ugly people. As in: 'Just look at that bloke – he must've fallen out of the ugly tree.' The proper response to such a remark is: 'Yeah, and got hit by all the branches on the way down!'

un-Australian

Some suggest this expression is a recent political invention, and others that it's un-Australian to call something 'un-Australian'. But the word 'un-Australian' appears in both the *Macquarie* and *Australian Oxford* dictionaries, meaning: 'not in accordance with the characteristics ... said to be typical of the Australian community'. The sociologists say that today 'un-Australian' means 'incivility and foreign influence'. Most people don't know that the word 'un-Australian' first appeared a hundred years ago. In the first half of the 20th century it referred to communists, fifth-columnists or radicals. But it's also a word used in fun. A citation from 1965 refers to a gadget as 'very un-Australian'. And there's a folk band who released a CD called *Un-Australian Songs*. So, while Americans may take being un-American very seriously, Aussies seem to think that 'un-Australian' means not being able to barbecue a steak properly.

Uluru

A giant sandstone monolith on a plain 450 kilometres south-west of Alice Springs in the Northern Territory. It was first recorded in 1872 and named 'Ayers Rock', after a premier of South Australia. In 1974 its Aboriginal name was restored, and both the rock and the surrounding national park were handed back to the care of the traditional (Aboriginal) owners. 'Uluru' is an Aboriginal sacred site. The rock stands over 300 metres tall and is the largest monolith in the world.

Unco

This is a double-barrelled insult invented by Aussie kids. In *Kidspeak* (a dictionary of Australian children's words, expressions and games) June Factor says that 'unco' can mean:

1. Clumsy, as in 'You're so unco you can't ride a bike'. This seems to make the word an abbreviation of 'uncoordinated'.
2. An unwanted outcast from the neighbourhood (or school) community, as in the insult, 'You're an unco loser!' With this meaning, the word looks like an abbreviation of 'uncool', although some think it comes from the same source as before – 'uncoordinated'.

Underground mutton

Rabbit. From the Great Depressions of the 1890s and 1930s, when whole families survived by trapping rabbits, either for their own consumption or for sale.

Unleaded

Medium alcohol beer.

Upya

'An exclamation of contemptuous rejection' says *The Australian National Dictionary*, thus finding polite words to record an impolite utterance. In his novel *The Shiralee*, D'Arcy Niland has the following memorable line of dialogue: 'Upya for the rent!' (A truculent refusal, you understand, to pay the rent.)

Ute

A utility (what the Yanks call a 'pick-up truck').

V

Vandemonian

The term 'Vandemonian' emerged in the 1830s. Initially, it was a fairly neutral term for a person born in, or resident in, Tasmania (or Van Diemen's Land, as it was then known), but it slowly took on darker undertones as it came to mean a convict who had served a sentence in Tasmania, or who had escaped from prison in Tasmania. These Tasmanian (or Vandemonian) convicts were heavily criticised for their unruly and wild behaviour, and those who were sent to Port Phillip colony in 1836 as a labour force were resented by the free settlers. So much so that their presence gave rise to an anti-transportation movement. In 1852 a *Convicts Prevention Act* was passed which excluded from Victoria all holders of conditional pardons from Van Diemen's Land – the much-feared Vandemonians.

Vegemite®

Vegemite® is a salty spread that's both a national institution and a registered brand name. It was invented by food technologist Dr Cyril P. Callister in 1922 for the original manufacturer Fred Walker, who ran a competition to find a name for this 'vegetable extract'. Vegemite® was the winning entry. However, in order to compete with an existing British product called 'Marmite' it was relaunched in 1928 as 'Parwill'. It was a joke, you see: if Ma might, then Pa will! (Not a very good joke, I grant you.) The relaunch fell flat and Vegemite® went back to being Vegemite® – as it has been ever since. In World War II it became part of the survival rations of Aussie soldiers, and in 1954 an advertising agency came up with a jingle for the product that put the phrase 'happy little Vegemites' into Aussie English.

Vegemite moment

Visitors don't always react as enthusiastically to this thick, salty, black sandwich spread as the native-born. Upon trying some delicious Vegemite on toast visitors have been known to screw up their noses and ask us how we can eat that stuff. Well, this response has given rise to the expression 'a Vegemite moment' – which is a moment, a point in your personal experience, that you absolutely love or absolutely loath. In other words, there is no middle ground. That 'love it or loath it' response is what makes the moment 'a Vegemite moment'.

Vegie

A stupid person (as in 'I've met broccoli brighter than that bloke').

Veranda

Originally an Anglo-India word (appearing in various forms in both Hindi and Bengali) meaning 'railing, balustrade or balcony'. Brought to Australia by Britons moving from one bit of the Empire to another, it took on special importance in Australian architecture because of the climate. (An alternative spelling is verandah, with an 'H'.) The *Oxford English Dictionary* says the special Australian sense of the word is: 'A roof-like structure built along the side of a building, esp. one built over the pavement outside the business premises.' But I'm not so sure. For a start, we've never called shop awnings 'verandas', and in the second place they were often built around more than one side. The homestead on a remote cattle station might have deep verandas on three, or all four, sides. The deeper and more extensive the verandas, the cooler the building was kept during the fierce heat of summer. In fact, those extensive verandas-on-all-sides homes gave rise to the following expression …

Veranda bum

A spare tyre of fat that goes 'all the way around the building' – a fat backside merging into a fat stomach and fat hips, all overhanging the belt in every direction.

Vermin

Wild animals that destroy crops (such as rabbits) or attack sheep (such as dingoes).

Versing

Australian sporting journalism appears to have given birth to the word 'versing'. It turns up on those sporting programs on radio and television in which blokes named Jacko and Cruncher preview next weekend's clash-fixture-events. They have trouble referring to the Sharks versus the Bears because 'versus' comes from Latin, and, anyway, it's two syllables. So they say, 'the Sharks verse the Bears' (that is, when they're not saying 'the Sharks vee the Bears'). This shortened form of 'versus' has been taken up by school slang and turned into a verb, as in the expression, 'Who are we versing this week?' In other words, 'versing' is not writing poetry, but playing another team. One school teacher discovered how far this had gone when she marked an assignment about the battle of Marathon which, the student said, was a case of 'the Persians versing the Greeks'.

Vino collapso

Cask wine – so named because the bladder collapses as the wine is drawn off.

Waddy

An Aboriginal weapon – a wooden club (from the Dharuk language).

Wait-a-while

A colloquial name for a number of prickly, thorny plants; for the obvious reason that you can't just brush past them – they make you wait a while as you carefully pick the prickles out of your clothes or skin.

Waler

A type of Australian horse – short for 'New South Waler'. Said to be light and fast, they were much favoured by the Australian Light Horse in World War I. It was Walers the Light Horsemen rode to victory in the last great cavalry charge of modern warfare at the battle of Beersheba on 31 October 1917. First bred for export to India for use by the Indian Army from the mid-1800s.

Walkabout

Originally this mean a journey on foot by an Aboriginal Aussie to spend some time in their home country, living off bush tucker in the traditional way; today when anyone goes for a bit of a wander you can say they've 'gone walkabout'.

Walla Walla

The name of an Australian trotting horse (1922–52) so successful that he was given increasingly large handicaps. So someone who is starting from a long way behind might be said to be 'starting further back than Walla Walla'.

Wallaby

A name loosely given to many of the smaller kangaroos. The name 'wallaby' came from the Port Jackson Aborigines.

Wallaby track

It used to be said that itinerant bush workers were 'on the wallaby track'. The term was used from 1849 for the well-worn tracks that led from one bush town to another. The term wallaby track comes from the fact that wallabies left clear tracks through the long grass and scrub, and early settlers found these ready-made tracks easier to use than pushing through new tracks of their own. Henry Lawson wrote a famous bush ballad called 'On the Wallaby':

> I am out on the wallaby humping my drum,
> And I came by the tracks where the sundowners come.

And the expression now turns up in Aussie nursery rhymes, such as:

> All of the wobbly wallabies
> Are out on the wallaby track,
> Wobbling away to the back o' Bourke,
> To the back o' Bourke and back.

From 19th-century itinerant bush workers to nursery rhymes – that's the journey of the expression 'wallaby track'.

Waltzing matilda

Carrying a swag; 'humping a bluey' or 'humping your drum' on the wallaby track. This, of course, is what the jolly swagman is up to in Banjo Paterson's classic bush ballad (Australia's best-loved song):

> Waltzing matilda, waltzing matilda,
> Who'll come a waltzing matilda with me?
> And he sang as he watched and waited till his billy boiled:
> Who'll come a waltzing matilda with me?

Waratah

A small native shrub (*Telopea speciosissima*) that produces a large, bright-red flower head. The floral emblem of New South Wales.

Warrambool

A watercourse that floods after rain, but is dry most of the year. Borrowed into Aussie English from an Aboriginal language (the Kamilaroi language). First recorded by William Ridley, a Presbyterian missionary in northern New South Wales, in 1875. Always of limited use, and now, perhaps, fading.

Warrigal

Some dictionaries of Aussie English will tell you that 'warrigal' is just another Aboriginal name for a dingo. But this is not strictly correct. Both are dogs, but the linguists seem to think that 'dingo' was used only of the domesticated dog, the camp dog, while what we think of as a dingo (a wild dog) was called a warrigal. Once adopted by Aussie English, both words developed a range of meanings. The essential characteristic of the warrigal was seen by European settlers to be its untamed nature. And the word could be extended from dogs to other animals, and even to people. Thus, until the 1930s, in some parts of Australia 'warrigal' was another name for a wild horse or brumby. And a person who chose to live wild, outside the boundaries of civilisation, could also be labelled a warrigal.

Wattle

Today we think of wattle 'as any of the very numerous Australian species of *Acacia*, shrubs or trees with spikes or globular heads of yellow or cream flowers' (*Macquarie Dictionary*). However, the word 'wattle' originally referred to a style of building: a wattle wall or fence was made from an intertwining, or weaving, of rods or stakes with interlaced twigs or branches. This practice of 'wattling' goes back over a thousand years. It was possible to build a modest hut out of wattle and daub: using wattled walls (branches woven through rods or stakes which were driven into the ground), the whole thing then being covered in mud (particularly mud with a high clay content) and whitewashed, once dry. This building technique was used in the early colonies of Australia, and the local bushes and shrubs that were most suited to this employment came to be called 'wattles'. And that's why our *Acacia* shrubs and trees are called wattles.

The Golden Wattle, with its distinctive clusters of small yellow flowers, is the national floral emblem of Australia. For many years the first day of August was known as 'Wattle Day'. It was inaugurated in 1909 by the Australian Wattle League of New South Wales, in order to 'encourage national sentiment as symbolised in the native flower'. The League used to mark the day by handing out sprigs of wattle to the public, and by planting wattle trees.

This traditional nod to our national floral emblem was revived in 1992, when 1 September was formally declared 'National Wattle Day' by the then Minister for the Environment, Ros Kelly, at a ceremony at the Australian National Botanic Gardens. (The scientific name of the Golden Wattle is *Acacia pycnantha*.)

And the whole business of having a national 'Wattle Day' led to the following Bush Ballad (or, possibly, Floral Doggerel):

Oh, the wattle! The wattle! The wonderful wattle!
It grabs at my throat and starts to throttle.
In fact, I almost choke with pride,
My heart begins to swell up inside,
When I think of this sunburnt golden land,
With the Golden Wattle on every hand.
As I walked in the park, eating my lunch,
I saw the wattle and picked a bunch.
I heard a voice say: 'No you shan't,
The wattle my lad's a protected plant.'
'But Officer Plod (policeman bold),
I am in love with the wattle gold.'
'It's no use, lad, it's off to the brig,
For picking a piece of wattle sprig.
You're not the full quid, you're not the full bottle,
If you go around picking public wattle;
You'd have to be an Aristotle,
To escape the charge of—picking wattle.'
Oh, the wattle does so captivate,
That the plant I love—but the Day I hate:
Because the plant I love to pick,
By Wattle Eve I'm in the nick!

Were you born in a paddock with the sliprails down?

This is what someone says when you walk into a room and leave the door open behind you (they're telling you to close the door). The correct answer to this question is: 'No, in a hospital with swinging doors.' An alternative challenge to compulsive door-openers is: 'Were you born in a tent?'. To which the correct response is: 'Yes, what's the flap?'.

Westies and others

'Westie' has long been a derogatory term used by some to label others they see as uncultured – the unsophisticated wearers of mullet haircuts and flannelette shirts. But such expressions are regional, 'westie' being chiefly heard in Sydney. The same person in Queensland would be called a 'bevan' and his girlfriend a 'bev-chick'. In Melbourne they can be called a 'mocca' or a 'scozzer' or a 'feral'. In Western Australian (and elsewhere) this unsophisticated kid is a 'bogan', while a younger bogan is a 'barry' (short for 'Barry Crocker' = 'shocker'). In Tasmania they could be called 'chiggers'; in Adelaide, 'boonies'; in the ACT, 'charnies'; and in the Riverina, 'gullies'. The female version is sometimes called a 'Charlene' or a 'Charmaine'. (See also **Bogan**.)

Wet sheep

A widespread belief among shearers is that shearing a wet sheep will give you rheumatism. An older belief said that the shearer could be poisoned by the vapours rising from the wet wool.

Whacko-the-diddle-oh

An exclamation of pleasure or approval; used elsewhere, but first recorded here in Australia in 1937. Often abbreviated to just 'Whacko!'

Whales

The large, fresh-water fish called the Murray cod, so called because of their size. They've been nicknamed whales since at least the 1870s. A large Murray cod can weigh as much as a man, and live as long.

Whaler

A swagman who sticks to tracks close to the Murray–Darling river system, and creeks and tributaries leading into it, so that he can supplement his diet with Murray cod. That pattern of travelling was called 'whaling' – hence the folk song 'Whaling Down the Lachlan'.

Whitewash

1. To shear a sheep (or lamb) lightly, because discoloured wool is taken off, making them look whiter.
2. To cover up an embarrassment (hiding it under 'a coat of whitewash').
3. To decisively beat an opponent in a sporting event, because it looks as though their side of the scoreboard is unmarked whitewash.

Whinge

Complain; grizzle; moan; carry on like a gate with a squeaking hinge. Aussies are supposed to be experts at whingeing. If whingeing was an Olympic event (so it's said), Aussies would win the gold every time.

Who's robbing this coach?

This is a way of saying 'Stop interfering with what I'm doing – and don't tell me what to do.'

Wide brown land

The famous description of Australia coined by Dorothea Mackellar (1885–1968) in her poem 'My Country':

I love a sunburnt country
A land of sweeping plains,

Of ragged mountain ranges,
Of droughts and flooding rains.
I love her far horizons,
I love her jewel-sea,
Her beauty and her terror –
The wide brown land for me!

Willy-willy

An Aboriginal name (from the Yindjibarndi language) for the whirlwinds of the outback. An eyewitness account from 1898 says:

> They usually begin upon a very small scale … a dancing column of dust, dung, dead flies and old paper. Give them time and they will show sport. But the willy-willy has no perseverance; he lacks continued effort, and the slightest opposition in the shape of a tin hut or a telegraph pole so destroys his symmetry that he dies of disgust in a heap of refuse. But with plenty of room he becomes rampant. When he gets over 50 feet high his power is vast.

Wino

A wine drinker – intended as a disparaging term and coming from the era when real blokes drank only beer or spirits. Wine, in those days, was only drunk by sheilas and derros. With the rise of the Australian wine industry the term has largely disappeared, although it still occasionally turns up as a synonym for 'derro'. (See **Derro** and **Sheila**.)

Witchetty grub

A white, wood-boring grub that can be eaten after being cooked in the ashes of the campfire; a juicy bit of bush tucker. This dietary habit led Eric Jolliffe to label his long-running series of cartoons about remote Aboriginal life 'Witchetty's Tribe'.

Wobble board

Musical instrument invented by Rolf Harris when shaking a painting on a sheet of thin hardboard. He was trying to get the oil paint to dry when he discovered the distinctive 'whoop, whoop' sound of the wobble board. It was popularised by his 1960 hit 'Tie Me Kangaroo Down'. Interest was revived by the use of the wobble board on Rolf's 1993 version of the Led Zeppelin song 'Stairway to Heaven'. The first ever World Wobble Board Championship was held in Bassendean (Western Australia) in 2001 as part of their centenary celebrations. Prizes were awarded for the best playing and the best artistic decoration. (See also **Tie Me Kangaroo Down, Sport.**)

Wobbly boots

What you're wearing after you've drunk too much grog. Celebrated in a song called 'Wobbly Boots', most famously sung as a duet by Slim Dusty and Rolf Harris.

Wogs in the west

The Western Australian government has decreed that the words 'wog', 'pom' and 'ding' are not to be regarded as offensive terms under the state's racial vilification rules. Of those three, 'ding' was one I'd never come across before. It turns out to be an abbreviation of dingbat and back in the 1920s it was used to label an Italian immigrant. Well, 'ding' seems to have survived in the west, and to have been put on this list of 'safe' words. The original of 'wog' is unknown, and all those claims about it meaning 'wily oriental gentleman' are linguistic urban myths. The old rule use to be that 'wogs' could use 'wog' but the rest of us couldn't. But in the west it is now open slather on 'wog'. (For **Pommy,** see the entry on that word.)

Wombat

A wombat is a thickset, burrowing marsupial native to Australia. The word is also a native; it came into English from the Dharuk language, and has since branched out into a whole metaphorical forest. As early as 1905 a slow or stupid person could be called 'a bit of a wombat'. In World War I, infantrymen who were set to work digging tunnels were nicknamed 'wombat's. In the 1980s the Costigan Royal Commission was told about 'wombats' on racecourses who illegally transmitted prices to an operator outside the track, using pocket radios. Now wombat has become an acronym: in the computing world a wombat is someone or something that's a 'Waste of Money, Bandwidth and Time': W.O.M.B.A.T.

Wonky

1. Unstable, unreliable.
2. Not feeling well; off your feed.
3. Mad; crazy.

Wood-and-water joey

An unskilled labourer, especially in the bush. Water and wood are the basic necessities of life in the bush, and this label probably comes from the Bible's reference to 'hewers of wood and drawers of water' (Joshua 9:21). The earliest reference is from 1882. Susan Butler says the 'joey' part of it comes from the goldfields, from the troopers and other representatives of the Governor Charles Joseph La Trobe who were nicknamed 'joes'. From there it became a general term for one serving a master. The larger expression ('wood-and-water joey') came to have a positive sense, meaning a useful, if menial, worker.

Wool away!

The shearer's call to the picker-up to clear away the fleece just shorn.

Woomera

Woomera is an Aboriginal word from the Dharuk people, and was first recorded in 1793. A woomera was originally a throwing stick, about a metre long, which hooked on to the end of a spear to propel the weapon with greater speed and force. The 'woomera' was, in effect, an extension of the spear thrower's arm, and an inventive piece of simple technology. On 24 April 1947 this word, 'Woomera', was chosen as the name for the town associated with the new rocket range set up jointly by Australia and Britain – an exercise that needed a large, remote area in which to test new weapons systems. Then in 2001 the Woomera Detention Centre was opened just outside the village – filling the headlines with the Dharuk word for 'throwing stick'.

Woop Woop

'Woop Woop' is what the dictionaries like to call a 'jocular formation'. It's been constructed along the lines of those Aboriginal languages that use reduplication in place names such as Wagga Wagga or Woy Woy. Looking into *The Australian National Dictionary* (published in 1988) we find the earliest citation is from 1918 (from a book called *Back to the Bush* – 'I once went to church in Woop-woop') and the most recent listed is from 1986 (a citation that describes a session of the Federal Parliament as being 'like council night in Woop Woop'). *The Australian National Dictionary* suggests that the name might have been coined from the earlier expression 'wop wop', meaning a careless bundle of something, or the person making the bundle. A citation from 1904 explains: 'A new name now given to the rouseabout … (in a shearing shed) is "wop-wop". The term is said to have originated from the peculiar sound ("wop-wop, wop-wop") caused by the picker-up running up and down the shearing board carrying fleeces to the wool tables during shearing time.'

Wowser

'Wowser' is an Australian word that means 'a puritanical person' – usually in the most negative sense. John Norton, editor of the Sydney *Truth* newspaper in the late 19th and early 20th centuries, claimed to have coined the word, but *The Australian National Dictionary* says it goes back to an English dialect word, 'wow', meaning 'to howl or whine like a dog'. In other words, it is the doggy expression 'bow wow', shortened to 'wow' and then extended to become 'wowser'. When John Norton claimed ownership of the word he pretended to have coined it from the acronym 'We Only Want Social Evils Remedied'. But this was a piece of inventive fiction on Norton's part. Originally, a wowser was anyone who made a noise about anything, but by the early 20th century it had come to be restricted to those who noisily complained about lewdness, crudeness and the general disappearance of common courtesy and civility from Australian society.

Wriggly tin

A nice bush nickname for corrugated iron.

Wrinkly

An old person is 'a wrinkly' (at least in the eyes, and the language, of young Aussies).

XPT

A fast train that travels between Sydney, Melbourne, Brisbane, Dubbo, Grafton and Casino. ('XPT' is short for 'Express Passenger Train'.)

X-ray painting

A style of traditional Aboriginal rock painting that shows the bones of the fish, birds or animals painted.

Yabba

Chatter, talk, conversation – perhaps rapid or garbled conversation. Often used in a reduplicated form: 'yabba yabba'. First recorded 1855. Some suggest it's a corruption of the English word 'jabber', but E. E. Morris in his *Dictionary of Austral English* (1898) is convinced it's of Aboriginal origin. (A verb as well as a noun: for example, 'yabbing', or 'yabbing on'.)

Yaffler

A loudmouthed or talkative person. A Tassie term. According to the experts, this began life as a British regional dialect word and now survives in Tasmania and nowhere else in the world. (Bass Strait, it appears, protects the rest of the world from yafflers.)

Yabby

Small freshwater crayfish; you can often catch yabbies in the dams on farms. This tasty creature is also spelled 'yabbie', and is known by a host of other names, depending on which bit of Australia you are in at the time: 'clawchie', 'crawchie', 'craydab', 'crayfish', 'jilgie', 'lobby', 'lobster', 'marron'. The word 'yabby' comes from the Aboriginal language Wemba-Wemba (Victoria/NSW): *yabij*. The activity of catching yabbies is called 'yabbying'. Very small yabbies, obtained on mudflats or sandy beaches using a yabby pump, are used as bait. I have caught yabbies in a farm dam by simply dangling a bit of meat on the end of a line in the water (no hook is needed): the yabby grabs the meat in its claws, refuses to let go, and can be hauled in and dropped in the bucket with all the other yabbies, to be cooked later.

Yakka

Good solid work, strenuous labour, is called 'hard yakka' in Aussie English, and it's an expression you'll find nowhere else on Earth. It's hard to know how long it's been around, because it tends to be part of the spoken, rather than written, language. The earliest citation is from 1888, but people might have been talking about 'hard yakka' long before that. 'Yakka' was borrowed from the Yagara language (spoken in the Brisbane region) and it spread rapidly across the country. So well known did it become that 'yakka' was adopted as a brand name by a company making overalls and work clothes. While some of the old Aussie expressions might be fading away, 'yakka' seems to be as strong as ever. It might, these days, be used in a half-joking fashion, but it is still being used!

Yarra

1. The river that flows through Melbourne – allegedly always filled with brown water, giving rise to the old Sydney joke: 'The Yarra is the only river in the world that flows upside-down.'
2. A type of Australian tree that grows near watercourses, and gives the Yarra River its name.
3. Insane, or stupid (from the name of a psychiatric hospital at Yarra Bend in Victoria).

Yarn

'Yarn' is Aussie slang for a talk or a chat, a conversation – first recorded from 1852. But behind it is a piece of British nautical slang: to 'spin a yarn' – referring to tall tales told by sailors. The literal meaning of 'yarn', of course, is spun fibre. One of the things that sailors did on ships during long voyages was to work with, or make, rope by (literally) spinning yarn. My guess about the storytelling expression 'to spin a yarn' is that it's the sort of tale-telling sailors engaged in to pass the time while they were rope-making (literally, yarn spinning). The nautical slang came to Australia with the first settlers as part of the 'flash talk' employed by the convicts (and recorded by convict author James Hardy Vaux in his *Vocabulary of the Flash Language*). Over the next few decades it was adapted by the early bushies to mean any chat or conversation or sharing of news.

YMCA dinner

A meal made from leftovers: 'Yesterday's Muck Cooked Again'.

Yobbo

A lout, hooligan or hoon. The standard evaluation of most of the younger generation by your average grumpy old man (see **Chutney**).

Yoe

In the earliest versions of 'Click Go the Shears' the old shearer gets his hands on a 'bare-bellied (or blue-bellied) yoe', where 'yoe' is said to be an Irish pronunciation of 'ewe'. In later versions of the song, singers tended to replace the puzzling word 'yoe' with 'joe' – an odd way to refer to a sheep, but it avoided a puzzle and made it easier to sing along. (See also **Click go the words**.)

Yonks

In Aussie English, 'yonks' means 'a long time': 'Oh, that happened yonks ago!' The *Oxford English Dictionary* says only 'origin unknown', but it does tell us that it's of fairly recent origin, the earliest citation being from 1968. Several of the authorities I consulted seem to think 'yonks' is a corruption, or abbreviation, of 'donkey's years', also meaning 'a long time'. The origin of 'donkey's years' is simple enough: it's a joke. You see, donkey's ears are long, so (by way of a rhyming joke) 'donkey's years' are also long. The problem is understanding what sort of verbal construction could get us from 'donkey's years' to yonks. Here's another possibility. Perhaps the elision of the words 'years' and 'long' would account for it. If you take the first and last letters of 'years' and the insert the diphthong from 'long' you'd end up with 'yongs', and 'yonks' just tidies that up. Well, it's possible.

Youse

Said to have come from Irish English, but common in Australia as the non-standard form for the second person plural pronoun. (Well, it's logical, isn't it? If 'you' refers to one person, and a plural is normally constructed in English by adding an 'S', then the plural of 'you' must be youse.) A thousand years ago the singular form of the second person pronoun was 'ye', and 'you' was the plural. Over time 'ye' slowly disappeared (it still occasionally turns up until the 1800s), leaving 'you' to do both jobs – both singular and plural. Hence, the confusion that gives rise to 'youse'.

Yowie

A legendary monster; an ape-like human two and half metres tall, said to roam in parts of the outback.

Zack

Back in the days before decimal currency was introduced (on 14 February 1966) there was a coin called a sixpence – five cents in today's money. And 'zack' was the nickname for a sixpence. Johnny Devlin had a hit song in the early 1960s called 'Got a Zack in the Back of My Pocket'.

Zigzag

The pattern of railway tracks built in Australia to deal with steep gradients. The track looked like a set of Zs drawn on the slope, with buffers and points at the end of each stretch of line, allowing the train to switch from line to line as it made its way up (or down) the steep slope. What is perhaps the most famous of such zigzag tracks still exists in the Blue Mountains west of Sydney.

Zonked

Tired; exhausted; worn out.

Zonkerpede

An all-purpose name for an unidentified insect of vaguely sinister appearance.

Zs

Sleeping is 'punching out a few Zs'.

Acknowledgments

The publisher and author acknowledge the following for their permission to reproduce extracts:

The Dorothea Mackellar Estate for permission to quote from *My Country*, by arrangement with the licensor, The Dorothea Mackellar Estate, c/- Curtis Brown (Aust) Pty Ltd

John O'Grady for permission to quote from *The Integrated Adjective*

John Williamson for permission to reproduce lyrics from his songs *Old Man Emu* and *True Blue*

Mushroom Music Publishing for permission to reproduce lyrics from the Humphrey B. Bear theme song

Mushroom Music Publishing for permission to reproduce lyrics from *(Give Me A) Home Among the Gum Trees*, written by Bob Brown and Wally Johnson

Rolf Harris for permission to reproduce lyrics from his song *Six White Boomers*

Hadley Records for permission to reproduce lyrics from *Redback on the Toilet Seat* by Slim Newton

Tom Thompson for permission to quote from Judith Wright's *Scribbly Gum* from *A Human Pattern: Selected Poems* (ETT Imprint, Sydney, 2010)